BEYOND HASHTAGS

CRITICAL CULTURAL COMMUNICATION

General Editors: Jonathan Gray, Aswin Punathambekar, Adrienne Shaw
Founding Editors: Sarah Banet-Weiser and Kent A. Ono

Beyond Hashtags

Racial Politics and Black Digital Networks

Sarah Florini

NEW YORK UNIVERSITY PRESS

New York

NEW YORK UNIVERSITY PRESS
New York
www.nyupress.org

References to Internet websites (URLs) were accurate at the time of writing. Neither the author nor New York University Press is responsible for URLs that may have expired or changed since the manuscript was prepared.

Library of Congress Cataloging-in-Publication Data
Names: Florini, Sarah, author.
Title: Beyond hashtags : racial politics and black digital networks / Sarah Florini.
Description: New York : New York University Press, 2019. | Includes bibliographical references and index.
Identifiers: LCCN 2019012051| ISBN 9781479892464 (cl : alk. paper) | ISBN 9781479813056 (pb : alk. paper)
Subjects: LCSH: African Americans and mass media. | African American mass media. | Race in mass media.
Classification: LCC P94.5.A37 F57 2019 | DDC 302.23089/96073--dc23
LC record available at https://lccn.loc.gov/2019012051

New York University Press books are printed on acid-free paper, and their binding materials are chosen for strength and durability. We strive to use environmentally responsible suppliers and materials to the greatest extent possible in publishing our books.

Manufactured in the United States of America

10 9 8 7 6 5 4 3 2 1

Also available as an ebook

CONTENTS

Introduction

On the night of November 24, 2014, St. Louis County prosecutor Robert McCulloch announced the grand jury's decision not to indict Police Officer Darren Wilson for the shooting death of unarmed Black teenager Mike Brown. I was in a car on I-64 driving through West Virginia, listening to a live stream of McCulloch's press conference provided by the independent media company This Week in Blackness (TWiB!) via their custom mobile app. After the press conference ended, the hosts of TWiB!'s flagship podcast *TWiB! Prime*—TWiB! founder and CEO Elon James White, TWiB! Senior Legal Analyst Imani Gandy, and TWiB! sound engineer Aaron Rand Freeman—discussed the verdict and took listener phone calls. While unrest gripped Ferguson, Missouri that night, I watched events unfold on Twitter, as information from journalists, activists, and local Ferguson residents circulated through my social media networks.

I had relied on the same digital networks for information the previous August, when protests broke out in Ferguson in the immediate wake of Brown's death. On August 9, Brown's name, in hashtag form, had appeared on my Twitter timeline within hours of his death. Before long, many Twitter users whom I follow had begun retweeting information from Ferguson locals who were on scene. Retweets of Hip-hop artist and Ferguson resident Tef Poe brought me the image of Brown's step-father, Louis Head, holding a makeshift cardboard sign reading, "Ferguson Police just executed my son!"[1] Other tweets contained links to Alderman Antonio French's Vine account, where he was recording and sharing six-second videos of the protests and the police response. In the days that followed, as local leaders and citizen journalists emerged on the streets of Ferguson, users in my Twitter network crowdsourced and compiled lists of reliable sources of information. Users also created the hashtag #IGotTheTalk to organize discussions of the conversations parents must have with Black children about how to safely interact with police officers. Meanwhile writer, activist, and mental health social worker Feminista Jones used her well-established social media presence and the hashtag #NMOS14 to organize a National Moment of Silence on August 14 in over one hundred locations across the United States to honor Brown and other victims of police violence.

As the protests unfolded in Ferguson, TWiB! and many other Black podcasters provided information and commentary. On August 10, the day after Brown's death, *The Black Guy Who Tips* (*TBGWT*) podcast made the hashtag #IGotTheTalk the title of that day's show, which continued the conversations taking place on social media.[2] Based in the St. Louis area, the podcast *Straight Outta LoCash* recorded an episode on August 14 titled "We ARE ALL #MikeBrown, We ARE ALL #Ferguson," contextualizing Brown's death and the subsequent protests within the local political climate and the area's history of racial tensions.[3] These and other podcasts such as *Insanity Check* and *Where's My 40 Acres?* (*WM40A?*) discussed the emotional and psychological impact of Ferguson. Such talk-radio-style podcasts, with their multiple channels for audience participation, including live chatrooms and active social media engagement, allowed listeners and hosts to come together and analyze and interpret the events as they transpired.

TWiB!, at the behest of their audience, made trips to Ferguson on August 13–16 and 18–23 to report live. Once in Ferguson, TWiB! used its existing broadcast-style podcast network and robust social media networks to give voice to local accounts of the events, offering a narrative that stood in opposition to that created by much of the cable news media. When, in the early morning hours of August 19, White and several others were tear-gassed by Ferguson police in a residential area, I listened helplessly to TWiB!'s live stream as they ran and hid. The following day, White released a recording of the incident through his social media networks. Eventually, both the clip and White made their way to the *Melissa Harris-Perry Show* on MSNBC, where he broke down as he relived the trauma of the experience.[4]

The way information circulated through these digital media networks during the events in Ferguson encapsulates many of the issues at the heart of this book. It exemplifies how Black Americans have been able to create and use multimedia, transplatform digital networks to articulate their experiences, cultivate community and solidarity, mobilize political resistance, and both bypass and intervene in legacy news media coverage.[5] Though Ferguson and the subsequent protests made such Black digital networks more broadly visible, these networks did not coalesce in that moment. They were built and maintained over the course of years through much less spectacular, though no less important, everyday use, including mundane social exchanges, humor, and fandom. Moments like Ferguson provide important and compelling examples of how such networks can be leveraged at times of turmoil and political crisis. But this is only one way these networks serve as a resource for participants, who make use of the flexibility offered by a multiplatform network to address issues throughout their day-to-day lives.

This book explores these everyday practices and their relationship to larger social and cultural issues through an in-depth analysis of a multimedia, transplatform network of Black American digital and social media users and content creators between 2010 and mid-2016. In these crucial years, leading up to and including the emergence of the Movement for Black Lives, Black Americans used digital networks not only to cope with and challenge day-to-day experiences of racism, but also as an incubator for the discourses that the movement propelled onto the national stage.

The network at the heart of this project has three anchoring elements—the independent media company This Week in Blackness, an informal network of independent Black podcasters, and the network known as "Black Twitter"; these form the core of the network analyzed here but are not coterminous with it. Using an interdisciplinary approach that draws from critical digital studies, media studies, cultural studies, African American studies, and critical race theory, I examine this digital assemblage and interrogate how Black Americans use it to create a space of distributed sociality and discourse production. In this networked space, participants blend elements of mass communication and sociality to reject dominant racial discourses, reassert and redefine their racial identities, forge community, organize politically, and create alternative media representations and news sources.

Digital networks are most often visualized as linear connections between a series of nodes. While this approach is an effective way of mapping the structure of a network, it fails to represent the dynamic and complicated social and cultural practices that both take place in and shape digital networks. My wish to emphasize the latter is reflected in the selection of Shinique Smith's "Out of Body" as the cover art. Her work conveys the vibrance and complexity of the network I write about in this book. "Out of Body" is alive and energetic, complex and multilayered. The lines, materials, and colors are interconnected, forming a cohesive whole, Yet, they are also varied and heterogeneous—a mix of colors, materials, and textures. It captures the kind of fluid beauty—chaotic yet intentional—that I have observed in the contingent and creative practices of the Black digital network that is the focus of this project. The bright colors, sweeping calligraphy and graffiti inspired lines, and multimedia materials represent the energy and creativity of the network described here in a way that standard network maps erase. It is the visualization of this network that I hope to instill in readers as they come to know it through the pages of this book.

I make three contributions to the field of critical digital studies. First, I emphasize the multimedia and transplatform character of this network, exploring how users employ platforms and technologies simultaneously and in tandem. I examine how users participate in debates, discussions, and sociality within the network by moving across platforms and employing combinations of text-based, audio, and visual media. Much critical digital studies research focuses on one particular technology or platform. Research on Black American digital media use in particular tends to be bound by platform, with great attention devoted to Black Twitter. Despite the inarguable value of such scholarship, it obscures an important element of digital practice—namely, the simultaneous and integrated use of multiple media and platforms.

Media studies scholars focusing on digital cultural production have long recognized the need for such analyses, given that convergence culture is characterized by the unexpected ways media move across platforms and devices.[6] Much research has been produced about transmedia storytelling, fandom, and branding.[7] Scholars have noted the way content creators, both independent and within the media industry, rely on a range of platforms to create their star images, gain audience support for independent projects, and do the now-essential work of connecting with audiences to generate sales.[8] Stuart Cunningham and David Craig have examined the rise of what they call "social media entertainment" (SME), which they define as "an emerging proto-industry fueled by the professionalation of amateur content creators using new entertainment and communicative formats, including vlogging, gameplay, and do-it-yourself (DIY), to develop potentially sustainable businesses based on significant followings that can extend across multiple platforms."[9] SME creators produce a range of content across platforms, including YouTube, Facebook, Twitter, Instagram, and Snapchat, choosing how to use each based on the affordances it provides. However, such scholarship examines these practices predominantly through the lens of the production, consumption, and circulation of mass media–style texts, leaving how these processes are imbricated with larger patterns of transplatform sociality relatively unexplored.

André Jansson and Karin Fast have pointed "to how social practices (in addition to texts per se) are molded by and negotiated through different platforms and devices."[10] Jillian Baez's work on DREAMers' use of digital media to construct alternative understandings of citizenship examines how they create visual, aural, and textual discourses, which are then spread through social media channels. This, combined with DREAMers' offline direct action, allows them to use multiple digital tools in tandem to express themselves and connect with one another.[11] Here, I undertake an analysis of how different media and platforms are used strategically in ways that best suit the exigencies facing the network of Black Americans described earlier in this chapter.

The second contribution of this study is how it foregrounds the value of cultural specificity in understanding emerging media. Networks are not just technologically but also culturally "programmed"—imbued with certain goals, values, and normative practices generated from "ideas, visions, projects, and frames" shared by members of the network.[12] Yet, the role these cultural values play in shaping users' practices is often overlooked.[13] As Miriam Sweeney points outs, "Hardware, software, content, representations, user practices, and interpretation are all the outcome of complex social processes shaped by cultural values and ideology."[14] She argues that each interface is "a cultural point of contact shaped by ideologies that are manifest in the design, use, and meaning of the technology."[15] Often scholarly attention to technological affordances focuses on how the materiality of technology—such as interface or design choices—shapes user behavior, an approach that has been criticized by some as verging on technological determinism. I embrace Peter Nagy and Gina Neff's concept of *imagined affordances*, which highlights how affordances arise "between users' perceptions, attitudes, and expectations; between the materiality and functionality of technologies; and between the intentions and perceptions of designers."[16] The term thus captures the contingent and shifting nature of affordances as well as the influence users have in the emergence of affordances. This conceptualization of affordances foregrounds the importance of cultural specificity in digital media research. Without the requisite cultural competencies, researchers are ill prepared to understand users' practices or their role in shaping the affordances of a given technology. At a moment when academics, journalists, and tech developers are intrigued with the possibilities of "big data," the kinds of "deep data" or "thick data" offered by critical/cultural studies analysis and ethnography are essential.[17]

Third, and most important, I make the aforementioned interventions while centering Black users. With a handful of important exceptions, it has only been in the last four or five years that scholars have devoted sustained attention to Black users, who had previously been mostly erased from discussions of technology due to a general presumption of non-participation.[18] When Black users have been the focus of analysis, such work is often taken up in the academic world for its insights into race or Black culture, ignoring the insights about technology that are offered through consideration of Black users' practices. The network at the center of this study is comprised predominantly by Black people and shaped by their perspectives and experiences and, therefore, certainly has much to teach about the contemporary issues surrounding race. However, it is of interest not solely for this reason. If affordances are imagined through the interaction between users' understanding and practices, designers' intentions, and the materiality and functionality of technology, then a consideration of marginalized users' practices can yield diverse and innovative ways of imagining affordances and, thereby, understanding the possibilities of technology. Though the intersection of racial politics and technology is central to my research, I also use the analysis of Black networks to demonstrate that marginalized users have much to teach us about technology, and not simply about marginalization.

The following sections begin with an explication of the contemporary US racial landscape that outlines the dominant discourses within which the network at the center of this project operates. I then explore how the same neoliberal discourses that have shaped racial ideologies have also influenced the development of digital and social media technologies, thereby necessitating negotiation by the Black users who traverse this technological terrain. Next I highlight how longstanding Black epistemologies, communicative practices, and aesthetics map easily onto the digital landscape, despite having different underlying logics and values. I offer a brief description of the network that is the focus of this book and my rationale for carving out this specific digital assemblage for analysis. After a brief discussion of methodological and representational issues, I conclude with an overview of the remainder of the book.

Technology and Neoliberal Racial Regimes

Contemporary US racial formations are characterized by the contradiction between discourses of progress and the persistence of structural racial inequalities. While a Black man was elected to the highest office in the land (twice), simultaneously there remain race-based disparities in educational attainment, health outcomes, unemployment, incarceration, and even infant mortality. This incongruence is obscured, however, by neoliberal racial discourses such as colorblindness that proffer nonracial explanations for racial outcomes. Further, the current technological landscape is one in which convergence and participatory media are more prevalent than ever and social media connect and circulate information at unprecedented speeds. This presents powerful opportunities for people of color and other marginalized voices, while simultaneously allowing existing mechanisms for erasing, silencing, and denying those voices to be adapted and extended into the same technological terrain. The emancipatory possibilities of digital and social media are constrained by the ways these technologies were shaped by the same neoliberal values that produce and maintain colorblindness as the dominant racial discourse.

With the rise of neoliberalism in the latter half of the twentieth century, race has been recast as a solely personal, rather than social, identity. David Harvey defines neoliberalism as "a theory of political economic practices that proposes that human well-being can best be advanced by liberating individual entrepreneurial freedoms and skills within an institutional framework characterized by strong private property rights, free markets, and free trade."[19] Neoliberalism has rearticulated the liberal humanist discourses of individualism and egalitarianism, intensifying the longstanding prioritization of individual freedom and autonomy in US culture and harnessing these discourses to free market logics.[20] This shift has led to the development of the discourse of colorblindness, which valorizes the idea of "not seeing race" and conflates the obscuration of difference with the achievement of racial equality. Colorblindness, while doing little to remove structural causes of inequality, allows racial disparities to be explained through nonracial mechanisms that focus on individual shortcomings, rather than systemic inequalities. Refracted through the lens of neoliberalism, racial identity has been divorced from politics, histories of oppression, and economic opportunities and transformed into an individual characteristic.[21] Race has effectively become "privatized," shifted from the public to the private realm of social life. Neoliberal racial discourses inhibit political uses of race while encouraging "citizens to 'do' race through market consumption and interpersonal relationships."[22] Rather than being a legitimate basis for political action or collective identity, racial difference becomes "emptied out and resignified as cultural commodities indicating mere 'lifestyles,'" as racial and ethnic identities become recast as simply niche markets or taste cultures.[23]

While it is still possible to acknowledge race in a superficial way, using race to assert collective identity or to articulate group demands "violates the cherished notion that as a nation we recognize the rights of individuals rather than group rights."[24] Racism and discrimination have become "problems to be confronted *only* at an individual level."[25] Thus, policies meant to ameliorate racial inequalities can now be opposed because they are "group based" rather than "case by case."[26] Race is understood as an insignificant social force and reframed as a "category at odds with an individualistic embrace of formal legal rights."[27]

Starting in the 1980s, neoliberalism attacked all forms of social solidarity. Framing collectivity as a problem, it instead asserted the importance of "individualism, private property, personal responsibility, and family values."[28] Neoliberalism imbricated individualism with market logics, redefining individual freedom as synonymous with the freedom to compete in the market. Consequently, "Any political movement that holds individual freedom to be sacrosanct [has become] vulnerable to incorporation into the neoliberal fold."[29] Thus, neoliberal individualism has been central to reimagining race in the post–Civil Rights era. Civil Rights Movement language and discourses—such as Martin Luther King Jr.'s admonition that people should be judged "not by the color of their skin, but by the content of their character"—have been rearticulated by conservative forces as mantras of neoliberal individualism. Imbricated with a prioritization of individual freedom and autonomy, the egalitarianism advocated by King has been transformed into a means of sustaining white privilege and power in seemingly race-neutral ways.[30]

The obscuration of structural racism and the individualization of race, racism, and racial identity have resulted in a variety of discourses that allow Americans to understand racial issues as the result of nonracial mechanisms. Colorblindness conceals the role of race in structuring our social world and explains events and patterns using any cause possible other than race.[31] Such nonracial explanations usually have their roots in core beliefs of US national identity, such as like meritocracy and rugged individualism. Notions that Americans can "pull themselves up by their bootstraps" and earn success through hard work recast racial inequalities as the result of individual failures.[32] These supposed individual shortcomings on the part of people of color are often seen as deficiencies that they themselves can rectify simply by working hard, being respectful, and always having their "superior humanity on display for whites to observe."[33]

But even as the space to acknowledge and challenge racism has been eroded, racial inequalities have not. Americans of color born and raised after the sociopolitical movements of the mid-twentieth century are told that their quality of life and access to opportunity are better than that of previous generations.[34] White Americans increasingly deny the very existence of racism, even going so far as to claim that they are now a victimized population.[35] Yet, only 67 percent of "Hispanic" Americans over the age of twenty-five have high school degrees,[36] compared with 93 percent of white Americans, 89 percent of Asian Americans, and 88 percent of Black Americans. Less than 50 percent of Native American students graduate from high school.[37] The median adjusted income for Black and "Hispanic" households is $28,000 below white households and $34,000 below Asian American households. Both Black and "Hispanic" Americans are twice as likely as whites to be poor, and one in four Native

American and Alaska Natives live in poverty. The Black unemployment rate is double and the "Hispanic" unemployment rate one and half times that of whites.[38] Of Natives living on tribal lands, the unemployment rate is near 50 percent.[39] Both Black and "Hispanic" populations are significantly overrepresented in the US prison population.[40] Though data shows Asian Americans meet or outperform whites when it comes to education, employment, and income, when this demographic is broken out by subgroups, it is clear that this prosperity is not evenly distributed. Household incomes of Burmese ($36,000), Nepalese ($43,500), Hmong ($48,000), and Bangladeshi ($49,800) are near or below those of Black and Hispanic Americans. Unemployment for Asian Americans in the aggregate is 3.6 percent—lower than white (4.5 percent), "Hispanic" (7.2 percent), and Black (10.3 percent). However, unemployment for Hmong and the Burmese is 28.3 percent and 35 percent, respectively.[41] Simultaneously, highly visible high-achieving people of color such as Barack Obama, are held up as examples of the success possible for those who work hard and make "good" personal choices.[42]

The discursive constraints created by neoliberal racial paradigms around issues of race were clearly illustrated by many of the responses to the tragic shooting at Emanuel AME Church in Charleston, South Carolina in 2015. On Wednesday, June 17, Dylann Roof attended a Bible study in the historic Black church, at the end of which he murdered nine people. According to a survivor, Roof explicitly stated that he was there to "shoot Black people," and during the executions, he said, "I have to do it. You rape our women, and you're taking over our country. And you have to go."[43] Within twenty-four hours, images emerged of Roof posing with a gun and the Confederate battle flag and of him wearing a jacket bearing the former flags of South Africa and Rhodesia, both symbols of white colonialist domination. As the country dealt with the tragedy, the national discourse grappled with how to understand this overtly racist act through the interpretive lens of colorblindness.

The following day, several elected officials and political commentators proffered a colorblind explanation of the massacre, seemingly seizing on any nonracial explanation for Roof's actions. Several conservative politicians, such as South Carolina Senator Lindsey Graham, suggested anti-Christian sentiment as the reason for the murders. Similarly, the morning show *Fox and Friends* and television personality Elizabeth Hasselbeck both referred to the shootings as an "attack on faith." As time passed, Roof's racist motivation became undeniable and colorblindness became an unworkable interpretive framework, the analysis shifted to reassert race and racism as individual, not collective, traits. Roof was cast as an *individual* racist who was unrepresentative of the larger culture. *Fox News* personality Bill O'Reilly minimized the impact of the ideologies Roof professed, calling Roof a "sick terrorist" and an "idiot," who "represents ooo.1% [sic] of the population." His guest, *Fox News* contributor Juan Williams, pointed to discussions about white supremacy as "cheap rhetoric," which was "taking advantage of a very emotional and upsetting moment in America." These sentiments permeated *Fox News*'s coverage and were not limited to the conservative-leaning news channel.

While the aftermath of the Charleston massacre is a heightened example, it illustrates the sociocultural context Americans of color must struggle with daily. From police brutality and racial profiling to day-to-day microaggressions, people of color are faced with navigating a society so heavily invested in obscuring racism that the clearly stated racial motives of a self-proclaimed white supremacist are viewed with skepticism. Within this sociocultural context, merely making structural racism visible is a significant challenge, as racial discourses keep power structures intact by limiting possibilities for critique.[44]

Neoliberalism and Technological Ambivalence

Thus, fighting racial oppression in the contemporary neoliberal context requires strategies for making race and racism visible, not merely as an individual trait, but in ways that refuse the erasure of the collective racial categories that profoundly shape our social lives. Media can be a potent terrain for such endeavors. Lori Kido Lopez demonstrates how Asian American media activists are engaging with media industries and creating independent media as a means of claiming both Asian American collective identity and cultural citizenship. She argues:

> Asian American media activists view cultural citizenship as a collective endeavor that cannot be accomplished at the level of the individual. This pushes back against assumptions that our neoliberal media landscape is inexorably moving citizenship toward the individual, and opens up space

for exploring the way that Asian Americans in particular are using media to create networks of cultural citizenship that seek to impact their broader community. . . . This perspective on the way that Asian Americans are responding to media representations also serves to challenge a ubiquitous postracial media discourse that insists upon race as merely an individual quality.[45]

Digital media are often praised as potential spaces for resistance, counter-discourse production, and the dissemination of alternative information. Much has been written about the possibilities of digital and social media for allowing marginalized users to bypass traditional media outlets and to create and circulate their own content.[46] Convergence culture has led to the blurring of distinctions between media producers and consumers and given users more control over how they interact with media.[47] Digital networks facilitate the spread of media content, and social media allow for a range of peripheral participation that includes users' roles in sharing, and thereby curating, media content.[48]

Despite the undeniable possibilities created by digital media technologies, their potential is tempered by the ways neoliberal discourses have impacted the development of technology. André Brock has pointed to the ways that the internet is "constrained by the values of individualism and articulations of 'color-blind' ideology."[49] This is in large part because neoliberalism and its attendant form of individualism were central in shaping the development and growth of digital media technologies and creating a digital and social media landscape that emphasizes the individual and reproduces colorblind discourses. Thus, despite digital media's potential to provide a space for the experiences of people of color, such media are still shaped by the same logics that silence and erase those experiences. Consequently, using them to construct counter-discourses around race is not an uncomplicated endeavor.

The same neoliberal discourses that reshaped US racial paradigms have also been important in the development of digital technologies, helping shape the fundamental organizing logic of digital media. Neoliberalism was integral to technological development, yielding digital media architectures and modes of sociality that bear the marks of neoliberal discourses. Thus, these racial discourses map comfortably onto digital networks because normative imagined affordances replicate larger social formations.

Technological development was shaped by neoliberal values. Wendy Chun argues that the personal computer has been central to the process of "individualization and personalization" and that the development of user-friendly interfaces has been important in "empowering and creating 'productive individuals'" in line with neoliberal ideals.[50] The internet became mainstream in the 1990s, concurrent with the solidification of neoliberalism as the dominant discourse in the United States.[51] Neoliberal individualism was a key force in the development of the internet in this period, both technologically and discursively, and the "California Ideology" that emerged among Silicon Valley tech developers embraced the free-market entrepreneurialism and of neoliberalism.[52] Neoliberal impulses to privatize led to the strengthening and expansion of intellectual property rights with a focus on online piracy and the creation of digital rights management technology.[53] In the twenty-first century, neoliberal individualism has been an important element in shaping social media platforms. Alice Marwick's ethnographic study of the California tech scene highlights how it embraces neoliberal individualism and adheres to neoliberal philosophies of deregulation and free-market economic policies.[54] The affordances intended by the designers and therefore reflected in the materiality and functionality of the social media platforms developed in this milieu have been shaped by this value system and have thereby allowed for the infiltration of market logics into everyday digital social relations.[55]

Digital media sociality has also developed to foreground the individual, allowing neoliberal individualism and related racial discourses to graft easily onto social media networks. Scholars such as Lee Rainie and Barry Wellman have argued that digital, social, and mobile media have facilitated and accelerated a shift away from clearly bounded groups or communities to loose and shifting networks of individuals, a phenomenon they've termed "networked individualism."[56] Instead of the group being the center of social life, the autonomous individual is at the center as she reaches across geographical and temporal distances to form complex networks with others around similar interests or beliefs. Marwick argues that "social media is intrinsically focused on individuals" and that the organizing logic of user-generated content "models ideal neoliberal selves" and "rewards those who adopt such subjectivities."[57] When it comes to the use of social media for politics and activism, Lance Bennett and Alexandra Sergerberg have noted a similar move away from collective logics—with their reliance on collective identities—to "connective" logics that are based on "personalized content sharing across media networks."[58] Thus, the prioritization of the individual is inscribed into the very structure of our digitally mediated interactions.

Within the paradigms of both networked individualism and contemporary racial discourses, race can be reduced to a personal characteristic around which an individual user can shape her network. Black users might create predominantly Black networks or networks that explicitly center on race, but without these being necessarily indicative of the existence of any community or collective identity. Racial identity instead functions more akin to a taste culture than a sociocultural group, reconstituted in a way that is compatible with individualist market-driven logics.

Moreover, notions of virtual disembodiment that suffused late twentieth-century technocultural discourses aligned closely with discourses of colorblindness. In the 1990s, technological utopians argued that digital interactions could lead to a new era of increased democracy and the obsolescence of power hierarchies based on identity categories as users "cross-dressed" and played with identity, leaving their bodies and thereby their embodied identities behind.[59] In 1996, responding to such rhetoric, Kalí Tal provocatively asserted, "In cyberspace, it is finally possible to completely and utterly disappear people of color." She argued that obscuring corporeal markers allows discussions of the internet to "elide questions of race" and reinforce whiteness as normative.[60] Such erasure was demonstrated quite clearly by Lisa Nakamura's ethnographic work on the text-based virtual world LambdaMOO. Nakamura argues that in the absence of corporeal signifiers of race, users were assumed to be white unless otherwise specified—an assumption that effectively reaffirmed whiteness as the invisible unmarked norm. Additionally, she noted that though participants were seemingly able to create any virtual embodiment they desired, this was largely an illusion. Participants of color who constructed their characters in racial terms were received with hostility for bringing the "divisive" issue of race into the digital space.[61] Only performances of race that reified longstanding racial stereotypes, reinforcing rather than challenging racial hierarchies, were accepted.[62]

Tal and Nakamura were writing of the early text-based internet. With its limited graphics capabilities, users were required to literally write their identities into existence via text. Today, the increased prevalence of images and videos online, while still making it possible to obscure identity markers, reinserts the body back into online interactions in ways that change the racial dynamics of digital spaces. However, though corporeal signifiers of race are more visible than on the text-based web and racialized bodies may have gained visibility via Instagram, Vine, YouTube, and other such platforms, the construction of race as a personal trait rather than social category allows colorblindness to continue to function without necessitating the disappearance of racialized bodies.

Users of color seeking to intervene in dominant racial discourses via these technologies must find ways to negotiate this terrain, a task that is often deeply ambivalent and rarely uncomplicated. For example, Lopez notes that while Asian American YouTube celebrities use the platform to create media that "renders Asian American identities legible and disseminates Asian American narratives and voices" that are rarely represented in legacy media, despite their contributions to the overall visibility that is at the center of claims for cultural citizenship, these creators are motivated more by the desire for individual personal success than for social change. Careful not to alienate any of their core audience with anything too controversial, they largely avoid explicitly addressing race or even Asian American identity.[63] As such, these creators employ what Ralina Joseph has termed "strategic ambiguity" as a means of resisting discrimination within the codes of neoliberal colorblindness. This involves "foregrounding crossover appeal, courting multiple publics, speaking in coded language, and smoothing and soothing fears of difference as simply an incidental side note." Thus, the "failure to *name* racism" is used to claim inclusion. While Joseph frames strategic ambiguity as a means of achieving individual success, she asserts it is not "simply the safe choice," but "a subtle form of resistance that balances on an escape hatch of deniability" and that allows the oppressed to "gradually chip away at hegemony" while seeming to acquiesce to it.[64] Lopez asserts that, despite their personal entrepreneurial approach and conservative approach to issues of race and identity, the Asian American YouTube celebrities she analyzes still contribute to "the larger project of Asian American media activism and a collective form of cultural citizenship" through their collaboration with and cultivation of Asian American audiences. These audiences not only makes Asian Americans intelligible in the larger media landscape, but also do so in a way that reifies Asian American identity, a collective and politicized identity that did not exist before the 1970s, prior to which Asian immigrants identifyed with their individual ethic identities.[65]

Though less interrogated than visual media, sound technologies have also historically worked to reify colorblindness in the United States. While race is associated with the visual, Jennifer Stoever's work on the sonic color line details the aural equivalent to the white gaze, the listening ear. She demonstrates that whiteness is in part an auditory construction, constituted through sonic markers and "sounded exclusions."[66] She details the role sound played in the racial regimes of the nineteenth and early twentieth centuries as Americans were disciplined to "'match' certain sounds, voices, and [sonic] environments to visual markers of race." Stoever asserts that radio was particularly important in the emergence of colorblindness, because during its Golden Age it was "uniquely suited to make the optics of race disappear through omission." However, as with colorblindness writ large, this served only to obscure, rather than undo, racial discrimination. The racialization of sound "continued to make the abstraction of race *palpable*—both blackness and whiteness—even when it could no longer officially be 'seen,'" and this in turn allowed "conservative, liberal, *and* progressive whites a method of continuing to perceive race and enact discrimination without *seeming* to do so."[67] The recognition of aural signifiers of race continues in digital terrains, as demonstrated by Kishonna Gray's work on linguistic profiling on Xbox Live.[68] Podcasts—as both sound media and products of the networked digital landscape—are doubly embedded in the logics of neoliberal colorblindness.

However, despite the imprint of neoliberalism on digital architecture and modes of sociality, digital networks are discursive formations as much as they are technological ones. Thus, though users of color exist within the technological structures that promote networked individualism as the primary social "operating system," these users can program their digital and social media spaces with cultural logics and communicative strategies that negotiate and, to varying degrees, resist neoliberal regimes of race and technology.

Black Americans, Race, and Technology

The network at the center of this project draws on traditions of Black expressive culture, cultural production, and sociality to reimagine the affordances of digital technologies in ways that negotiate and sometimes resist normative imagined affordances and the way they reinscribe neoliberal logics of race. Black American users are particularly adept at such reimaginings because much of Black epistemology, communicative practices, and aesthetics have characteristics that are well-suited to digital terrains, though with different underlying logics. Black culturally inflected imagined affordances have the potential to create a networked space that resists and undermines dominant neoliberal racial discourses—particularly individualism and colorblindness—despite how those discourses are endemic to the normative imagined affordances of technologies.

Technological adoption and innovation has long been part of Black cultural practice, and many Black epistemologies and expressive cultures closely mirror those of contemporary digital culture. This is perhaps because, as Marisa Parham argues, there "is something endemic or inherent to diasporic experience itself that reproduces some of the technical structure of what we otherwise call the digital"; in other words, "Black diasporic existence is a digitizing experience."[69] The people of the African Diaspora developed many of the philosophical orientations and expressive practices associated with digital culture at least a century before digital technologies existed. Because of the trauma of enslavement, Black Americans developed many of the theoretical concerns associated with postmodernism as early as the nineteenth century, producing intellectual frameworks that closely resemble those of European thinkers such as Jean-François Lyotard and Jacques Derrida.[70] Thus, as Tal observes, Black critical theorists were grappling with "the problem of multiple identities, fragmented personae, and liminality," anticipating the major theoretical questions of the digital age by over a century. By the twentieth century, Black thinkers had already long grappled with the problems raised by the emerging digital landscapes. She points to W.

E. B. DuBois's concept of double-consciousness and the work of Black intellectuals such as Henry Louis Gates Jr. and Toni Morrison as offering fruitful paradigms for analyzing the digital.[71]

Further, Black communicative practices and expressive cultures are well suited to digital environments. Catherine Knight Steele notes how the historic importance of orality in Black American culture aligns with the secondary orality—that emerges from and is dependent upon literate culture and writing—that characterizes patterns of online communication. Electronic media signaled a shift back to orality in the dominant US culture, and that shift intensified with the internet. The "additive, redundant, and polychromic nature" of blogs and social media are hallmarks of the ongoing importance of orality online. Thus, Steele argues, "Given the continuing significance of orality among those of African descent, it is not surprising that African Americans readily participate in social networking and blogging."[72] Moreover, Black Americans who participate in such digital spaces already possess longstanding and sophisticated strategies for communication grounded in the logics of orality.

Moreover, for centuries, Black Americans have cultivated complex processes of cultural expression grounded in principles that have become central to digital media use. Participation, remediation, and bricolage, hallmarks of digital cultures, have historically been central to the expressive cultures of Black American communities.[73] Black American musical traditions are an illustrative example. In Black American communities, music has always functioned as a participatory group activity with a fluid boundary between performer and audience, who were expected to engage and contribute.[74] Repetition, revision, and recontextualization have always been integral to Black musical genres like jazz and Hip-hop.[75] Thus, Black cultures have long been characterized by the participatory impulse attributed to contemporary convergence culture and the recombinant meaning-making processes central to digital vernaculars like memes.[76] Parham, who describes turntablism as an example of these predigital practices, asserts that early Hip-hop pioneers found ways to make an analog technology behave as if it were digital.[77]

It stands to reason that Black Americans would be innovators in digital environments that facilitate these communicative and expressive strategies. However, while Black American practices may be congruous with the materiality and functionality of the technologies they use and may even resemble normative practices, they are often grounded in epistemologies, assumptions, and intentions that differ from and even directly conflict with the understandings and intentions of designers. Thus, the imagined affordances produced in the network discussed here work to reaffirm Black subjectivities, validate Black experiences, and enable forms of Black sociality that resist the ways dominant racial paradigms are reproduced by emerging media technologies. Given that Black American cultures have, over the course of centuries, developed complex practices of participatory creativity, remediation, and remix, the culturally specific and historically grounded modes of interaction and meaning-making that Black users bring to their online practices are particularly well suited to digitally networked contexts. While digital cultures produced by hegemonic whiteness often deploy such practices in ways that reproduce networked individualism, connective logics, and a colorblind erasure of race, Black users in this network employ similar practices, but with different underlying logics of community, collectivity, and color-consciousness.

This book explores the strategies through which Black users of digital networks deploy norms and cultural practices that allow them to contest the rearticulation of race and racism as merely individual personal phenomena. They resist colorblindness and instead foreground and celebrate complex and heterogeneous Blackness. Drawing on longstanding traditions of Black media-making, expressive culture, and communicative practices, these users contest dominant racial discourses and claim the networked space to replicate and circulate Black epistemologies.

The Network

This book focuses on a digital assemblage comprised of three overlapping but distinct elements—a large informal network of Black podcasters, the independent media company This Week in Blackness (TWiB!), and the related subgroup of the predominantly Black network of Twitter users known as "Black Twitter." These serve as core communicative sites for the network, but do not comprise its entirety. Users also employed platforms such as Instagram, Facebook, Vine, YouTube, Google+, email, and instant messaging. Thus, I do not limit my analysis to the three core elements, but have used them to anchor and establish the parameters of my research. Below, I briefly describe each of these three constitutive components of the network.

In recent years, Black podcasting has flourished. When I began this project in 2012, my searches yielded only about ten Black produced podcasts. Between 2012 and 2014, there grew to be more than I could keep track of. By the time *Serial*, the podcast that is credited with kicking of the current podcast boom, debuted in October 2014, Black podcasters were already well ahead of the trend. Because I seek to analyze a specific transplatform network, however, I limit my project to podcasts that are part of the specific network I analyze here. This narrows my focus to a collection of independent podcasts based in the United States, which have some sustained interaction with one another and with the other elements of the network examined in this project.

For this reason, I do not include podcasts that are not independent, that have no sustained relationship to the larger network, or that began in 2015 or later. By "independent," I mean podcasts that are not produced by a media company or created by an established legacy media personality.[78] Thus, I do not include *The Combat Jack Show*, which began in 2010 and was a pioneering podcast, or *The Read* because they are properties of The Loud Speaker Network.[79] Similarly, I exclude *Two Dope Queens* and *Another Round* because they are produced by WNYC and Buzzfeed, respectively, and because they have no consistent connection to the other elements of the network examined here. Given my focus on US racial politics and US-produced podcasts, Canadian-based *Chonilla*, a popular and long-running podcast, also falls outside the scope of the study. The parameters of the study result in a predominantly male cohort of podcasters, though Black women do have a prominent voice. While there is a sizable number of LGBTQ people in the audience and the network more broadly, with a few exceptions, the podcast hosts skew strongly straight and cisgender. If I were I seeking to do a series of case studies of Black-run podcasts, I would have a more inclusive selection of shows. Because I seek to focus on interconnected networks, many such podcasts were excluded—a fact that is worth noting and that represents a limitation to this research.

Some of the first podcasts in the network I study—*Blacking It Up!* (now *TWiB! Prime*), *Insanity Check*, *The Black Guy Who Tips*, and *Where's My 40 Acres?*—began between 2008 and 2010. All of the podcasts in the network produce talk-based programming, though they vary greatly in their production value and the regularity of their output. The podcasts range in size from *TWiB! Prime*, the flagship podcast of This Week in Blackness, which averaged between 1 and 1.5 million downloads a month by 2015, to smaller shows with audiences in the hundreds. This network of podcasters is held together by informal affiliations and reinforced by social media interactions. The podcasters frequently collaborate and share heavily overlapping fan bases. However, the network is neither monolithic nor univocal.

Three of the oldest podcasts in the network—*Insanity Check, The Black Guy Who Tips*, and *Where's My 40 Acres?*—used the term "Chitlin' Circuit" as early as 2010 to describe their then-small cohort of Black podcasters, and I use it to refer to the podcasts discussed in this book as well. The podcasters' choice of this term reveals much about how they conceptualized their practices. During the era of segregation, the name "Chitlin' Circuit" referred to venues that allowed Black musicians, comedians, and actors to perform, and it continues to be used by some comedy clubs and theaters that market themselves for Black audiences. While the term "Chitlin' Circuit" had largely fallen out of use among these podcasters by 2015, I have chosen to retain it because of its historical connotations. It positions the podcasts and their audiences in a long history of racial exclusion and resistance and highlights the legacy of Black entertainers creating for Black audiences outside of the white gaze. Additionally, the word "circuit" emphasizes the paths along which materials travel, making the term appropriate for describing the digitally networked nature of these podcasters and their audiences.

The second anchoring point of my analysis is the independent media company This Week in Blackness. While TWiB!'s primary content is podcasts—thereby imbricating it with the Chitlin' Circuit podcasts described above—it produces a range of other media and also serves as a professional news organization, making it distinct from the other Black podcasters discussed in this book. White started TWiB! as a web video series in 2008, and by the end of 2015 TWiB! had grown into a multimedia company producing the original video series, seven different podcasts, a blog-style website, and an eight-episode run of *A Black Show* for Free Speech TV.

TWiB! also differs from the other podcasts in its connections to both large-scale corporate news media and independent progressive media outlets. White has made appearances on MSNBC, CNN, Al Jazeera, and Current TV and written for the *Huffington Post*, *Salon*, the *Root*, and the *Grio*. Other TWiB! personnel, such as Gandy and L. Joy Williams, maintain professional connections to political and activist organizations. Thus, TWiB! forms an important point of articulation between the digital network at the center of this book and established legacy media, mainstream politics, and activist organizations.

The final focal point of my analysis is Twitter, specifically a subset of the network that has come to be known as "Black Twitter." Black Twitter can be thought of as a meta-network, comprised of smaller subnetworks that emerge from interpersonal connections and shared interests.[80] Black Twitter has evolved into a dense and active network that has been leveraged to mobilize users around various political and cultural issues.[81] It has also become an important resource in circulating information and mobilizing political action in recent years. It was a key force in bringing Trayvon Martin's death into the national news cycle, and, as Martin's death and the subsequent acquittal of his killer became galvanizing moments, Black Twitter emerged as an important element of the movement commonly referred to as "Black Lives Matter." In fact, the iconic hashtag #BlackLivesMatter was created by Alicia Garza, Patrisse Cullors, and Opal Tometi in response to the acquittal of Martin's killer.

The Black Twitter network is too vast to be fully addressed here. Thus, I limit my purview to subsections of the network that are in some way connected to the podcasts discussed above or to TWiB!. This includes the podcasters, their listeners, their guests, and those with who they interact in publicly available social media. Many of the podcasters, such as White and Gandy from *TWiB! Prime* and Rod Morrow from *TBGWT*, are also high-profile participants in the Black Twitter meta-network. They have significant visibility because of their high follower count and have often been responsible for creating hashtags that organize conversations within the larger Black Twitter network. Additionally, this visibility has allowed their Twitter accounts to serve as points of articulation between the network and those outside it, including media industries, politicians, and advocacy and activist groups.

Black podcasters and their listeners sit at the intersection of two groups that use social media, particularly Twitter, at higher rates than the general population. Podcast listeners spend more time online and engage with social media more than nonlisteners.[82] Similarly, Black Americans have higher rates of social media use on many platforms. While 23 percent of all internet users and 21 percent of white internet users are on Twitter, 27 percent of Black internet users are on the platform.[83] In the eighteen-to-twenty-nine year-old demographic most likely to listen to podcasts, 40 percent of Black users are on Twitter, compared to 28 percent of their white peers.[84]

Additionally, Twitter functions as a central clearinghouse to circulate materials posted on other platforms. Users rely on Twitter to share and circulate links to blog posts and news coverage as well as posts on Instagram, Tumblr, Facebook, and Vine. It is standard practice for podcasters to tweet links to their latest episodes. Thus, in many ways Twitter serves as a hub connecting the three anchoring elements of the network to each other and to other social media platforms.

In many ways, this network is an iteration of the participatory media-making that characterizes the contemporary digital landscape—as people express their frustration with or resistance to mainstream corporate media through more independent and collaborative media creation.[85] It has become common for communities and social networks to form through and around such media. YouTube, for example, has long been a site for participatory culture, with users "contributing content, referring to, building on and critiquing each other's videos, as well as collaborating" and using the interactive commenting features to build community.[86] Similarly, independent online content creators often use social media networks to connect with current and potential audiences and to generate support for their projects.[87] While the network explored in this project does integrate content creation with interactive affordances and social media platforms, it did not coalesce around the content creators nor does it operate primarily in the service of audience creation and content circulation. In 2010, when my analysis begins, TWiB! and a handful of podcasts were the only content creators in the network. The majority of the podcasts began between 2012 and 2014, and many of these podcasters attribute their interactions in the network with inspiring them to become creators themselves.

The network combines much of the ethos of noncommercial community-based media with the practices, though not always the intentions, of entrepreneurial media creators. With its emphasis on creating a Black cultural space, the network falls within the tradition of what Clemencia Rodríguez has termed "citizens' media," which she defines as a collective enactment of citizenship that seeks to actively intervene and transform the established mediascape by contesting social codes, legitimized identities, and institutionalized social relations in ways that empower the community involved.[88] The network at the center of this book combines this underlying ethos with the interactive transplatform practices of creators of SME and other aspirational uses of digital media. Some participants in the network, particularly TWiB! and some of the more visible Twitter micro-celebrities, fall more on the entrepreneurial end of this spectrum. But across the entirety of the network, the goal diverges from neoliberal practices that are common among SME and other digital content creators.

While Cunningham and Craig's description of SME captures the transplatform nature of the network discussed here and points to the same kinds of conflation of content production and sociality, they focus mainly on SME as a developing industry and its relationship to capitalist media markets. They understand SME as a "huge experiment in seeking to convert vernacular or informal creativity into talent and content increasingly attractive to advertisers and brands."[89] They point to a recurring career trajectory from hobbyist to professional among SME creators. However, many of the participants in the network analyzed here, particularly among the Chitlin' Circuit podcasts, have not pursued such a transition, and those who have, such as TWiB! and some Twitter micro-celebrities, have done so in ways that overlap heavily with SME but do not fully share emphasis on entrepreneurialism. Additionally, while SME entails the absorption of social networks into the creation of mass media–like entertainment, the network at the center of this project uses mass media–style content creation as part of sociality. The broadcast-style content operates as both media text and utterance within ongoing social interactions.

As a result, many theorizations of digital labor—such as venture labor, hope labor, and aspirational labor, in which unpaid and underpaid labor are common—cannot fully explicate this network's dynamics.

Though each is distinct, these forms of labor all emerge from neoliberal discourses that prioritize individual self-expression, self-branding, self-sufficiency and shift risk from the employer to the individual.[90] Additionally, they share a forward-looking orientation, in which productive work is undertaken with the anticipation that it will yield future professional or financial benefits. While the forms of labor that power this network's content production are often un- or under-compensated, they frequently lack the temporal orientation of the above forms of digital labor. Further, when participants in the network do undertake creative labor with the intention of generating a future benefit, individual aspirations are inextricably bound with collective benefit. They engage in this labor with the hope of personal success *and* of doing something positive for Black people in general.

While scholars of online cultural production have highlighted the ways that creators utilize the interactive affordances of various platforms, these discussions have been largely limited to asynchronous interactivity. Lopez writes of the comment function of YouTube as a place that allows the audience's ideas to coexist with that of the creator.[91] Even Cunningham and Craig's description of SME is focused largely on interactivity that does not take place in real time. They conclude their book by predicting the rise of a new phase of SME, enabled by "synchronous interactivity between social media users appearing in and commenting on video."[92] Here again, the network discussed here has been ahead of the curve. TWiB! and many of the Chitlin' Circuit podcasts avail themselves of various platform affordances that allow real-time participation from their audience, often by cobbling together platforms that are used simultaneously.

Finally, though this book focuses on Black Americans, the network discussed here articulates and interacts with larger global networks. Black Twitter, in particular, includes a significant number of users from Africa and across the African Diaspora. Further, these transnational networks often function as spaces for solidarity between Black Americans and the Global South. Throughout the twentieth century, Black American radical movements in the United States formed alliances with anticolonial movements across the Global South. This solidarity was predicated on an understanding of a shared source of oppression—namely, imperialism and colonialism.[93] Such transnational solidarity can be seen in the connection between the Movement for Black Lives and Palestine. In the mid-twentieth century the Black Power movement—including the Student Nonviolent Coordinating Committee and the Black Panther Party—aligned with Palestinians, viewing the Israeli/Palestinian conflict through an anti-imperialist and antiracist framework. Contemporaneously, when unrest spread across Ferguson in August 2014 and police began to teargas protestors, Twitter users in Palestine tweeted both messages of support and practical advice on coping with tear gas. During the Ferguson October protests that followed that year, a group of Palestinians traveled to Ferguson to participate, marking their actions via social media and protests signs with the hashtag #Palestine-2Ferguson. There they were welcomed by the Organization for Black Struggle (OBS) because of the ongoing work of the St. Louis Palestine Solidarity Committee (STL-PSC).[94] These transnational relationships, while not explored in depth here, should be kept in mind as part of the broader context in which this network operates.

Methodology and Terminology

This book is based on thousands of hours of podcast listening and on participation in social media networks between 2010 and 2016. I ground my analysis in podcasts, videos, blogs, and social media timelines as well as in ethnographic data drawn from participant observation and interviewing. I have worked closely with TWiB! since 2012 and have spent a week with the company in-studio in Brooklyn in March 2013 and at its Berkeley studio in March 2014. I also attended Netroots Nation, an annual progressive grassroots organizing conference, with TWiB! from 2013 to 2016 and traveled with the company as it covered the 2016 Democratic National Convention in Philadelphia.

Though I am a long-time fan who has participated in the network as it has grown, as a white woman operating in this explicitly Black social space, I remain an outsider in ways that implicate my work within a troubling history of white scholars writing about Black cultural practices. My whiteness brings with it a number of ethical issues I have attempted to address through a self-reflexive methodology and a collaborative relationship with those I write about, including providing them with drafts for feedback prior to publication. In the appendix, I have outlined these ethical concerns and the collaborative methods I employed. My choice to place this discussion in the appendix derives from my efforts to navigate these ethical challenges. This network is a Black space, and my participation is contingent on my understanding and accepting that my perspectives, communicative norms, and opinions will not be prioritized. While I do not deny, nor do I wish to obscure, the complex ways that subjectivity and positionality function in my research, I also seek here to honor a very simple core tenet: this is not about me. Though I believe in the value of highly situated and reflexive research, I have chosen to foreground the voices and practices of the participants in this network and relegate my methodological reflections to the periphery of this text.

In seeking to foreground the voices of the members of this network, I have made several representational choices. First, I use the term "Black," which I capitalize, rather than "African American." This choice mirrors a preference for the term "Black" within the network I am writing about. Further, when I mention someone by name, it should be presumed that he or she is of African descent unless otherwise specified. In dominant US culture, whiteness is invisible, and individuals are presumed to be white unless otherwise specified. I invert this hegemonic norm, and, because the network is an explicitly Black space, take Blackness as normative. I indicate an individual's race in only two situations: (1) when the person is not of African descent and (2) when the person has asked to be identified in a specific way, as when a biracial person who is Black and Native American prefers to be identified as such.

Second, I use direct quotations whenever possible to highlight the voices of the participants in the network. In doing so, I am faced with orthographic choices about how to represent speech. Many of the individuals I quote use a vernacular, and I have opted not to change their language to conform to Standard English. I retain the original grammatical structures and elements of pronunciation, particularly the shortening of multisyllabic words (such as "e'rybody" as the pronunciation of "everybody") or when speakers leave the letter "g" off of the end of words. However, because this is not a linguistic study, I do not attempt to capture accents, tonal inflections, or other such elements. Additionally, for the sake of clarity, I have removed vocalized pauses (such as "um" and "uh") and stutters or false starts from some quotations taken from spoken communications, including podcasts and interviews.

I refer to individual users by the names they have chosen to employ online, be that a legal name, a first name only, a pseudonym, or a username. While some of the participants in the network use their legal names, particularly those working for or with TWiB!, the majority use pseudonyms, which are often also their usernames on social media platforms such as Twitter. Frequently, privacy concerns drive the choice to obscure one's identity. Many of the participants in the network have "day jobs" and have employers and colleagues who might not look favorably on the opinions they express or the tone with which they express them. To avoid jeopardizing their livelihoods, they choose to remain identified by only a pseudonym. Additionally, given the frequency and aggressiveness with which marginalized people are harassed online and the increasing commonality with which such harassment follows users into their offline contexts, many of the participants see anonymity, or at least pseudonymity, as important to their personal safety and well-being. Thus, I refer to participants in the network by their chosen public name, adopting their strategy for maintaining their privacy as the standard for this project.

Finally, for the sake of clarity, I distinguish between Black Lives Matter and the Movement for Black Lives. Black Lives Matter is the name of the official organization founded by Alicia Garza, Patrice Cullors, and Opal Tometi. The phrase "Black Lives Matter," was coined by Garza after the 2013 acquittal of George Zimmerman in the death of Trayvon Martin as part of what she called "a love letter to Black people," which she posted on Facebook.[95] Cullors turned the phrase into a hashtag on Twitter, and Garza, Cullors, and Tometi went on to found an organization by that same name. But the phrase and hashtag were relatively unknown until the unrest in 2014 in Ferguson following Mike Brown's death, when local residents, many of whom are now activists but had no prior experience with organizing, took to the streets. The protests initially embraced the chant and hashtag "Hands Up, Don't Shoot," referencing reports that Brown had his hands up at the time he was killed. Gradually, as the protests went on, the phrase "Black Lives Matter" came to more prominence and became a short-hand for the larger ongoing movement that was born in Ferguson.[96] Since then, any contemporary collective of Black people protesting or organizing is now often referred to, particularly in the press, as "Black Lives Matter." However, the movement writ large includes a number of organizations—Black Youth Project 100, the Dream Defenders, the Organization for Black Struggle, Hands Up United, Millennial Activists United, and Lost Voices, to name a few. Other activists who are not affiliated with any organization, often deliberately as a matter of principle, see themselves as part of the movement and are often also referred to as "Black Lives Matter" activists, despite having no connection to the organization.

A fair amount of confusion has ensued as a result. For example, in October 2016, several news outlets reported a meeting between Hillary Clinton and "Black Lives Matter" activists.[97] Members of the Black Lives Matter *organization* made a clear public statement that "Black Lives Matter," meaning *their* organization, did not meet with Clinton.[98] Meanwhile, people who identified as part of the larger movement, who had in fact met with Clinton, responded by asserting they felt excluded by the conflation of the movement and the organization. Members of the broader movement have tried to change the name of the movement to the Movement for Black Lives or revise the acronym BLM to stand for Black Liberation Movement. To avoid confusion here, I refer to the movement as the Movement for Black Lives, reserving Black Lives Matter for the organization of that name.

Structure of the Book

Each chapter illustrates the strategies users in this network deploy to address and navigate the challenges of being Black in the United States in the age of colorblindness. Chapters 1 and 2 focus on mapping the network and foregrounding how participants reimagine the affordances of the technologies they are using. The first chapter outlines the structure of the network and its discursive construction as an explicitly Black space. I argue that its multimedia, transplatform character allows it to function as a "network" in the dual sense of the term—as a broadcast-style network and as a digital social network—making it a flexible, multilayered space in which to negotiate racial discourses. I then analyze an exchange between TWiB!'s White and the Harlem-based Reverend James David Manning to demonstrate how deeply interconnected the elements of the network are and how conversations move across the network via a range of platforms and media.

Chapter 2 argues that the network functions as an oscillating networked public. I draw on the work of Catherine Squires and danah boyd to examine how different affordances of the network allow, and sometimes force, users to shift between creating digitally enabled enclaves and directly debating dominant discourses forwarded by those outside the network. I contextualize the network in the history of Black alternative media production, particularly radio, as well as within the tradition of Black social enclaves such as barber and beauty shops and churches. Because digital media often blur mass and interpersonal communication, these different traditions are intertwined in the context of the network. I argue that the intimate qualities of radio-style audio combined with a conversational style and the use of Black vernaculars and Black cultural commonplaces evoke and reproduce a sense of being in Black social enclaves and allow podcasts to serve as important resources for listeners as they navigate a hostile racial landscape. I then move on to explore moments when the more visible elements of the network, particularly TWiB! and Twitter micro-celebrities, serve a counter-public function to directly challenge mainstream legacy media and elements of the political establishment. I analyze three examples—debates over the racial dynamics of the Occupy Wall Street movement, *Game of Thrones* fandom under the hashtag #DemThrones, and criticism of some of Senator Bernie Sanders's supporters' desire to minimize the importance of racial issues in the candidate's platform during the 2015 presidential primary, expressed by the #BernieSoBlack hashtag. Each example demonstrates how the participants exploit or work around platform design and functionality to shift the network between enclave and counter-public.

Chapters 3 and 4 then examine how this transplatform digital assemblage gets utilized in specific situations or in response to specific exigencies, with particular attention to the discursive work that takes place in the network. Chapter 3 examines roles of memory and history in the network. Remembering is never an end in its own right; rather, it is a means of asserting power, legitimizing social relations, and validating political traditions.[99] Because it is generally the powerful in a society who make the choices about what is remembered and what is forgotten, the dominant US history has been constructed in ways that generally leave the mechanisms of racial oppression intact, ensuring their continuation while asserting their disappearance. This chapter explores how participants in the network actively resist these dominant historical narratives and reassert accounts of the past that highlight ongoing racial oppression and resistance. I examine how the TWiB! podcast *Historical Blackness* hosted by Dr. Blair L. M. Kelley uses history as a resource for reinterpreting the present in ways that undermine dominant racial discourses. The remainder of the chapter then focuses on complex ways in which the legacy of Martin Luther King Jr. is deployed for neoliberal political ends. The network has developed three metaphors to encapsulate these strategies—the idea of "MLK fan fic," MLK as Pokémon, and MLK as the "Big Joker" in the card game Spades. The chapter concludes with a discussion of how King has been invoked to condemn the tactics of the Movement for Black Lives and how the movement has reclaimed and re-remembered King in ways that position its members as the inheritors of his legacy.

While the events of Ferguson in the summer of 2014 sparked the national protest out of which the Movement for Black Lives emerged, the digital and social media networks that became of great importance to the movement coalesced years earlier. It was the death of Trayvon Martin in 2012 and the subsequent acquittal of his killer in 2013 that prompted existing Black digital networks to deploy their connections around political issues. Chapter 4 explores the role these networks played at moments of racial trauma, particularly the Zimmerman acquittal, the death of Mike Brown, and the subsequent unrest in Ferguson. I argue that the flexible, malleable character of the network allowed it to be deployed for a number of simultaneous, overlapping, yet distinct activities, including creating community and solidarity through catharsis and collective grieving, circulating oppositional interpretations of events, organizing responses and political engagement, and both bypassing and directly intervening in mainstream corporate media narratives.

Finally, I conclude with a brief discussion of the radical changes that have taken place since mid-2016, several months before the presidential election, when I stopped gathering data. Since then, many of the phenomena I analyze have shifted dramatically. In the conclusion, I explore the current state of colorblindness, including the changes to the dominant racial discourse that seem to be underway. I then address the decreased visibility of the Movement for Black Lives. Black Americans are still being shot and killed by law enforcement, and activists are still protesting and organizing. But the movement has largely fallen out of the news cycle, largely to make way for the constant coverage of Donald Trump's presidency and his unprecedented violation of US political norms. Finally, I end with a discussion of the interstitial mode of production used by most of these podcasters in my study, touching on issues of sustainability and monetization.

1

Mapping the Transplatform Network

On January 28, 2016, Nicju, co-host of the *What's the Tea?* podcast tweeted, "HOMIE DOWN CODE 10" to Elon James White, founder and CEO of This Week in Blackness (TWiB!), and Rod Morrow of The Black Guy Who Tips (TBGWT) podcast franchise.[1] She had used Twitter's quote function, which allowed her to share a tweet and add her own 140-character commentary. The tweet was from Harlem Pride and read, "BREAKING NEWS! Homophobic Pastor's Harlem Church Up For Public Auction Over Unpaid Debts."[2] The homie in question was Reverend James David Manning, who has been an ongoing source of both outrage and amusement for the network at the center of this project since early 2014, when an image of the sign in front of Manning's ATLAH Ministries had circulated on social media. The sign read, "Obama has released the homo demons on the Black man. Look out Black woman. A white homo may take your man." The sign and a related YouTube video, in which Manning elaborated on the threat of "homo demons," became a viral sensation, prompting White to use TWiB!'s video series to create a response. The video, in which White sought to highlight and rebut Manning's homophobic claims, became the first in a series of video interchanges between White and Manning. Nicju's use of the term "homie" was a call-back to one of Manning's videos in which he addressed White directly using the term "homie" repeatedly. The phrases Manning bellowed throughout the video, including, "HEY, HO-MEY!" and "I got the BI-ble, homie!" became ongoing jokes in the network as, over the course of several days, the network followed, shared, and discussed White and Manning's exchanges across multiple platforms and using various media.

The incident with Manning demonstrates how the network at the center of this project is distributed across digital media platforms and how participants interact using a range of media—text, image, video, and audio—that they both create and circulate. Members of the network are connected via multiple platforms, some broadcast-style and others more private and interpersonal—including Twitter, Facebook, Tumblr, Instagram, Google+, and instant messaging—which they use both simultaneously and in conjunction. This network serves as a crucial resource for its members as they navigate the United States as racialized subjects, providing them with everything from mundane social interaction to emotional support and solidarity during moments of social and political crisis. It offers participants the ability to both produce and consume content that prioritizes Black perspectives and experiences, and it serves as a space where users can collectively interpret and respond to dominant discourses about race and Blackness.

Digital technologies blur conventional boundaries between public and private, producer and audience, and mass and interpersonal communication.[3] This fluidity undermines distinctions between communicative practices and genres that were conceptualized as separate domains in the predigital era. The result is a complex and flexible network of social and material connections that can be used for a variety of purposes—culturally inflected fan practices, community building, cultural critique, and citizen journalism—depending on the exigencies of any given moment.

The digital assemblage analyzed here has three anchoring elements—a network of over sixty Black independent podcasters, the independent media company This Week in Blackness (TWiB!), and the predominantly Black network of Twitter users that has come to be known as "Black Twitter." These three deeply imbricated, yet distinct, elements do not constitute the full extent of the network, but they do serve as its core. The participants that constitute this multimedia, transplatform network are predominantly, though not exclusively, middle-class Black Americans between the ages of twenty-five and forty-five. The members are diverse and heterogeneous, coming from a wide variety of backgrounds and geographic locations.

But regardless of differences, all those in the network share an unapologetic rejection of colorblindness and a prioritization of Black perspectives. The network is a place where Black users and content creators do not have to obscure or minimize their racial identities. The rejection of colorblindness is readily apparent in names and avatars, many of which are explicitly racially marked. For example, many podcasts have names such as *The Black Guy Who Tips* (*TBGWT*), *Nerdgasm Noire Network*, *Black Girl Nerds*, and *Black Astronauts*. The podcast *Where's My 40 Acres?* (*WM40A?*) takes its name from the land redistribution plan proposed after abolition but never brought to fruition.[4] While digital technologies make it possible for users to obscure their racial identities by choosing avatars and usernames that contain no signifiers of race, many participants in this network reject such practices. For example, *TWiB! Prime* co-host Imani Gandy has long blogged under the name "Angry Black Lady," which is also her Twitter handle (@AngryBlackLady), and *WM40A?* co-host uses the pseudonym Phenom Blak. Avatars are frequently pictures of the users themselves or other images that reference Black identity, such as racially accurate cartoon versions of the user. Even if the content or individual is not explicitly racially marked, interactions and content often employ Black vernaculars, a range of cultural common places, and culturally specific knowledge. The participants refuse to codeswitch in ways that might make their communicative practices more accessible to audiences or interlocutors less familiar with Black cultural and linguistic practices and instead communicate as they would in exclusively Black spaces.

In this chapter, I map the network, following two major conceptual threads throughout. First, I emphasize the interconnected nature of the network. In addition to content moving throughout the network, conversations and discussions also unfold across platforms, often involving the sharing, remediating, or remixing of previous content or utterances. This interconnectedness reflects a deeply communitarian ethos that functions in opposition to neoliberal individualism. Second, the network extends and adapts, rather than departing from, predigital practices of Black cultural production and sociality. This strategy aligns the network with Black cultural practices and discourses that predate neoliberal colorblind discourses of race.

I begin with a description of each of the three anchoring components of the network, highlighting both their interconnection and the ways in which they are distinct. I then examine how the network blurs the boundaries between mass and interpersonal communication. I argue that the network can be conceived of as a network in the dual sense of the term—as a broadcast-style network and as a network of technologies and people. After outlining this duality, I explain how it allows the network to combine in one space a multiplicity of Black community-based media traditions with longstanding and culturally significant modes of Black sociality. Finally, I conclude by returning to the encounter with Manning to demonstrate how the fluidity and flexibility of the network is used in practice.

The Podcast "Chitlin' Circuit"

Over the six years of this study, independent Black podcasts have flourished. Through them, podcasters and their audiences are able to create and consume media free from the limitations of dominant racial discourses that simultaneously erase and deride their Black identities. The podcasts provide content that foregrounds Black perspectives, offering an alternative to mainstream legacy media, which participants generally see as failing or even outright antagonizing Black audiences. The podcasts share an emphasis on audience interaction, making them not only broadcast-style content but also a locus for social engagement, which is enhanced by the deep collaborative and communitarian ethos of the network.

The podcast Chitlin' Circuit is a network of independent Black podcasters connected via informal affiliations and social media interactions. There is no central focal point, and not all of the podcasters interact directly with one another. The network is not homogenous or monolithic. Many of the podcasts take progressive political positions, and the two largest and most popular podcast franchises in the network—TWiB! and The Black Guy Who Tips—take an explicitly feminist/womanist and pro-LBGTQ stance. However, some of the podcasts express more normative conceptions of gender roles and LBGTQ issues. Despite this, participants in the network have become more progressive over time, and many have credited their participation in the network as helping them recognize and begin to reject their own sexism, misogyny, and homophobia. Though the relationship between the podcasters is largely supportive, disagreement and conflict are not unusual, and some participants have tense or even antagonistic relationships.

Many of the podcasters have single, stand-alone podcasts. However, increasingly, Chiltin' Circuit podcasters have been forming podcast networks, which run multiple podcasts under a single franchise. These franchises include TWiB!, The Black Guy Who Tips, Movie Trailer Reviews Network (MTR), The Black Astronauts Podcast Network, Where's My 40 Acres? (WM40A?), Black Girl Nerds (BGN), and The Cold Slither Podcast Network (CSPN). Among these, the CSPN, for example, had nine different podcasts as of 2016—*The Good and Terrible Show*, *The Baker-Bone and Rome Bad Advice Show*, *Crown and Collards*, *The Gridiron Gals Podcast*, *The Comic Book Chronicles*, *The WrassleCast*, *Blipster Life*, *Know the Score*, and *Classick Team-Up!*—each of which operated under the large brand umbrella of Cold Slither, including being available for download through the same feed. Many of podcast networks began with one show, from which the network took its name and which remains its flagship show. For example, TBGWT produces a podcast of the same name as well as several other shows, as do WM40A? and The Black Astronauts.

All of the podcasts in the network are in the style of talk radio, though their production value and the regularity of their output vary greatly. Most are categorized as comedy by podcatcher services, largely because of their eclectic topics of conversation and their irreverent tone. Some podcasts are ostensibly focused on one theme. For example, *WM40A?* initially focused on Hip-hop, while *Spawn on Me* and *Gaming and Then Some* are devoted to video games. But it is not uncommon for these podcasts to cover a variety of topics, ranging from television to politics to the latest social media dustups. Although, like podcasting in general, the network skews more heavily male, Black women are a strong presence.[5] Each of TWiB!'s podcasts has at least one woman co-host. Beyond this, there are also many all-Black women podcasts, such as *Nerdgasm Noire Network*; *Whiskey, Wine, and Moonshine*; The Black Astronauts's *Ladies Launch*; *Black Girl Nerds*, CSPN's *The Good and Terrible Show*, and *Black, Sexy, Geeky, and Mental*.

The Chitlin' Circuit podcasts largely eschew the tightly formatted character of most legacy media, opting instead for an informal, flexible approach. Though the hosts have topics or news stories that they are prepared to cover, they do so via free-form conversation that is generally not limited by time constrains. It is not unusual for shows to be two or three hours long, with hosts moving from topic to topic through organic conversation rather than predetermined segments. Receiving little to no editing, the shows present the discussions in their entirety. The podcasts embrace a range of Black vernaculars and regional accents. Irreverent, humorous, and conversational, the podcasts make heavy use of Black American cultural commonplaces, linguistic practices, and communicative norms, which mark the space as culturally Black.

The podcasts all use similar distribution mechanisms and share a strong prioritization of audience interaction. Many of the podcasts stream live at prescheduled or announced times via their websites or streaming services such as Spreecast (now defunct), TuneIn, or Stitcher Radio. The show producers make their content available in multiple ways, including embedding audio in the podcasts' official websites and offering shows for download on iTunes, Stitcher, TuneIn, and Podomatic, or via RSS feeds. The largest podcasts, *TWiB! Prime* and *TBGWT*, feature chatrooms during their live streams, which allow listeners to interact in real time during their shows. TWiB! has a chatroom built directly into its website, while *TBGWT* streamed live via Spreecast and used that site's built-in chatroom feature until the site became defunct in 2016, at which point it moved to Crowdcast. Almost all of the podcasts have multiple channels for listener feedback and interaction, including email, voicemail, and social media accounts. Podcasters and their listeners interact heavily on social media, particularly on Twitter and Facebook.

The relationships between the podcasters is highly collaborative, fostering a communitarian ethos. In many ways, the Chitlin' Circuit podcasts have retained the "horizontal" approach described by Richard Berry in his work on podcasting in the early 2000s, wherein "producers are consumers and consumers become producers and engage in conversations with each other. . . . There is no sense of a hierarchical approach, with Podcasters supporting each other, promoting the work of others and explaining how they do what they do."[6] As podcasting became more popular and more professionalized over the years, this sense of collectivity has remained among the Chitlin' Circuit podcasts. They often promote one another, appear as guests on each other's shows, and share heavily overlapping fan bases. *TBGWT*, hosted by husband and wife team Rod and Karen Morrow, has been a key force in connecting and maintaining the network. Rod and Karen frequently have the hosts of other podcasts on their shows, including the hosts of *3 Guys On, TWiB! Prime, The Spann Report, Insanity Check, Hey You Know It!, The*

Three-A-Negroes Podcast, WM40A?, The Black Astronauts, The Dream Team, and *The Mundane Festival*. Rod and Karen are also frequent guests on other podcasts, at times doing multiple guest appearances a week. iTunes reviews written by TBGWT listeners frequently include the names of other Chitlin' Circuit podcasts to which the show has introduced them, highlighting *TBGWT*'s emphasis on supporting other podcasters. In addition to cross-promotion and collaboration, Rod and Karen help other podcasters in concrete technological ways. They are frequently contacted by beginning podcasters asking for technical assistance getting their own show started, and, Rod explains, "I try to help everybody that I can."[7] For example, when Jess Wood and Josh Homer, formerly of the *After Black* podcast on TWiB!, decided to start their own show, *The Ratchet Hatchet*, Rod helped them with their technological set-up. Nic and Reg from *What's the Tea?* have gone so far as to dub Rod and Karen as their "podcasting parents" and several podcasters have referred to Rod as the "podfather."[8]

While the spirit of cooperation and mutual support is central to the ethos of TBGWT, it is far from alone in this approach. The Black Astronauts Podcast Network started the "Support Ya Own Movement," which "encourages reciprocal support among peer groups" within "urban podcasting."[9] The Black Astronauts also maintain a list of fellow Black podcasters on their website, as does WM40A? and TBGWT. TWiB! has maintained long-term connections with many of the podcasters in the network. Both Kriss from the MTR Network and Rod from TBGWT have been frequent guest hosts on TWiB! podcasts since 2011. In 2014, White started the Black Podcasters United group on Facebook with the goal of connecting Black podcasters, and TWiB! has also collaborated with other podcasters, such a *Black Girl Nerds*, *What's the Tea?*, and *Back 2 Reality*.

The podcasts also share heavily overlapping audiences. You will find many of the same people in the chatrooms of various podcasts or leaving reviews and listener feedback for multiple Chitlin' Circuit podcasts. Highlighting this relationship, on one episode of *What's the Tea?*, co-hosts Nicju and Reggie introduced their guest and fellow podcaster with, "for the like 1 percent of our audience that we *didn't* steal from these other podcasts, this is Mike from *Where's My 40 Acres?*"[10] Many of the podcasters themselves are heavy listeners to other podcasts within the network. Rod and Karen often discuss their fandom of other podcasts, and Aaron B. from The Black Astronauts has asserted he is "a fan first" when it comes to podcasting.[11]

The interconnectedness of the podcasters and their audiences is in line with what we know about the listening habits of podcast consumers. Data show that podcast listeners are what could be called "superlisteners." While the average American consumes roughly four hours of audio per day, podcast listeners consume an average of six hours and six minutes.[12] Of weekly podcast listeners, 37 percent consume five or more podcasts a week, with an average consumption of six per week.[13] However, within the Chitlin' Circuit network both the podcasters and their audience seem not only to be consuming podcasts at a "super-listener" rate, but also to be choosing podcasts that are connected, thereby building and maintaining the network.

The Chitlin' Circuit podcasters and their listeners often note that they see Black podcasts as an alternative to legacy media, which, they assert, under- and misrepresents Black Americans. Legacy news media in particular are often criticized as framing Black Americans in problematic and often damaging ways. Following the Charleston massacre in 2015, Rod initiated a discussion on Twitter about the crucial role Black podcasts play in many listeners' lives. Contrasting podcasts to mainstream media, he tweeted, "Black Podcasts are a much safer space for black people than the mainstream news and radio."[14] He continued, "I've been watching so much pain go down my timeline for the last week and seems like the media is complicit in this," and then added, "It can make you start to feel crazy. Like 'Am I the only one who sees this shit?' Black podcasting is a good balance."[15] He argued, "So get y'all some black podcasts in your rotation so you can enjoy being supported. Nothing wrong with seeking out your own."[16] Rod's followers on Twitter, several of whom self-identified as *TBGWT* listeners, echoed his observations.

The desire for a "safe space" extends beyond news and current events and also manifests in the Chitlin' Circuit podcasts' sustained engagement with popular culture and fandom. Discussion of movies, television, and mass media are common across all of the podcasts. Many podcasts offer movie reviews and television show recaps. Some do this irregularly, such as *Whiskey, Wine, and Moonshine*, which did six shows reviewing the television show *Being Mary Jane*.[17] For others, it is a regular component of their output. In 2013, WM4oA? began a new show called *TheBoobTube*, where it recaps and discusses television shows including *Love and Hip-Hop, Catfish, Orange Is the New Black*, and *Girls*. TBGWT has popular recaps for *The Walking Dead* and *Game of Thrones*. In addition, a notable number of podcasts in the network is devoted exclusively to nerd culture. These include *Nerdgasm Noire Network, Black Girl Nerds, Black Tribbles, Blerds on Nerds, Geek Soul Brother*, and *For Colored Nerds*, as well as TWiB!'s *We Nerd Hard* and TBGWT's *The Nerd Off*. These shows review, discuss, and debate all elements of nerd culture, ranging from comic books to sci-fi to video games.

The podcasts provide important spaces where the podcasters and their listeners can engage in fan practices without anxiety. The importance of having a Black space for fan practices was highlighted by Rod, who explained:

> It's so sad the compromises Black people have to make in general. Right? . . . Black people who like sports typically have to listen to sports radio that don't like Black people. "I don't like any of the athletes. I don't like any of the culture. . . . I hate your music. I hate your clothing. I hate everything about you." But guess what? You don't have anywhere else you can get your local sports talk from other than fifty-year-old white men who kinda don't like young Black dudes. And you have to deal with that every day, and every day to get the update on what's going to happen with Julius Pepper you also have to hear them call him a lazy good for nothin' . . . You have to basically listen to them call him an uppity nigger . . . and it wears on you.[18]

While the fan practices engaged in by the podcasters and their listeners sometimes address issues of race, often this content makes no explicit reference to race. However, such activities take place in an explicitly Black space that, in addition to enabling Black users to engage in fandom and mundane interactions without being marginalized or facing racial and/or gendered aggression, also provides an arena for Black users to engage with media texts in culturally resonant ways. In her discussion of colorblind television casting, Kristen Warner argues that reaffirming racial identity depends not only on explicit references to it or on the presence of marginalized bodies, but also on tone and the use of commonplaces that resonate socially and culturally.[19] The fan practices engaged in by the Chitlin' Circuit podcasters and their audience allow for such cultural specificity, creating a space for Black fans to identify with fan cultures without conforming to the normative whiteness common in such practices.

Most of the Chitlin' Circuit podcasts have demonstrated little desire to move away from their status as hobbyists. With the exception of The Black Guy Who Tips, which has successfully monetized by offering premium content, it is clear that the majority of the Chitin' Circuit podcasts are not working to "break into" the media industry or to turn podcasting into a career. They eschew the practices that lead to the monetization of content creation online. First, most do not promote their work beyond their own social media posts and appearances on each other's podcasts, where they do remarkably little to "plug" their projects and instead bolster the strength and interconnection of the network. They also rarely employ standard promotional strategies, whether that be simply asking friends and followers to share information about their project or specific PR efforts to get blogs and online magazines to write about the shows. Moreover, the primary content created by the network is podcasts, perhaps the least spreadable and monetizable media available to them. Podcasts are long form, and, while short audio segments can be edited to make circulation via social media channels (i.e., spreadability) easier, they are not the media that are most likely to "go viral." Further, while Google offers ad monetization for both websites and YouTube, which provides a straightforward, if not extremely lucrative, means of monetizing blogs and videos, podcasts have no such option. In fact, most of these podcasters pay for their own hosting with services such as Libsyn and have their shows distributed through less easily monetizable outlets such as iTunes and the Google Play Store. None has cultivated Instagram followings that would qualify them as "influencers" or allow them to sign up for services that would match them with promotional deals through which to generate revenue. While internet content creators are making significantly less money than the celebratory discourses of "doing what you love" and bypassing media gatekeepers would lead one to believe, there are clearly available strategies that this network is simply opting out of.

This Week in Blackness

Although This Week and Blackness (TWiB!) can be considered part of the Chitlin' Circuit and although its podcasts have much in common with those discussed above, it is distinct in several important ways. While its primary content is podcasts, TWiB! also produces a range of video and electronic print content. Additionally, whereas the Chitlin' Circuit podcasts serve primarily as alternatives to, or even havens from, legacy media, TWiB! has a more complicated relationship with such media, in that its mission has always included actively shifting the dominant discourse in ways that are not a priority for most other Chitlin' Circuit podcasts. While TWiB! has consistently sought to disrupt stereotypical notions of Blackness and to serve Black audiences, it initially attempted to do so in conjunction with, rather than wholly alternative to, established media outlets.

Started as a web video series in 2008 by Elon James White under the banner of his Brooklyn Comedy Company, by 2015 TWiB! had grown into a large multimedia company that produced the original video series and a range of other digital content. TWiB! introduced its first podcast, *Blacking it Up!*, for a short run in 2009 and then brought it back permanently in 2011, changing the show's name to *TWiB! Radio* (June 2012–February 2014) and then to *TWiB! Prime* in 2014. While *TWiB! Prime* remains its flagship show, as of 2016 TWiB! has produced seven podcasts covering a range of topics including politics, popular culture, sex positivity, and sports. It briefly published blog-style electronic magazine called *Valid*, and, in 2014, the company completed an eight-episode run of *A Black Show* for Free Speech TV. By early 2016, *TWiB! Prime* had become an hour-long news and current events show produced in video and aired on Free Speech TV as well as being available as an audio podcast.

Initially, *Blacking It Up!*'s format and approach shared the free-form, fluid, conversational style of the other Chitlin' Circuit podcasts. From early on, its hosts of *Blacking It Up!*, who collectively went by the name "Team Blackness," often joked that they were not "CNN Negro" or "N(egro)PR"—a joke that freed them from the conventions of "professional" journalism and political analysis. They swore, joked, and offered off-color commentary. While its current iteration continues to allow for comical and absurd conversational tangents, which are referred to as the show "going off the rails," *TWiB! Prime* functions primarily as a professional news outlet and has developed a more tightly formatted structure closer to those of standard radio. By mid-2015, *TWiB! Prime* had a set length, regular commercial breaks, and prerecorded news briefs. This evolution emerged from the ongoing negotiation of TWiB!'s relationship to established media outlets and the ways the organization functions as both alternative to and interlocutor with those media. In particular, as TWiB!'s impact grew and audience members increasingly said TWiB! was their main sources of news and commentary, White felt a growing responsibility to provide content that would be interpreted as professional and polished. Thus, TWiB! prides itself on producing carefully researched and nuanced analysis of the topics it covers and often brings in experts, including academics, lawyers, politicians, and activists, to provide context and analysis.

From the start, TWiB! deliberately resisted hegemonic constructions and representations of Blackness by offering diverse representations of Black people and nuanced political and cultural criticism that privileged Black perspectives. Its mission is guided by a desire to challenge the rhetoric of colorblindness that often functions to obscure ongoing racism and to disrupt the dominant representations of Blackness that flatten out and homogenize Black communities.

TWiB!'s output was intended to cater to a largely overlooked and underserved Black audience. In June 2011, White explained that every aspect of TWiB! was designed "to prove a point"—the point that there is a clear and strong audience for the programming TWiB! was creating. He described the intended audience member as someone "who is smart, who is politically engaged, who is technologically engaged, who can enjoy the ratchet just right alongside intelligent shit. Who can quote 50 Cent and Nietzsche within the same sentence."[20] L. Joy Williams, then co-host of *Blacking It Up!* asserted that TWiB! sought to undermine the myth that Black people "are this monolith that all watch BET [Black Entertainment Television], drink Kool-Aid, and occasionally got to jail." She added that the independent Black media produced by TWiB! can work to "break down that myth and say that you can program differently because we have a different audience within our people."[21]

At first, White intended to alter the media landscape by integrating TWiB!'s approach and perspective into corporate media, rather than functioning as a wholly independent alternative. In the early years of TWiB!, White sought to form a partnership with larger, more visible, and established media outlets. For example, when White rebooted *Blacking It Up!* in 2011, it was with the, ultimately abandoned, intention of pitching the show to SiriusXM Radio. During this same time period, White had talks with Interactive One, the parent company of *NewsOne*, which declined to work with TWiB! because, according to White's contact, "Black people don't listen to podcasts."[22]

Until 2014, TWiB! was completely dependent on unpaid volunteer labor. Starting as a small-scale operation, with both videos and podcasts produced in White's Brooklyn apartment (which he shared with his now wife Emily Epstein-White), TWiB! also relied on listener donations to stay afloat between 2011 and 2014. Then, in 2014, it introduced "The TWiBularity," a name that with puns on the idea of a "singularity" and refers to one master feed where all TWiB!'s projects converged. As a "freemium" service, it was designed to combine free and subscription-only content. *TWiB! Prime* streamed live Monday through Thursday via the TWiB! website and other podcast applications such as TuneIn and Stitcher. Afterward, it was made available for free download via iTunes, Stitcher, and other applications. Conversely, TWiB!'s six other podcasts—*TWiB! after Dark*, *We Nerd Hard*, *SportsBall*, *Historical Blackness*, *Academic Shade*, and *This Tastes Funny*—were available for free only when they streamed live at their scheduled time; otherwise, on-demand listening and downloading were available through a monthly subscription. "The TWiBularity" is also the name of a custom mobile app created by TWiB!, available on iOS and Android operating systems, that allows subscribers to live stream both audio and video content, listen to older episodes of TWiB!'s podcasts, check TWiB!'s live-streaming schedule, and receive messages from the company. The free counterpart to the TWiBularity app is named "the TWiBulari-free" and provides access only to TWiB!'s nonpremium content.

For the first several years of TWiB!'s existence, White believed that it could secure entry into the established media industry by creating high-quality content and garnering a sizeable audience. It was the cancelation of NPR's *Tell Me More* in June 2014 that finally disabused

White of this belief and solidified TWiB!'s need to be financially self-sufficient.[23] *Tell Me More*, a current events–focused talk show designed to appeal to Black listeners, was canceled because NPR affiliate stations were not ordering the show or were running it in late-night timeslots.[24] *TWiB! Prime*, which covered the story, concluded that the failure *Tell Me More* did not bode well for TWiB!'s ability to partner and collaborate with established media, especially given its deeply irreverent approach and rejection of the NPR aesthetic. Sound engineer and *TWiB! Prime* co-host Aaron Rand Freeman described the polished and professional style of *Tell Me More* as a "perfectly manicured Negro situation." He encapsulated his dismay at the cancelation, saying, "NPR-dipped Negros can't stay on the air? NPR flavored? Of aaaall the Negros? I understand Elon can't stay on the air. Elon tells everybody to go fuck themselves all up and down. I get it. But NP—really? Really?"[25] The fate of *Tell Me More*, a show that adhered to the professional standards and practices of NPR, was understood by TWiB! as an indication that TWiB!, with its less conventional, more brash style, would never become part of the existing corporate media landscape. In considering its long-term financial options, TWiB! turned to its audience, asking listeners to "step up" and support the organization financially to ensure its future. Shortly after this, the TWiBularity was born.

Gina Neff has referred to the kind of un- or undercompensated labor on which TWiB! depended as "venture labor"; it involves "an investment of time, resources, and labor into a job" for the purposes of "a future payoff other than regular wages."[26] For their part, Kathleen Kuehn and Thomas Corrigan speak of "hope labor," or work undertaken as a means to future employment or monetization.[27] Similarly, Brooke Duffy has written of the aspirational labor of Instagram influencers, the productive activities they undertake in the hopes of future social or economic capital.[28] From the start, TWiB! certainly fell into the category of these future-oriented forms of labor. White created and grew TWiB!, particularly its podcasts, with the intention of developing it into a media company with fully paid staff. Eventually, between its freemium service and other smaller sources of revenue, TWiB! was able to offer staff some compensation. However, it is extremely difficult, if not nearly impossible, to establish a wholly independent media company that generates enough revenue to fully compensate all of its participants at market value, and TWiB! has never been able to fully do so. But even as TWiB! staff sought experience and visibility that might benefit them in the future, they also worked for TWiB! because they believed in what it was doing—or as Freeman once explained to me, people continued to work "because [TWiB!s] mission is so damn noble." While the labor that powered TWiB! clearly possessed a future-looking orientation—like venture, hope, and aspirational labor—this future benefit was not seen as solely individual. TWiB! was conceived not merely as a project that could lead to professional careers, but as a media intervention on behalf of Black people, who have been chronically erased or misrepresented by US media. They were engaging in labor with the hope of personal success *and* of doing something positive for Black people writ large by ameliorating the impact of legacy media.

Whether seeking media partnerships or not, intervening in and shifting dominant discourses has always been central to TWiB!'s mission. Targets of such interventions could be legacy media outlets or other Black Americans who asserted hegemonic discourses of misogyny or heteronormativity, such as Manning. White sees this as a core difference between TWiB!'s approach and that of many other podcasters. Asserting that TWiB!'s goal was to "try to change how the conversation is happening nationally," he pointed to this as the reason for TWiB!'s substantial funding needs:

> As a podcast space, we're probably doing just fine. Like, actually, we're doing way better than most podcasts. . . . But because we are a bigger space, we have more people involved. We're attempting to do more things. I mean, that's why we produced a TV show. That's why what we're seeking in funding is very different from, like, let's say if you started a show tomorrow about ice cream. You probably wouldn't have to go through the same funding situation as what we're doing.[29]

One key manifestation of this difference is TWiB!'s on-location reporting of events, particularly those associated with the Movement for Black Lives, such as the unrest in Ferguson, Missouri. On August 9, 2014, Mike Brown, an unarmed Black eighteen-year-old, was shot and killed Ferguson Police Officer Darren Wilson, setting off protests lasting for days. During this turmoil, there was often a vast difference between the coverage provided by the mainstream news media, particularly cable news channels, and the accounts that were emerging from Ferguson community members and protest organizers via social media. Local residents claimed media coverage overemphasized the destruction of property, playing into narratives of angry, dangerous Black "rioters" rather than reporting the police violence directed at the crowd. TWiB!, at the behest of its audience, traveled to Ferguson, where it leveraged its existing broadcast-style network and social media networks to give voice to local accounts of the events, offering a narrative that stood in opposition to the picture created by mainstream media.

In addition to this kind of journalistic coverage, TWiB! also engaged in public debate with those holding differing opinions. White and Imani Gandy, co-host of *TWiB! Prime*, were often challenged or even outright insulted on Twitter, and despite colloquial wisdom to "not feed the trolls," they did engage with those users in public debate. White has explained that he does so with the specific understanding that the user he is interacting with is representative of many others who hold similar opinions. He sees himself as working to inform and possibly change the views those onlookers.

While other Chitlin' Circuit podcasts do engage those outside the network, particularly on social media, it is not with the goal of expanding their audience, intervening in dominant discourses, or creating dialogue with outside communities. This is exemplified by Rod's response to the attention he garnered after creating the hashtag #BernieSoBlack, a critique of Bernie Sanders supporters' approach to race during the 2016 Democratic presidential primary. The hashtag reached the national trending topics on Twitter, an algorithmically produced real-time list of the most tweeted-about subjects, and Rod found himself at the center of a great deal of attention. The Bernie Sanders for President sub-Reddit, a forum on the website Reddit, suggested that they host Rod for an "Ask Me Anything" (AMA) question and answer session, to which he replied, "'No, that's more work.' . . . I mean, no offense. But, maybe Elon would do that. He loves educating ignorant motherfuckers. I'm not really a fan. Not that these people are jerks or anything. I just don't like being an educator because I'll fuck around, cuss somebody out. I'll be like, 'Damn, I just fucked up the cause.'"[30] Rod's reference to TWiB! indicates how it functions as part of the larger conversations happening in the network while also serving as a point of connection that moves the network's discourses out beyond its boundaries, an issue I address further in the next chapter.

Black Twitter

The third element in which I anchor this study is the network of predominantly Black Twitter users who have come to be known as "Black Twitter." Black Americans were early adopters of and innovators on the Twitter platform. Within three years of Twitter's debut in 2006, Pew Research found that 26 percent of Black American internet users used Twitter or another similar status update service, compared with 19 percent of whites.[31] Many of these users came from networks that existed on other platforms, such as MySpace, Facebook, and Black Planet, who migrated together to the new platform. By 2010, others outside the network had started to note the large Black presence on Twitter,[32] in part because the trending topics feature made Black discourse visible to non-Black users on the platform.[33] By July 2015, the *LA Times* had hired a reported to cover "Black Twitter."

It is important to note that Black Twitter does not exist in any unified or monolithic sense. Just as there is no "Black America" or single "Black culture," there is no "Black Twitter." What do exist are millions of Black users networking, connecting, and engaging on Twitter with others who have similar concerns, experiences, tastes, and cultural practices. Meredith Clark describes Black Twitter as a meta-network, comprised of smaller networks centered on users' personal connections and common interests.[34] Black Twitter is conceptualized by many of its participants as "a series of neighborhoods" that can merge and act in concert around issues of concern across Black communities.[35]

Like the Chitlin' Circuit podcasts and TWiB!, Black Twitter and its constitutive neighborhoods are explicitly and unapologetically Black spaces. Clark notes that racial identity has played an important role in Black users' adoption of the platform and in the way Black Twitter participants discursively construct and understand the network. She found that the participants she interviewed unanimously saw Black Twitter as a space that centers Black perspectives and experiences, representing an "online convergence of ideas exchanged within the cultural context of the Black experience in America."[36] Thus, while it is crucial that discussions of Black Twitter avoid reductively flattening out and homogenizing the network and its participants, it is equally important to avoid imposing colorblind discourses on the network and thereby erasing the importance of race and culture in this context. The conversations on Black Twitter are characterized by cultural specificity, and display of cultural competencies is an important mode of performing Black racial identity in the network.[37]

Black Twitter has been able to leverage its densely connected networks to engage around a range of political and social issues, often successfully intervening and altering the outcome of events. For example, Black Twitter was instrumental in creating the visibility and pressure that resulted in the indictment and prosecution of George Zimmerman in the killing of Trayvon Martin. On February 26, 2012, Trayvon Martin, an unarmed Black sixteen-year-old, was shot and killed while returning to his father's house from a nearby convenience store. Zimmerman, a self-appointed neighborhood watchman armed with a 9-mm handgun, saw Martin and believed his presence in the neighborhood to be suspicious. By the time police arrived on the scene, Martin lay dead from a gunshot wound to the chest. Initially, Zimmerman, who claimed self-defense, was not arrested or charged. In the weeks that followed, public outcry mounted, as many Americans doubted the veracity of Zimmerman's account. On March 8, 2012, a Change.org petition to bring charges against Zimmerman was started and subsequently became the fastest growing petition in the site's history, with an average of one thousand signatures per minute. One month after Martin's death, when the petition was delivered to authorities, it had over two million signatures.[38] Twitter was a major resource in circulating information about the case and the link to the petition. The hashtag #Trayvon made multiple appearances in the United States' national trending topics.[39] After Zimmerman's acquittal, Twitter was used to organize protests, and the hashtag #BlackLivesMatter, which would become the rallying cry for the subsequent movement against police brutality and institutional racism, was born.

TWiB!, the Chitlin' Circuit podcasters, and their listeners reside in a "neighborhood" on Black Twitter, and many are influential users with large followings that function as hubs in the Black Twitter meta-network. The affinity between the podcasts discussed above and this

Twitter network is so strong that Rod described Black podcasting as essentially moving "Black Twitter to audio form."[40] In addition to participating in the Black Twitter network, the podcasters bring discussions from Black Twitter into their broadcasts, often covering conversations and events taking place in that network.

It is not unusual for podcasters to spawn hashtags that galvanize the larger Black Twitter network and gain mainstream visibility. For example, Feminista Jones, writer, activist, and mental health social worker, was not only a prominent figure on Black Twitter, with over 57,000 followers as of 2016 (a number that increased to 158,000 by 2018), she also co-hosted TWiB!'s sex-positive podcast *TWiB! after Dark* from June 2013 to November 2014. Jones has created numerous influential hashtags, such as #YouOKSis to discuss street harassment of women of color and #NMOS14, an abbreviation of "National Moment of Silence," which was used to coordinate moment of silence commemorations of Mike Brown in over ninety US cities on August 14, 2014. White has also created several hashtags that have garnered national visibility. Two notable examples are #DudesGreetingDudes, which challenged dismissals of street harassment as mere greetings with parodies of what similar greetings would look like between men, and #TheEmptyChair, a response to the *New York Magazine*'s cover featuring thirty-five of the women who accused Bill Cosby of rape and an empty chair to signify the women who had not come forward. Both hit the US trending topics on Twitter and were reported by journalists and bloggers, with #TheEmptyChair being covered by the *Washington Post, CNN*, and NPR.[41]

For the network that is the focus of this project, Twitter functions in several interlocking ways. First, it serves as a platform for interpersonal and social interactions, creating and maintaining personal connections within the network. Second, Twitter is also a space for immediate real-time discussion, whether that be live-tweeting a television show or responding to breaking news as it unfolds. And third, because Twitter is publicly available and because the trending topics feature can call broader attention to those topics, often in the form of hashtags, Twitter is a point of connection between the network and those outside it.

The #BernieSoBlack hashtag from July 2015 exemplifies each of these uses. The hashtag emerged from a personal exchange between TBGWT's Rod and *TWiB! Prime*'s Imani Gandy. On July 18, 2015,

Black Lives Matters protestors disrupted the Presidential Town Hall at Netroots Nation, a progressive grassroots organizing conference. The event featured Democratic primary candidates Martin O'Malley and Bernie Sanders. After the protest, Sanders was the target of heavy criticism for his refusal to engage with issues of systemic racism and for answering questions about structural racism with economic solutions. Many Sanders supporters responded by noting that Sanders had attended The March on Washington in 1963 as a way of delegitimizing any criticism of Sanders around issues of race. The following morning, after almost a full day of Sanders's supporters pointing out his Civil Rights Movement bona fides, Gandy tweeted, "If I see one more Bernie acolyte mention that he marched with MLK, I'm going to burn the Internet to the ground."[42] The tweet initiated an exchange between Gandy and Rod, who facetiously responded, "Hold up! Bernie Sanders marched with MLK? This changes EVERYTHING!"[43] Gandy added, "Pretty sure Bernie played spades with Stokley Carmichael at a Jackson 5 concert once," prompting Rod to tweet the following jokes in quick succession:[44]

#BernieSoBlack HE teaches you how to Cha Cha Slide!

I heard Bernie Sanders showed Redd Foxx how to put dice in a Crown Royal bag! #BernieSoBlack.

I actually heard it was Bernie's idea to march in Selma. MLK wanted to do the march in Hawaii. A destination march. #BernieSoBlack.[45]

What was initially an interpersonal exchange as part of a larger discussion about a news story quickly scaled up as the hashtag picked up momentum and hit Twitter's US national trending topics. It also became part of the media narrative around the Netroots Nation protest, covered by Reuters, the *Guardian*, Bloomberg News, MSNBC, CNN, and *Slate*.[46] Rod gave interviews to *Vox*, the *Los Angeles Times*, and the *Daily Beast*, and ultimately found himself sharing the Vox.com front page with Hillary Clinton and Donald Trump.[47] In this way, Twitter often acts as a point of articulation between the network and mainstream media and establishment politics.

Finally, Twitter is a useful locus of analysis for this study because it functions as a central hub through which participants disseminate materials from other social media platforms. Twitter is used to share links to new episodes of podcasts, to news stories and blogs, and to content on other social media platforms such as Instagram and Vine. These practices are part of the day-to-day use of Twitter, but become particularly visible at moments of crisis and political engagement such as the uprising in Ferguson in August 2014. Many people on the ground in Ferguson used Instagram (both images and videos) and Vine to capture events as they unfolded. Twitter became a central clearinghouse for this material as users tweeted links to other social media posts, a practice that is facilitated by various social media apps that enable simultaneous posts on multiple platforms. Thus, a focus on Twitter allows my analysis to include other social media platforms used by the network.

While the three constitutive elements of the network I discuss above are distinct, they are deeply interrelated, and the boundaries between them are often blurry. Together, they form a large Black network created and maintained by collective discourse production. Yet, each offers different imagined affordances that allow participants to engage in a range of communicative practices, simultaneously and in tandem.

The Duality of the Network

The digital assemblage outlined above possesses characteristics of a "network" in both senses of the term as a broadcast-style network producing content for distribution and a digitally enabled social network. Although the distinction between broadcast-style network and social network is blurry at best, the dual nature of the network allows for adaptations and translations of longstanding practices of Black cultural production and sociality in the same networked space.

This is true of the Chitlin' Circuit podcast, of TWiB!, and of the Twitter network in which both are embedded, as each of these three element are often used simultaneously in ways that resonate with both understandings of the term. This duality is apparent in the podcasts created by the network, which are broadcast-style media content produced for distribution and circulation. Podcasts are a predominantly audio medium (though video is increasingly common) characterized by portability and seriality and employing many of the same conventions as radio. The similarities between podcasts and radio are apparent from the fact that most popular podcasts are downloadable episodes of radio shows such as *This American Life* and *Radio Lab*. Like radio, podcasts use the one-to-many logic of broadcasting,[48] and the podcasters in this network often employ the language of broadcasting—referring to their live streams as "broadcasts" or going "on-air"—as do the platforms that provide access to their content—such as Stitcher Radio, TuneIn Radio, or Blog Talk Radio. Several of the podcasters in this study—including TWiB!, TBGWT, Movie Trailer Reviews, The Black Astronauts, and Cold Slither—operate what they refer to as "podcast networks." These networks are analogous to broadcast networks in that they produce several different podcasts series as part of an overarching brand.

The podcasts in this network are in the style of talk radio and share talk radio's emphasis on listener participation. Like talk radio, many of the podcasts include listener call-in segments. However, digital media technologies offer additional avenues for audiences to participate in live shows, allowing a level of interactivity and geographical reach unavailable to previous generations of Black media producers. Several of the podcasts that stream live provide a chatroom where listeners can log-on and interact in real-time. Listeners offer commentary, and hosts often interject comments from the chatroom into "on-air" discussions. The chatroom is of such importance to TWiB! that it sold t-shirts listing the chatroom alongside the names of the three hosts of *TWiB! Prime*—"Elon & Imani & Aaron & the Chatroom"—effectively giving it the status of co-host. Twitter is often used similarly. Many listeners tweet while listening live, and the hosts include comments from Twitter in the shows.

However, social media, particularly Twitter, do not merely augment broadcast-style content; they also possess characteristics of such mass communication. Many early researchers of Twitter characterized it as a platform where users broadcast, or at least narrowcast, to their followers.[49] Some theorists have made comparisons between Twitter and podcasting's parent format, radio, pointing to Twitter's immediacy and making analogies to ham radio and CB radio.[50] Kate Crawford, in her analysis of Twitter as a mode of listening, argues that users can engage Twitter as they do radio, employing "background listening" and "tuning in" when something catches their attention. She asserts that the flows of information on Twitter, like radio, "can circulate in the background, a part of the texture of the everyday."[51]

In addition to functioning as a broadcast-style network, it is also a network of people and technologies. It is a space for sociality that is imbricated in but not dependent on the media texts produced by and circulated within it. Such interactions are not the same as those that take place in "fan" networks in the traditional sense. Thus, not only do participants regularly engage in interactions that are not directly tethered to the podcasts, but some participants in the network do not listen to the podcasts at all. Additionally, the social media networks in which these podcasts are embedded did not coalesce around them; rather the social media element of the network predated most of the podcasts. Often podcasters attribute their participation in the network with inspiring them to create their own content.

The network's intertwining of broadcast-style media and sociality reflects the contemporary digital media environment. The emergence of social media has made "audiences more visible" to media producers.[52] Whereas mass media removed the audience from physical co-presence and made it an abstraction, social media has increased the accessibility of the audience not only to the producer, but also to each other.[53] This shift in the producer-audience dynamic can be seen in the ways that podcasters integrate users from their social networks in their media production process, which, in turn, imbricates their podcasts more deeply in the broader conversations taking place in the network.

The podcasts are so deeply intermeshed with social media that, in addition to providing broadcast-style content, they contribute to broader social media–enabled conversations. Podcasters often use their shows to participate in larger conversations in the network, weighing in on discussions happening on social media and or continuing a conversation that they engaged in on Twitter or Facebook. In effect, the podcasts often become interlocutors in discussions that extend well beyond their direct audiences.

The dual nature of this multimedia, transplatform network makes it a powerful means for negotiating racial discourses. Digital media technologies often blur the distinction between the public and the private, and the configuration of this network brings together both public and private traditions of Black counter-public production.[54] The network functions as a contemporary iteration of longstanding practices of counter-public formation, in both Black independent media and everyday Black social spaces. As such, it serves as valuable resource for rejecting colorblind racial discourses and creating alternative imaginaries about race.

Rejecting Colorblindness and Constructing a Black Cultural Space

Given its dual nature, the network draws simultaneously on historical traditions of Black community-based media production—particularly newspaper and radio—and of Black social engagement in spaces such as barber or beauty shops and churches. Grounded in these traditions, the participants' communicative strategies construct the network in ways that define it as a Black space. They extend practices of Black cultural production and sociality from before the neoliberal era into the contemporary moment. These practices bring with them conceptualizations of race and racial identity that undermine colorblindness, particularly the construction of race as a personal trait rather than collective social category.

The network's refusal to fully connect with or court the cultural industries has likely shielded them from the compromises so often required by the structures of these industries. Professionalization is fraught for media content producers of color, often requiring them to compromise some aspects of their work just to gain entry into the industry, even at the fringe. Anamik Saha has demonstrated how people of color who create independent media content must find ways to work in and through established media industry practices, which can force them to accommodate problematic practices. In his study of an independent Asian dance music record label, he found that their marketing displayed "internalized corporate promotional techniques that steered it in a direction that ultimately led to self-exoticization."[55] Aymar Jean Christian discusses how the creators of *Broad City* struggled with the shift in expectations after they signed a deal with Comedy Central, noting how they were required to "sand [the] edges down so that more people can watch and enjoy."[56] Thus, because the network at the center of this project has avoided becoming imbricated in larger cultural industries, the kinds of Black cultural practices that might otherwise constitute an "edge" in need of smoothing are instead permitted to flourish.

The podcasts in this network, with their similarity to radio, can be located squarely within a long and rich history of Black independent media. Beginning in the 1820s, the Black press created and circulated oppositional frameworks, rearticulated Black identity, and disseminated information to Black communities.[57] With the advent of radio in the early twentieth century, Black media producers took these practices to the airwaves. Since the Civil Rights Movement, Black radio has been a site for political dialogue and debate.[58] In her study of Chicago's Black talk radio station WVON-AM, Catherine Squires finds that the station is continuing the legacy of the Black press by creating a Black counterpublic, addressing not just "Black" issues, but all issues while privileging and centering Black perspectives and interpretive frameworks.[59] The Chitlin' Circuit podcasts and TWiB!'s content function as digital iterations of these historical practices.

Podcasts' similarity to radio makes them particularly well suited for the task of reasserting a sense of Black collectivity in ways that undermine the individualism that permeates dominant racial discourses. Many scholars have pointed to radio's ability to constitute listeners as an imagined community.[60] Susan Douglas argues that radio has cognitive dimensions that "make radio's role in constructing imagined communities . . . much more powerful that what print can do."[61] Podcasts also have some of these same possibilities for building a sense of connection.

These podcasts interpellate their listeners by deploying cultural commonplaces, vernaculars, and modes of address to constitute a "Black audience." Vorris Nunely asserts that a "Black audience" is not merely a group of Black spectators or listeners; rather, it is an audience that "is persuaded by tropes, knowledges, and terministic screens anchored in African American life and culture." Performers are able to identify with this audience through "speech, gesture, tonality, organization, image, attitude, and ideas anchored in the deployment of African American knowledges, hermeneutics, and understandings of the world." The Black audience is not monolithic; instead, it is constituted by the use of "different hermeneutical frames emerging from different terministic screens constructed through distinctive experiences when it comes to crucial issues and interests related to African American life and culture."[62] The podcasts in this network refuse to be constrained by the listening ear and, instead, replace the normative whiteness of traditional radio-style audio with content that evokes the Black audience and allows listeners to hear themselves, rather than to be Othered.[63]

The talk-radio format enhances this sense of collectivity. In the early days of US radio, the inclusion of audience participation–based programming brought the voices of the "average" American to the airwaves, thereby not only constituting an imagined community of listeners, but also providing a series of performances that demonstrated "who 'the American people' were, what they sounded like, and what they believed in."[64] The podcasts in this network make use of a similar mechanism. It is not uncommon for TWiB! podcasts to take listener calls. Podcasts such as *TBGWT* and *WM4oA?* also have voicemail, where listeners can leave messages to be played on the shows. *In Deep Show* has a recurring segment called "Can I Talk My Shit?," which plays prerecorded audio sent in by listeners discussing issues that are important to them. These calls and messages serve as performances of who members of the network are. Far from presenting a series of individuals who "happen to be Black," callers similarly invoke a Black audience, often rejecting color-blindness and its emphasis on the individual, and instead constructing themselves as members of social group whose lives are shaped by the experience of structural racism.

Additionally, the talk-show format includes audience members' contributions not only as performances of "who listeners are," but also as co-creators of those representations. Squires argues that the talk-show format "allows the audience to participate in constructing social texts and assigning meanings" and therefore is "an opportunity for a dynamic process of joint creation of texts and reciprocal information sharing between audience, guests, and . . . staff."[65] Thus, radio not only creates a sense of community and provides performances that reflect the members of that community, but also allows audience participation in this process so that these performances become to some degree a result of collective meaning-making.

The network is also constructed as a Black space through the modes of sociality enabled by the imagined affordances of each platform. The sense of community and connection created by the radio-style audio of the podcasts is strengthened by the "ambient intimacy" created by the social media elements of the network.[66] Members of the network interact heavily on social media, particularly Twitter. These exchanges are often unrelated to the content produced by the network's content creators and focus instead on current events and the day-to-day lives of participants. The constant stream of information found across social media, much of it mundane, creates a sense of familiarity among members of the network. If, as Crawford notes, "access to the minutiae of a person's life is something normally reserved for family, close friends, and lovers,"[67] then such digital interactions work to strengthen feelings of connection.

On Twitter, the primary structural relationship—that between followers and those whom they follow—has been theorized as creating "personal publics."[68] In these personal publics, "news reporting and instances of professional communication can share the same space with personal musings, phatic communication, and social grooming." Thus, the network contains multiple overlapping personal publics, in which media content, such as podcasts, is circulated and consumed alongside conversations about politics, personal opinions about popular culture, and commentary about the daily goings-on of life. Personal publics are "characterized by the communicative mode of 'conversation,' where the strict separation of sender and receiver is blurred."[69] On Twitter, the @-reply feature allows this network to be utilized for "micro-" level interpersonal communication by allowing users to directly address each other.[70] Thus, users are not just broadcasting information to their personal publics, but also having conversational exchanges.

This conversational micro-level communication allows the network to host the kinds of everyday talk that Melissa Harris-Perry, argues "African Americans jointly develop understandings of their collective interests and create strategies to navigate the complex political world."[71] The social interactions enabled by the network translate this longstanding enclaved sociality into the digital arena, a phenomenon I explore in greater depth in chapter 2.

Homo Demons vs. Mrs. Elon James White

In this final section of the chapter I analyze the network's reaction to the exchange between TWiB!'s Elon James White and Reverend James David Manning of Harlem's ATLAH Ministries regarding the latter's antigay statements. In February and March of 2014, their "beef" set the network abuzz in ways that illustrate a number of characteristics of the network at the center of this project, including how deeply interconnected the three anchoring elements of the network are, as well as how the network brings communicative modes of broadcast and everyday social interaction together. The incident also highlights the distributed nature of the network itself and the discussions it enables, as conversations take place across multiple platforms and employ text, images, video, and audio content, which are often remixed or remediated. At the same time, it shows how the different elements of the network are distinct from one another—particularly how TWiB! attempts to directly shift broader cultural discourses, how the other podcasts in the network serve a more intragroup social function, and how Twitter, itself a central hub for multiple social media platforms, functions as the primary tool for both conversation and the circulation of content.

On February 28, 2014, Manning posted a video to YouTube in which he elaborated on the sign in front of his church warning of "homo demons." In the video, Manning asserted that President Obama was working to "convert" Black men to "homosexuality," causing the destruction of the Black family and leaving Black women to raise children alone. Manning argued that as Obama encouraged more Black men to embrace same-sex relationships, these Black men were then "being scooped up by white homos" who had moved "into Black neighborhoods" and were "looking for Black men that have been converted." Manning warned Black women of the difficulty they would face in trying to compete with gay white men for Black men's affections. A white gay man, he said, has "usually got money. A white homo usually has an American Express card. He usually has an opportunity at the theater. Homos love the theater. They love to go out to dinner parties. They love that kind of a thing." He stated that the sign in front of his church was a "direct action" taken against this threat to the Black community.[72]

TWiB!, which has always taken an unapologetically pro-LBGTQ stance, used its web video series to challenge Manning and his assertions. The video, titled "Blackness. Today: #Homodemons," was posted to TWiB!'s YouTube channel just two days after Manning's original video was released.[73] TWiB!'s response video opens with White sitting at a desk in the TWiB! studio and saying, "You know sometimes you hear or see something that you're just simply not prepared for?" The video then cuts to an image of the ATLAH Ministries sign accompanied by audio taken from Manning's video as he reads the text of the sign. White then spends the remaining two and a half minutes of the video critiquing and mocking Manning's assertions in equal measure. After pointing out that he, as a straight Black man, likes all the things Manning lists as characteristics of gay white men, White goes on to argue that as laughable as Manning's assertions might be to him or many in his audience, it would be a mistake to dismiss these statements as "crazy talk." He cites Harris-Perry, the Maya Angelou Presidential Chair Professor of Politics and International Affairs at Wake Forest University who hosted a show on MSNB at the time, who once said to him that calling things "crazy" minimizes what they are, which is "dangerous." White points out that Manning is not alone in his beliefs. He concludes,

> As opposed to worrying about the homo demons attacking Black men, why don't you worry about the actual people attacking Black men. I find it really hard to believe that Jesus would be co-signing you wasting time on homodemons when there are actual issues that you could be putting more time toward.

In addition to being posted to TWiB!'s YouTube channel, TWiB!'s video response to Manning was also posted on TWiB!'s website (ThisWeekInBlackness.com), Google+ profile, Tumblr, and multiple Facebook pages, as well as to White's personal Google+ profile, Tumblr, and Twitter. TWiB!'s video was circulated across social media platforms by members of the network, many of whom participated in critiquing Manning's homophobic stance, usually via sarcasm and humor. On Twitter, high-profile members of the network such as *TWiB! Prime* co-host Gandy and journalist and commentator Goldie Taylor retweeted the link to the video.

Challenging problematic discourses, both from within and outside Black America, has always been at the core of TWiB!'s mission. These challenges have varying levels of visibility and impact, depending on how they are taken up and circulated within and beyond the network. While some TWiB! videos circulate and fade without every drawing the attention of those being critiqued, this particular video came to the attention of Manning himself, who posted a rebuttal to TWiB!'s response on YouTube approximately one week later.

Manning's seven-minute response video, titled "Mrs. Elon James White," begins with the TWiB! video unedited in its entirety and then cuts to Manning sitting at a desk, from which he offers his rebuttal. Manning begins with challenges to White's masculinity and sexuality in terms that are grounded in dominant heteronormative discourses, calling White "Mrs. Elon" and asserting that he "appears for all intents and purposes to be bisexual." He goes on to critique White's failure to reference the Bible in his criticism of Manning's position, framing this as a fatal flaw that makes White's criticism inherently invalid. Saying that White's argument is "as empty as a pocket," Manning presents the Bible to the camera,

> But I have the Bible, homie. HEEY! HEY, HO-MEY! I HAVE THE BI-BLE. I HAVE THE WORD OF GOD. You can call me what ya want. You can say anything about me and my character that that you will. But what-cha gonna do 'bout this right HERE?

Continuing to hold up the Bible up, Manning goes on to claim that White isn't opposing him, but rather Jesus, and then devotes the last minute of the video to attacking Harris-Perry, calling her a "dyke" who "can't keep a man," and challenging the authenticity of her Blackness by proclaiming her to be the "most pinched nose white acting person you'd ever want to see." He insults Harris-Perry's "fake braids," comparing her to Bo Derek, the white actress who famously wore cornrows in the 1979 movie 10. Manning scolds White for quoting Harris-Perry rather than "someone with integrity." He chided, "You from Brooklyn, put up some statements from Shirley Chisholm. Or you don't know about her?"[74]

Manning's response video came to White's attention the same day it was posted, prompting White to tweet. "So apparently I got under Mr. #Homodemons skin. Does he really want to do this? Does he really?" By 11:00 p.m. EST that night, White had announced on Twitter that he was editing a video response to Manning's rebuttal. The following day, White posted "Dear 'Dr.' James David Manning . . . A.K.A. Dr. #HomoDemons" on YouTube, TWiB!'s website, and the same social media sites as the initial video.[75]

TWiB!'s six-and-a-half minute video featured White intercutting his commentary with clips from Manning's response to his initial video.

White's counterargument focused on a number of factual errors in Manning's video, including the fact that Shirley Chisolm was "an icon of equality for everyone" and "well known for her advocacy for gay rights," with a screen capture of the results from a Google search of Chisolm's name appearing next to White's head. Mocking Manning's disregard for factual information, White muses, "Maybe the Old Testament says, 'Thou shalt not Google.'" He concludes by saying, "Next time you want to call someone a dyke or just be generally ignorant and homophobic, ask yourself a question, 'What *would* Jesus do?' I'm going to assume he probably wouldn't get into YouTube beef."

Members of the network circulated the new video more extensively than TWiB!'s first response to Manning, often tweeting the link along with their favorite quotations from White's rebuttal. As members of the network discussed and retweeted the link, Rod, who has been a long-time listener of TWiB! and a guest host on several TWiB! shows, began a series of tweets satirically proclaiming his support for Manning. Rod asserted, "Dr. Manning hits on all the key questions I've asked about @elonjames and #TWiB for years."[76] He then enumerated twenty-one "concerns," including asking, "Heeeey Homeboy . . . how you gonna quote Melissa Harris Perry [sic] when she is a black gay Bo Derek?" and "What IS Elon gone do about 'dis here?'"[77] One longtime and active participant in the network organized and archived Rod's concerns using Storify, a now-defunct website that allowed Twitter users to embed chosen tweets along with added commentary to capture Twitter exchanges in a linear narrative form.[78] Once a Storify of Rod's questions had been created, users circulated a link to it, disseminating it through Twitter's fragmented, non-linear environment, where more and more participants joined the discussion, which lasted for several days.

White's and Manning's YouTube beef became a topic of discussion not only on social media, but eventually on other podcasts in the network, notably the March 9, 2014, episode of *TBGWT*, titled "#DrManning-Bars."[79] The podcast was initially live-streamed via Spreecast, a website that allows for a video conference call between hosts, which can then be viewed by audience members. Subsequently, the episode was available for download as an audio file. In addition to Rod and Karen, the show also featured Kriss from MTR Network. About twenty listeners actively participated in the chatroom built into Spreecast's interface, including many who were also TWiB! listeners and several who produce their own podcasts. Almost without exception, the chatroom participants were already familiar with White's and Manning's conflict, and many had already participated in discussing the incident via social media.

As Rod introduced the topic, listeners in the chatroom were already indicating their familiarity with the situation. Ms. Think Pretty Smart, co-host of the *Whiskey, Wine, and Moonshine* podcast, wrote, "best vid ever!!," and other listeners quoted the "Hey, Homie!" segment of Manning's video. Rod continued, explaining that Manning's video "was so good that I was like 'I wish I was doing the show right now.' . . . And people were like 'Y'all should cover this on your show.' And I was like 'We will.' I was like, it would be even better if we get Kriss here, and that was how this was born." While TWiB!'s videos were produced to engage directly with Manning's discourses and then Manning himself, *TBGWT* clearly had another goal—jokes. The hosts and listeners, while being critical of Manning's antigay position, never attempted to earnestly rebut Manning's argument. Opting to mock it instead, they created a space for intragroup discussion. After a brief summary of the conflict that precipitated Manning's response video, they began playing the audio of Manning's video, which begins with TWiB!'s initial unedited video in its entirety. *TBGWT* then played the audio from Manning's response, pausing it frequently to offer commentary.

At several points, the discussion between Rod, Karen, and Kriss explicitly addressed the differences between TWiB! and TBGWT or MTR's flagship podcast *Insanity Check*. For example, early in TWiB!'s original video, White asks, "Were there no gay Black men before Obama became president? Obviously not." At this point, Rod pauses the audio and says, "Here goes Elon with all this reason and shit. . . . Like this is his thing, like somebody says somethin' patently ridiculous, to which me and Kriss go 'Man, fuck that dude,' and Elon goes, 'Let's explain why this dude is wrong exactly.'" They continue this commentary a few moments later, after White, in his original video, notes that Manning's doctorate was awarded by an unaccredited school that Manning himself founded. Rod pauses the video and he, Karen, and Kriss have the following exchange:

ROD: See, Elon be using the Google.
KRISS: Right, he, you know, he's puttin' work in. . . .

ROD: That's his biggest weakness, by the way. Like, Elon wants to be
accurate.

KAREN: Tryin' do them facts, dog.

ROD: Like, Elon's gonna look the shit up. He's gonna be right. He gon
know. Like, he's gonna ask the right questions. He gon challenge
himself. Ask himself two, three times, like, "Is my opinion the most
correct one? How can I nuance this more?" And that's all well and
good, when you're tryin' to be factual. But dis ain't dat, Elon. [Laugh-
ing] Dis. Ain't. Dat.

These exchanges highlight differences between TWiB! productions and
other Chitlin' Circuit podcasts. While TWiB! actively seeks to intervene in what it sees as problematic discourses, such as the homophobia
forwarded by Manning, *TBGWT* and *Insanity Check*, along with other
podcasts in the Chitlin' Circuit network, are interested in mining such
situations for humor and creating an enjoyable or cathartic experience
for the hosts and their listeners. While the humor used in such instances
often contains implicit, and sometimes explicit, critique, its primary
intent is usually to address an intranetwork audience rather than to
directly rebut individuals such as Manning.

Additionally, the exchange between White and Manning and the
ways it circulated demonstrate several key characteristics of this network. First, it highlights the multimedia, transplatform nature of the
network. The entire exchange transpired using multiple media—images,
text, video, and audio—which were combined and recombined in ways
that facilitated discussion and sharing. Both the conversation and the
content circulated across multiple platforms—on YouTube, Twitter,
Facebook, Google+, Tumblr, Instagram, podcasts, and chatrooms.

Second, this example illustrates the deeply connected and collaborative nature of the network. TBGWT not only made TWiB!'s video and
Manning's response a topic of discussion on its podcast, but also invited
another podcaster, Kriss to participate in it. Additionally, by the time
TBGWT recorded the "#DrManningBars" episode, listeners of the podcast, many of whom were also listeners of TWiB! and who interacted
heavily on social media, were already largely familiar with the incident.
The network connections were made clear by comments in *TBGWT*'s
chatroom during the episode. At one point, Sojourner Verdad, co-host

of *Whiskey, Wine, and Moonshine*, commented, "I wish nicju was here. She found a video of him in an electric blue fancy robe," referring to the co-host of *What's the Tea?* who had earlier found footage of Manning that she had shared with the network. When Manning mentions White's wife, Emily Epstein-White in his video, longtime listener to both *TBGWT* and *TWiB!*'s podcasts, @cubicle_bc, noted that he remembered watching a video of White getting engaged, which took place at a live event for *TWiB!* in New York City and was both live-streamed and recorded.

While this example illustrates the interconnection of the network, it also highlights how each of the three constitutive elements is distinct from the others and furthers its own specific communicative goals. For *TWiB!*, that goal was directly challenging the problematic discourses put forth by Manning by offering a humorous yet well-reasoned and fact-based retort. While *TBGWT*'s coverage was not devoid of critique, it was more concerned with the intracommunity value of discussing the event. Twitter served both as a space to circulate content, such as the videos, and as a space for discussion of events as they unfolded, with podcasts later elaborating.

Additionally, throughout the discussion of the "homo demons" incident participants made heavy use of Black American cultural commonplaces and cultural references, speaking to a Black audience and reifying the network as a Black cultural space. First, the mere selection of the ATLAH sign, located in Harlem, and Manning's comments, connects the interaction to traditions of the Black church. White, at one point, speaking to the rhetorical traditions of the Black church, responded to Manning using the cadence often associated with Black Christian preachers. Additionally, the discussion in the network often relied on specific Black cultural references. For example, the title of *TBGWT* episode "#DrManningBars" is a reference to Hip-hop, in which the word "bars" refers to musical bars and is often used to describe lyrical delivery within the genre. The hosts discussed the exchange between White and Manning as if it were a Hip-hop MC battle, and, at one point, Rod even added the beat from Nas's "Ether," one of the most iconic Hip-hop dis tracks of all time, underneath Manning as he spoke.[80]

Thus, the network is marked as a Black space, both through explicit demarcation such as show names and through communicative practices. Its dual nature—as a broadcast-style network and a digital social network—allows for multiple longstanding Black communicative practices to operate together. Whether in broadcast-style communication, such as TWiB!'s video response to Manning, or in social spaces, such as TBGWT podcasts and their accompanying chatroom, the components function as contributions to larger distributed discussions happening across the network. This deeply interconnected multiplatform network offers participants a range of different affordances that can be leveraged depending on the needs of the moment. As such, aspects of the network can provide a space for both intragroup conversation and engagement with those outside the network. It is the oscillation between these two functions that I address in the next chapter.

2

Enclaves and Counter-Publics

Oscillating Networked Publics

In March 2014, HBO released a *Game of Thrones*–inspired mixtape titled *Catch the Throne*, featuring well-known Hip-hop performers such as Big Boi, Common, and Wale. Lucinda Martinez, HBO's senior vice president for multicultural marketing, described the effort to the *Wall Street Journal*, saying, "Our multicultural audiences are a very important part of our subscribers, and we don't want to take them for granted." But if HBO wanted to reach out to Black *Game of Thrones* viewers, they needed only to look to Twitter, where Black Twitter users have created a robust fandom using the hashtag #DemThrones. Though Twitter often facilitates the visibility of Black discourse, giving Black Twitter its leverage in broader cultural conversations, the African American Vernacular English (AAVE) inflected hashtag effectively conceals the network's activities, even to the robust data gathering mechanisms of HBO itself. #DemThrones participants are able to make use of Twitter's immediacy to engage in synchronous co-viewing and commentary while simultaneously forming a barrier to outsiders.

At times, participants in Black Twitter wish to capitalize on the visibility created by the platform, strategically using trending topics and other affordances to make their voices and experiences more widely known. Yet, at other times, these same affordances bring unwanted visibility, particularly scrutiny from dominant groups, in ways that inhibit Black users from participating freely on the platform. In response to this tension, participants in the network that is the focus of this book have developed a range of techniques for managing visibility and maximizing platforms for their communicative goals. This chapter explores how the network, conceptualized as a transplatform networked public, shifts between functioning as an enclave, which serves as a forum for unpoliced intranetwork conversation, and a counter-public, which engages directly in contesting and opposing discourses outside the network. The cultural practices, epistemologies, and subject positions of the users interact with the materiality of the technologies to create a set of imagined affordances that allow this oscillation between enclave and counter-public.

Digital media scholars often invoke "publics" in analyses of digital networks, though they may rely on different definitions of the term. In the original Habermasian concept of the public sphere, the term carries with it some kind of political valence, including active deliberation and explicit political discussion.[1] However, for marginalized groups, seemingly mundane activities often come to take on political importance. The performance of social identities and the "expression of one's cultural identity through idiom and style" can be an important mode of political engagement, regardless of whether there are direct and immediately discernable political consequences.[2] For Black Americans, who must operate within a white supremacist society, seemingly apolitical, mundane, or everyday activities are often de facto political because they resist white normativity.[3]

The public discussed here is a networked public—one that is constituted and structured by networked technology. In her theorization of networked publics, danah boyd asserts that they are both "(1) *the space* constructed through networked technologies and (2) *the imagined collective* that emerges as a result of the intersection of people, technology, and practice."[4] In much digital media research, the digital *space* of the public is treated as coterminous with the platform that is the focus of analysis. MySpace, Facebook, Twitter, and Tumblr have all been discussed as hosting publics of various kinds.[5] But it is also fruitful to consider the ways that the *collective* constructs a *space* that is not limited by platform. In doing this, we can begin to conceptualize different platforms not as separate and interlocking networked publics, but as elements of one multilayered public, the space populated by the collective, where imagined affordances can be strategically deployed in conjunction with one another. This approach is particularly suitable for elucidating Twitter, which commonly serves as a content aggregator and bridge between multiple platforms.

Conceptualized this way, the network at the center of this project comes into view as what Catherine Squires has called an "oscillating public." Squires is most frequently cited for her three-part model of publics as enclaves, counter-publics, and satellite publics, each of which she identifies by analysis of motivation, communicative practices, and behaviors. She observes that a public can separate itself from others, forming an enclave where "counterhegemonic ideas and strategies" can be hidden "in order to avoid sanctions." By contrast, counter-publics "engage in debate with wider publics," often "to test ideas and perhaps utilize traditional social movement tactics." Satellite publics are hybrids of the two, "seek[ing] separation from other publics for reasons other than oppressive relationships but . . . involved in wider public discourses from time to time." Such publics "aim to maintain a solid group identity and build independent institutions," while at times entering "into wider public debates when there is clear convergence of their interests with those of other publics" or when they experience "friction or controversies with wider publics."[6] However, her earlier work does not include satellite publics and instead refers to publics that shift their function as "oscillating." Squires describes this phenomenon saying, ". . . we can also imagine a public *oscillating* to engage in debate with outsiders, to test ideas."[7] I wish to recuperate Squires's notion of oscillating publics because, while satellite publics do engage wider publics from time to time, the concept of satellite publics does not fully capture the frequent, contingent, and multilayered shifts unfolding constantly in the network I analyze here. Thus, I believe the concept of oscillation has profound utility for understanding the function of publics in the digital landscape.

Referring to the three types of publics, Squires observes "institutional, political, and social contexts may make the use of one of these types of responses more prevalent at any given moment." She notes that enclave, counter-public, and satellite public are not absolute or stable states. But, in different moments the "discourse and cultural expressions of a public may employ all of these responses."[8] When moved to networked digital contexts, this fluctuation intensifies. Catherine Knight Steele explores this fluidity in her work on Black blogs by showing how they shift between these modes based on their theme.[9] Because the network at the center of this project brings together various media and platforms, the shifting both Squires and Steele highlight is more deeply pronounced. Given the way discourse is produced and flows across various digital platforms, which, while linked and intertwined, possess their own materiality and functionality, it is productive to think of one multiplatform network that shifts, or oscillates, between enclave and counter-public. Moreover, this networked public does not shift in its entirety. Various elements of the platform are often deployed simultaneously for different functions, with some elements serving as enclaves and others being used as counter-publics. These shifts are accomplished through the imagined affordances of various platforms, which sometimes align with developer intentions and sometimes circumvent them.

The network discussed here oscillates between both enclave and counter-public, deploying different imagined affordances and strategies, sometimes simultaneously, to do so. Thus, I argue that this network is an oscillating networked public, in which material affordances are combined with culturally specific communicative practices that create a space for both intragroup discussion and direct counter-public debate. The oscillation may be achieved through the movement of users from one platform to another or by maneuvering within platforms to imagine non-normative affordances. Futher, enclave and counter-public are not mutually exclusive states and may exist simultaneously, even inhabited by the same people as they use different platforms or deploy different strategies on the same platform in tandem.

I begin with a description of how the network functions to create enclaves through technological functionalities that create barriers, both formal and informal, to outsider participation. I then turn to how the network can simultaneously be used to disrupt and challenge discourses from outside the network. Finally, I conclude with a discussion of how the affordances of networked publics, particularly related to scalability and invisible audiences, allow and sometimes force the network to oscillate from enclave to counter-public.

Networked Enclaves

The network at the center of this project functions as a resource for creating enclaves away from the disciplining gaze of the dominant society, where marginalized groups can communicate and interact using non-hegemonic discursive practices. Squires uses James Scott's concepts of "hidden transcripts," the discourses and knowledges marginalized groups must obscure from the dominant group, to describe the type of communication that happens in enclaves.[10] Furthermore, as Karma Chávez demonstrates, these enclaves can also serve as essential spaces where groups can interpret external rhetoric about themselves and create new rhetorical strategies.[11] The racial hierarchies and power structures of the United States have long necessitated that Black Americans create such spaces for themselves—dating back to "hush harbors" formed in slave quarters, woods, and praise houses where Black people interacted with each other away from the white gaze and continuing in the traditions of Black churches and barber and beauty shops of today.[12] Such spaces not only allowed for safe and sequestered Black sociality, but were "at the core of the black critical tradition in America."[13]

Vorris Nunely demonstrates that such enclaves are crucial to the development and maintenance of Black epistemologies and subjectivities. He describes them as "lifeworlds" where "Black political rationality has been and continues to be privileged" and where "the unsaid in the public sphere gets said; where the unhearable gets heard; and where the filtering of American and African American culture and life occurs through African American hermeneutics."[14] These "camouflaged" spaces produce and maintain what Nunely terms "African American Hush Harbor Rhetoric (AAHHR)," which contains and conveys Black epistemes and rationalities. This rhetoric exceeds cultural difference and identity and involves the "manufacturing of ontology and knowledge."[15] AAHHR takes Black experience and knowledge as normative and serves "as a primary ground for manufacturing Black or African American subjectivities." Thus, he asserts, "Beneath the vernacular banter is a biopolitics that does not merely resist (which depends too much on the power and subjectivities it opposes) but, more importantly, produces distinct subjectivities." The enclaves and the AAHHR they produce "do more than challenge White, mainstream, and American knowledge on the political or social register; they challenge on the level of ontology and subjectivity . . . the very notion of what it is to be fully human."[16]

The network discussed here provides participants with a multimedia, transplatform, and mobile set of resources for creating enclaves in which AAHHR can thrive. Enclaves are created through podcasts and their channels for audience interaction, through private and closed Facebook groups, and through the use of nonstandard hashtags and AAVE to obscure conversations on Twitter. This technologically enabled iteration of hush harbor enclaves has a geographic reach and a mobility unavailable to previous generations. At the same time technology has also made these spaces available to the white gaze in new ways and thus posed new challenges for maintaining the boundaries of the enclave.

Of the various elements of the network, the Chitlin' Circuit podcasts function most effectively to create networked enclaves. Here podcasters and their listeners can engage in a range of communicative practices away from the white surveillance and dominant discourses that constitute whiteness as normative. These practices include community-building, catharsis, interpretation of outside discourse, fan practices, and everyday discussion. For Black Americans, operating within a society constrained by discourses of colorblindness, where their mere performance of race might illicit hostility, spaces for such practices must be actively created, maintained, and policed. As Rod said of *The Black Guy Who Tips* (*TBGWT*) podcast, "It's a safe spot, and we don't have a lot of safe spots in American media and in America as a whole."[17] He characterized the podcast as a "stress free" media space, saying, "Black people listen to our podcast because they're like, 'Here's a place where I don't have to worry about being attacked all the fucking time.'"[18] These podcasts allow participants to interact around a range of issues without having to conform to white norms and where AAHHR is the communicative and epistemological foundation. They interpellate listeners through the use of AAHHR, deploying cultural commonplaces, vernaculars, and modes of address to evoke the kind of "Black audience" described by Nunely.

Though podcasts often take many conventions from radio, the Chitlin' Circuit podcasts more closely resemble informal social interactions in their embrace of a free-flowing, flexible, and conversational style, including significant phatic communication and the use of a wide range of vernaculars. One comment left on iTunes by a listener described the discussions on *3 Guys On* using the term "chop it up,"[19] a vernacular expression common in Black communities that refers to friendly, informal conversation. For his part, Rod describes the *TBGWT* podcast format as "kind of just talkin'. But it's organized talkin'."[20] Often shows depart from the formal introduction that offers listeners the name of the podcast and the names of the hosts. It is not uncommon, for example, for the hosts of *Where's My 40 Acres?* (*WM40A?*) to get so wrapped up in conversations that they get twenty or thirty minutes into a show before introducing themselves. Some podcasts never introduce the hosts, leaving listeners to glean their names only through consistent listening.

The use of Black vernaculars is also central to the differences between the Chitlin' Circuit podcasts and radio. Podcasters in this network come from across the United States, representing a wide range of accents and vernacular variations. The podcaster who perhaps exemplifies this most is Karen from *TBGWT*, who has a pronounced southern accent that many listeners say reminds them of home or family. One iTunes review, titled "Country Play Cousin," described her accent, as "country. Like no shoes, dirt road, sharecropper country."[21] Black vernaculars and cultural commonplaces are prevalent, as are references to Black expressive cultures. This hails listeners as a Black audience by requiring them to have appropriate cultural competencies and related AAHHR frameworks to understand the discussions taking place.

This approach makes the podcasts unappealing for some who are looking for a more normative, radio-style production that has been made available as a podcast through asynchronous mobile technology. But to the majority of the Chitlin' Ciruit listeners, the approach creates a chemistry that invokes spending time with friends or family. The iTunes reviews of the podcasts in this network are filled with comments about how the shows feel like casual conversation with friends or family. For example, one reviewer described listening to *Whiskey, Wine, and Moonshine*, a podcast hosted by three Black women, as "sitting around with my sisterfriends having a talkfest along with drinks,"[22] while another reviewer noted that Nicju and Reggie, hosts of *What's the Tea?*, "have a great back and forth and will instantly become friends in your head."[23] *In Deep Show* and The Black Astronauts' show *Ladies Launch* were described as making you feel "part of your family" and "at home," respectively.[24] One iTunes review of *What's the Tea?* was titled "Break out those good plates!" and went on to describe the podcast as "like your favorite aunty and uncle visiting."[25]

It is not uncommon for the podcasts to be compared, by both listeners and the podcasters themselves, to iconic spaces of AAHHR such as the barber or beauty shop or church. For example, one early episode of TWiB!'s *Blacking It Up!* was explicitly titled "Barbershop." After Elon James White, co-host Aaron Rand Freeman, and several listeners who called in had a frank and in-depth conversation about Black men's experiences with the police, guest Luvvie Ajayi remarked that she felt like she was a "fly on the wall at the barbershop."[26] Comments left on iTunes by listeners of *TBGWT*, *3 Guys On*, and *The Black Astronauts* reiterate the assertion that the shows are reminiscent of the barbershop. One review for *TBGWT* was even titled, "Barber shop (or beauty shop) talk for you [sic] iPod and MP3 player."[27] Another review, this one of *3 Guys On* titled "am i in the barber shop?!," began, "'cause that's how i feel when i listen to y'all."[28] Prior to joining TWiB!, Shane Paul Neil, co-host of TWiB!'s *Sportsball*, described *TBGWT*, *WM40A?*, and *Insanity Check* as "bringing the barbershop to the internet."[29] Similarly, *What's the Tea?* has been compared in iTunes reviews more than once to going to church. One review says that the hosts, Nicju and Reggie, "come together each week to take you to pod church and you would do well to attend service regularly."[30] Another simply states, "They remind me of folks I went to church with and had great conversations with."[31] Such comparisons are noteworthy because, Melissa Harris-Perry argues, important ideological work, such as the construction of worldviews and collective identity, happens in everyday talk and interactions occurring in these Black social spaces.[32]

Podcasting's commonalities with radio strengthen the medium's ability to convincingly reproduce the feeling of Black social enclaves. Scholars have argued that radio is a deeply intimate medium. As Susan Douglas observes, "Listening often imparts a sense of emotion stronger than that imparted by looking," because "While sight allows us some distance . . . sound envelops us, pouring into us whether we want it to or not, including us, involving us."[33] This sense of being immersed in sound allows listeners to feel transported into the conversation they are listening to, feeling as if, as one iTunes review for *Straight Outta LoCash* describes it, they are "chilling with the homies and kicking it and having a good time."[34] With content that closely mimics the kinds of conversation that take place in traditional Black social spaces such as barber and beauty shops and churches, these podcasts "envelop" listeners with the sound of these Black enclaves.

Moreover the recreation of Black enclaves is intensified by mobile listening practices. Alexander Weheliye has demonstrated the ways sound can be used to produce a sense of private space.[35] Mobile listening allows listeners to reproduce a sense of these spaces on-demand wherever they are. Headphones in particular, which are sold as a means of sonic personalization by their manufacturers and often used as such by consumers, can be used to create a sense of personal space, simulating privacy.[36] Michael Bull's work on iPod listeners has shown that users often consume audio via mobile devices and headphones to "sonically individualiz[e] their experience of space."[37] He argues that mobile listeners use headphones to create a "sound bubble" around themselves as a means "to claim a mobile and auditory territory for themselves through a form of 'sensory gating.'"[38] Mack Hagood writes of Bose's QuietComfort noise-canceling headphones as *"soundscaping devices*, carving out an acoustically rendered sense of personal space."[39] Soundscaping offers a "sense of physical and psychological space" despite one's surroundings.[40]

Chitlin' Circuit podcast listeners have reported, via iTunes and Stitcher reviews and other channels for feedback, that they listen to the podcasts while commuting to work and while at work, using headphones in their cubicles or offices. Many listeners have also indicated that they are one of a few Black people, or even the only Black person, at their place of employment, a phenomenon so common that some podcasters dubbed such individuals "cubical Negroes," and there is a podcast in the network entirely devoted to office life titled *Operation Cubicle*. Black podcast listeners can use their mobile podcasts to soundscape their daily lives with sounds of Black sociality as they navigate the world.

More than simply cocooning listeners in the sounds of Black sociality, the podcasts aid in the reproduction of Black subjectivity constituted through AAHHR, which is "where Black meanings can be found, where Black folks go to rebaptize themselves in Black culture in ways often unavailable in the public sphere."[41] As Nunely argues, Black cultural commonplaces can exude "massive concentrations of Black symbolic energy. This symbolic energy moves African American audiences because it taps deeply into African American terministic screens, experiences, memories, and meaning."[42] Mobile listening allows for this process to become portable and on-demand. Through the use of Black epistemes and discourses, the podcasts produce the listeners' subjectivity in opposition to the dominant racial discourses that work to produce them as racialized, and therefore marginalized, subjects. They are sonically able to shut out the "hail" of the dominant discourse and instead cocoon themselves in sonic landscapes that interpellate them as fully human Black subjects.

Further, these podcast listeners demonstrate how users' cultural practices, expectations, and subject positions interact with the materiality of technology and the designers' intentions to shape the imagined affordances of a technology. While such Black podcast listeners soundscape to claim acoustic space and insulate themselves from their surroundings, their strategy is the inverse of how Bose seems to imagine their consumers. Hagood points to the underlying neoliberal logic of the Bose headphones' branding and advertising campaign, which feature white male business travelers attempting to find respite from the unwanted noise of jet engines, crying children, and women's voices while in transit.[43] He argues that QuietComfort headphones are designed as technologies of individualization built on the neoliberal logic "that problems must be solved individually and within the market rather than addressed as systemic issues."[44] These Black podcast listeners, however, soundscape with the sounds of Black sociality, cultivating not individualism, but collectivity. They seek not to isolate themselves, but to ameliorate their isolation in a white milieu. Their simulated private space is not one of individual privacy, but of the collective private spaces of Black enclaves.

Moreover, these podcasts are not always simply mimicking Black sociality. The digital and social media network in which the podcasts are embedded creates numerous avenues for listener participation. Chitlin' Circuit podcasts maintain various combinations of real-time chatrooms accompanying their live streams, a strong social media presence, and multiple avenues for listeners feedback, including email, comment sections, and voicemail. Shows that live-stream during the workday allow listeners to interact with the show and other listeners in real time. Often comments in the chatrooms or on Twitter are inserted into a show's discussions, allowing listeners channels for synchronous interaction and participation. To varying degrees, these feedback channels, particularly the chatroom, allow the audience members to become interlocutors in the conversations as they unfold on air. Thus, they are not merely enveloped in the AAHHR of the podcasts but are often active participants in its construction.

However, this process is not uncomplicated. Moving Black social enclaves to digital spaces increases the likelihood that the conversations will be "overheard" by outsiders, a phenomenon that occurs frequently on blogs and in social media where Black discourse is made available and visible to outsiders in a way it was not before.[45] Podcasts, however, are more resistant to easy intrusion and therefore ideal for creating enclaves, given how the medium's distribution and consumption model makes it difficult for the casual troll or harasser to penetrate. None of the podcasts in the network formally advertises beyond it; instead, they all cultivate their audiences through word of mouth, social media interactions, and guest appearances on other podcasts. Thus, to know that a podcast even exists, one must already have some contact with the network. This, along with the temporal commitment required by a podcast, increases the difficulty of intruding into the conversation, compared to Twitter or other social media, which are easily searchable and have algorithms that make discourses more visible.[46] The podcasts unfold in real time; you can't "skim" them as you might a text-based medium like Twitter or Facebook. At best, a listener can play the podcast at an accelerated speed to decrease listening time. But, given that it is not uncommon for the podcasts in this network to be over two hours long, this only minimizes the time commitment somewhat.

Additionally, unlike social media, podcasts are not searchable. While show titles and descriptions (to the extent that the show provides a description) are searchable, the actual audio content is not. Searchability is one of the four key affordances of networked publics.[47] The inclusion of podcasts as a prominent element of a transplatform networked public limits that affordance for a segment of the network. Thus, the podcasts form opaque pockets within the distributed conversation occurring across the network. Conversations that begin on social media are often carried over to the quasi-private spaces of the podcasts, where outsiders are deterred from participating. While podcasts are networked and disseminated in ways that transgress temporal and geographic boundaries, they still offer a barrier to intrusion by those who do not operate within the parameters of AAHHR rationalities and discourses.

Though podcasts serve an important function in enclaving, they are by no means the only part of the network deployed in this way. Because the podcasts are so deeply intertwined with the digital social networks of the podcasters and their listeners, they also serve as hubs around which social media enclaves are created. In the summer of 2015, both TWiB! and TBGWT created closed Facebook communities, which users must request permission to join. Though the moderators approve almost any request, the process can deter random people looking to troll and harass the group. By the end of 2015, TWiB!'s group had over 780 members and TBGWT's had over 1,100. Other podcasts have a followed suit, creating similar closed groups, all of which have significantly overlapping memberships.

These groups are not fan communities in which listeners discuss the shows and their content. Sometimes news stories or comments shared in them become topics of discussion on the podcasts, rarely vice versa. While these groups are another extension of the network, they are also enclaves in themselves—open to new members yet policed against hostile users. Thus, when White announced TWiB!'s group on Twitter, saying "Are you a fan of #TWiBNation?," he emphasized that "we've created a FB group that's moderated to keep it safe and awesome w/ EXCLUSIVE CONTENT"[48] Karen and fellow podcaster Aaron B., of the Black Astronauts Podcast Network, explained that she and Rod had worked to make TBGWT's group "a place that is safe and not hostile" for their fans.[49] This means that some boundaries have to be observed, Karen explained how TBGWT's Facebook group differed from individual's personal profiles, "You have to deal with that on your normal Facebook I was like not here that's why we made it private."[50] Apart from privacy, Rod said, "We literally only have one rule, don't be a dick." He continued by noting that anyone who listens to their show knows they don't want transphobia, sexism, or misogyny in the group, "You know, don't troll and harass our fans. Don't come in there spreading this stupid shit."[51]

Networked Counter-Publics

While some elements of this network function effectively to create enclaves, other elements serve a counter-public function and engage with those outside of the network, particularly those who further dominant racial discourses. Counter-publics operate by engaging other, often hostile, publics. According to Squires, they reject the performance of hegemonic communicative behaviors and "instead project the hidden transcripts, previously spoken only in enclaves, to dominant publics."[52]

This can involve testing the reaction of wider publics by asserting previously unstated ideas and opinions, rebutting or challenging dominant publics, or attempting to build coalitions with other groups. In the case of this network, it also functions to move AAHHR, and the epistemes and interpretive frameworks it contains, beyond the enclave to where it can directly challenge hegemonic discourses.

Twitter serves as an important site of counter-public engagement for the network due to the architecture of the platform, the visibility Black Twitter has gained in recent years, the micro-celebrity status of many participants, and the connection of several participants to news outlets and activist or advocacy groups. While Black Americans were active on Twitter from its inception, it was not until Twitter started its trending topics feature in 2009 that this presence became visible to users more broadly as Black Twitter users' heavy traffic began pushing their hashtags and tweets into the trending topics.[53] By 2010, the trending topics were often dominated by Black users live-tweeting events such as the *BET Awards*, and over the next few years, the network that has come to be known as Black Twitter received attention from bloggers and other online personalities.[54] Gradually, Black Twitter had garnered the visibility to exercise influence on the news cycle.

Twitter was an indispensable component in bringing the 2012 shooting death of Trayvon Martin to broader attention. By 2013, Black Twitter had become visible enough to be able to leverage the network to have an impact more broadly. This was the year of hashtags such as #PaulasBestDishes, which helped increase pressure on celebrity chef Paula Deen as she was being sued for creating a hostile work environment, and #JurorB37, a member of the jury that acquitted George Zimmerman in the death of Trayvon Martin and who had gotten a book deal to write about the trial. Black Twitter also became mainstay topic in the blogoshpere, the *Root* started its regular "Chateratti" feature, and Buzzfeed produced the first of its "Best Black Twitter Moments."[55] Thus, members of the Black Twitter network potentially have access to the visibility generated by Black Twitter itself.

Twitter is public and easily searchable, and it allows for simultaneous direct address and multilayered conversation.[56] This, combined with the visibility of Black Twitter and the micro-celebrity of many in the network, makes Twitter an ideal counter-public space. Finally, several of the podcasters function as gates to larger, more mainstream publications, allowing them access to venues as well as opportunities to push the counter-discourses of the network out to other publics. One early example of this use was a 2011 debate between White and several users who supported the Occupy Wall Street movement in which White rebutted attempts to assert colorblind discourses as the appropriate interpretive lens.

During November and December 2011, the movement was at its height. Incidents of police use of force against the movement, including the use of pepper spray, filled the news.[57] On November 15, the New York Police Department evicted Occupy protestors from their camp in Zuccotti Park in Manhattan. In response to the news coverage of police use of force on Occupy protestors, White tweeted, "'Oh? The NYPD are treating you badly? Violent for no reason? Weird.'—Black People."[58] White's critique highlighted how police violence experienced by Black Americans has been routinely ignored while the use of force against largely white Occupy protestors was receiving heavy media attention. His tweet was retweeted over 2,600 times, a large number for those early days on Twitter. Over the next couple of weeks, White created a multimodal argument elaborating on the sentiment expressed in his tweet, interweaving his Twitter timeline and an article he published on the *Root*. The article, which begins with a screen capture of his above tweet, outlined his frustrations with the stream of tweets and blogs expressing outrage over the police's action:

> Although I absolutely agreed with the sentiments, I had a nagging feeling in my stomach. I couldn't let it go. My inner militant Negro (whom I keep sedated with brunch and Modern Warfare 3) wanted to write in all caps: "OH, SO THE WHITE MAN GETS HIT AND NOW IT'S AN ISSUE! THE BLACK MAN HAS BEEN BEATEN FOR YEARS! WE DIDN'T LAND ON PLYMOUTH ROCK, PLYMOUTH ROCK LANDED ON US!!"[59]

While the Twitter conversation inspired the article, White also tweeted excerpts from the article, along with the link to it. For example,

> When minorities speak up & say there's an issue, we're told maybe we're doing something wrong.

The type of outrage that pops up now at what many of us have lived w/ on a regular basis for years feels insulting.

your newfound plight has been some peoples [sic] plight for generations. We just didn't have a catchy name for it.[60]

White tagged these tweets with #OWS, the hashtag that was being used by the Occupy movement and those discussing it. The hashtag functioned as a crucial tool for counter-public engagement by creating a point of articulation between this networked public and other publics, thereby enabling the debate and contestation that are central to counter-publics.

Thus, the conversation that began as a comment on Twitter from a micro-celebrity who was part of a highly visible network then migrated to a formal media outlet, the *Root*, because of White's existing professional connections. The inclusion of White's Twitter handle in the article enabled any reader to engage him directly, while White's use of the #OWS hashtag in the tweeted excerpts from his article made it visible beyond his followers. In this way, White was able to take a critique grounded in AAHHR and move it out to a broader public. In fact, the sentiment of his initial tweet was not unique to him, but reflected conversations taking place in the network more broadly. White and his Twitter account served as a locus of counter-public engagement through which the counter-discourses of the network could be deployed in other publics.

As a result, many supporters of Occupy challenged White on Twitter by using a colorblind framework and trying various tactics to minimize the role of race. The users who challenged White deployed three primary discourses. First, they asserted the primacy of class, and not race, in social oppression. For example, one user tweeted, "To be fair, it's about economics, regardless of color. Cops crack just as many skulls in trailer parks as in the hood,"[61] and another commented, "right now rich folks vs the rest of us trumps race."[62] Second, they asserted that the invocation of race was inherently divisive and problematic. One user replied to White, tweeting, "do u know where racism begins? with a racial identity! #selfsegregation is still #segregation."[63] Finally, these users rehearsed discourses about how race does not exist on a biological level.

One user tweeted to White, "Technically, there is only the human race. Genetics are too homogenous among all humans to differentiate into different races."[64] All of these discourses served to reinforce the dominant discourse of colorblindness.

White and his followers addressed such comments on Twitter, using the @-reply feature, which allows for direct exchanges. This allowed users to challenge White directly and allowed him to respond directly. Each of White's replies were also seen by his followers, many of whom joined the conversation. White and others in the network rebutted these comments in no uncertain terms. Thus, in response to claims that "self-segregation" and racial identity is the core source of racism, White responded directly to the user, "This is ridiculous."[65] Several of White's followers engaged the same user. For example, @solbutterfly, a member of the network and a racial justice organizer, specifically invoked colorblind racism, saying, "Colorblind racism (which is what that statement is) presupposed that race does not exist as a system of oppression 2day."[66]

In addition to directly rebutting the users challenging him, White used tweets without @-reply's to produce general, nondirected counter-discourse. For example, prompted by the responses he got, White used a series of tweets to address a longstanding tension between white progressives and Black communities around the prioritization of race in politics and activism. He specifically identified the erasure of race as a barrier, rather than path, to solidarity. White put forth his critique in a series of tweets, including

> Why do you need to bring up your race, huh? #BetterQuestion: Why are you so bothered by it?

> STOP TRYING TO ERASE RACE. Race doesn't separate us from you. You telling me that race is not important DOES.

> I refuse to play absolutes. I refuse to lose part of myself to make others comfortable. Either open your mind or be prepared to fight.

> So in order for the 99% to be as one we all have to strip ourselves of our identities? What type of one dimensional nonsense is that?

Understanding our difference within 99% will actually bring us together. Trying to erase them will only cause resentment.[67]

The use of a series of tweets to make an extended argument on Twitter, known as a "tweetstorm,"[68] was enhanced when Twitter began threading conversational replies in 2013. The thread feature, added in 2017, then made these conversations potentially more visible. At the same time, the structure of Twitter allows for discussion of public debates to take place on an individual's timeline. This was the case when White and Blair L. M. Kelley, Associate Professor of History at North Carolina State University and the host of TWiB!'s podcast *Historical Blackness* had a sarcastic exchange that highlighted the salience of race in the lives of Black Americans historically:

> KELLEY: Are they beating @elonjames with the "race isn't real" stick? It was real in the LAW until 1965. . . .
> WHITE: NOT BIOLOGICALLY . . .
> KELLEY: It was real enough to hold my ancestors in slavery for generations . . .
> WHITE: THAT'S JUST A CONSTRUCT MAN . . .[69]

This debate over race and Occupy Wall Street, which illustrates how the network can be used to directly confront discourses about Black communities, was relatively small in scale compared with the discussions that occurred during moments of racial turmoil, such as the 2012 death of Trayvon Martin, the 2013 acquittal of George Zimmerman, and the 2014 unrest in Ferguson. With regard to these, the network discussed here participated in leveraging Twitter to create a counter-public that contested racial discourses at a national level, as I discuss in greater detail in chapter 4.

Oscillating Networked Publics

Though Twitter and podcasting have architectures and functionalities that encourage their use as counter-public and enclaves, respectively, these elements of the network are not static. Users often oscillate from one function to another. Below, I outline two examples of oscillation.

The first concerns fan practices around *Game of Thrones* in which participants live-tweet using nonstandard hashtags, which obscure their activities from outsiders while allowing them the take full advantage of Twitter's affordances for synchronous co-viewing. The second example, the creation of and reaction to the #BernieSoBlack hashtag, illustrates that at times the network oscillates not because it chooses to do so, but because external pressures can force enclaves spaces to shift to serve a counter-public function.

#DemThrones: Thwarting Visibility on Twitter

Fandom is one of the most prominent day-to-day practices of the network, including TV show recaps, movie reviews, and live-tweeting. Since seemingly mundane interactions can function as a terrain for AAHHR, subverting white epistemes and reaffirming Black subjectivities, such fan practices have deep significance, and for many Black Americans fandom can be a political act. Rebecca Wanzo writes, that because of the lack of representation and persistence of problematic representations of Blackness, "Fandom has often been asked of African Americans and has been treated as an act of resistance necessary for the progress of the race. . . . In the African American community, film and television are often seen as having a great deal of importance."[70]

Fandom is complex terrain for Black fans, particularly for those who are women and/or LGBTQ. Fandom itself is often coded as white.[71] Further, the network discussed here is heavily invested in media that is considered "nerd culture," such as video games, comic books, and sci-fi and fantasy genre TV shows and movies. Nerd culture is often constructed in opposition to "coolness," making participation in nerd culture contentious for Black fans whose racial identity has long been coded as "cool."[72] Because nerdiness is coded as both white and masculine, Black women in particular can feel alienated.[73] One general response to these complications has been for Black nerds, many of whom have taken to calling themselves "Blerds," to create podcasts and websites devoted to their fan practices, including *Nerdgasm Noire Network*, *Black Girl Nerds*, *Black Tribbles*, *For Colored Nerds*, and TWiB!'s *We Nerd Hard*, to name a few.

In addition to simply providing spaces where Black users can engage in fandom and mundane interactions without being marginalized or facing racial and/or gendered aggression, spaces also allow Black users to engage with media texts in culturally resonate ways. The explicitly Black cultural space of the network allows users a level of cultural specificity in their fandom that would be impossible to achieve in normatively white spaces. Kristen Warner, in her work on Black women *Scandal* fans, asserts that "a fan community is created not only out of a shared interest in a love object but also out of similar approaches to demonstrating that love."[74] She highlights how *Scandal* fans layer expressions of Black culture over the media text by giving commentary, summarizing scenes, or rephrasing dialogue in AAVE to "fill in cognitive gaps" left by the colorblind racial discourse of the show.[75] This network's fandoms deploy similar approaches, creating Black spaces to engage in forms of fandom that allow for cultural specificity and the embrace of Black communicative practices.

One major component of the network's fan practices is live-tweeting, especially during television shows, including *Game of Thrones*, *The Walking Dead*, *The Strain*, *Arrow*, *The Flash*, *Love and Hip-Hop*, and *Scandal*, along with movies and shows available through streaming services such as Netflix. The network also participates in live-tweeting award shows, particularly the *BET Awards*, as well as political debates and sporting events.[76] Black Girl Nerds (BGN), which is an online community that includes a website, a podcast of the same name, and a strong social media presence, often coordinates such live tweets. BGN was created to allow "women of color with various eccentricities to express themselves freely and embrace who they are."[77] Past shows used for their synchronous viewing have included the 1980s cartoon *Jem* and cult classics *The Last Dragon* and *Coming to America*. Graveyard Shift Sisters, a website and a Twitter presence devoted to Black female horror fandom, coordinates asynchronous tweeting of streamed horror films every Friday night using the hashtag #FridayNightHorror. They have coordinated live tweets of movies such as *Scream*, *Night of the Living Dead*, *Friday the 13th*, and *Vampire in Brooklyn*.

Among the most popular televisions shows in the network is HBO's series *Game of Thrones*. The network has nicknamed the show "Dem Thrones," an AAVE-inflected version of the show's title that is also used as a hashtag for live-tweeting. The nickname "Dem Thrones" was created by the hosts of the *FiyaStarter* podcast during season 2 finale, and

#DEMTHRONES was included in the show notes for their July 7, 2012 show. The first occurrence of the hashtag on Twitter was in May 2012.[78] It was popularized by *TBGWT* during that same year and subsequently picked up and further popularized by other podcasts, in particular *Black Girl Nerds*. By the beginning of *Game of Thrones* season 3, in summer 2013, *TBGWT* inaugurated its regular weekly *Game of Thrones* recap segment with "Episode 443: Return of #DemThrones."[79] What began as a relatively short segment, clocking in at about half an hour for the first recap, has since grown into a regular in-depth discussion lasting sometimes up to two hours. By season 5, #DemThrones was making regular appearances in Twitter's US trending topics and was being used by high-profile Twitter users like director Ava Devernay and Ferguson protester Netta Elzie.[80]

The use of a non-standard hashtag is of note for several reasons. First, the majority of fans live-tweeting shows generally use a standardized hashtag, customarily created by the television industry. For *Game of Thrones* this is #GameofThrones or, more commonly, #GoT. The #DemThrones hashtag, which emerged from the network rather than from the marketing mechanisms of HBO, was largely insulated for many years from those outside the network. The AAVE hashtag #DemThrones effectively organized an enclave, whose members could take advantage of the platform's affordances to engage in synchronous co-viewing while obscuring their tweets from outsiders. Second, the use of AAVE marks the timeline as a culturally Black space, thereby hailing participants as a "Black audience" and signaling that the fandom will be grounded in Black interpretive frameworks. This ad hoc Twitter enclave, combined with podcast recaps, allows culturally inflected fandom, as well as Black readings of a text with a notable absence of Black bodies.[81]

This strategy is imperfect, however, because Twitter is easily searchable and uses algorithms, like the trending topics, that make content visible. As of season 5, the #DemThrones hashtag had garnered enough popularity to regularly appear in the US trending topics, increasing the likelihood that those outside the network would take note. This, in fact did happen in 2016, as evidenced by *Business Insider*'s article "If You're Using the 'Game of Thrones' Hashtag, You're Missing Out on the Show's Best Commentary," which quoted a number of tweets from the May 16 episode, including one by the Black Girl Nerds Twitter account, and noted the existence of many other "Black Twitter offshoots of mainstream hashtags."[82] The visibility of the hashtag has led to some low-level harassment targeting Black participants. For example, just a week prior to the *Business Insider* article, a user with the Gadsden flag as an avatar tweeted an image of a Movement for Black Lives march overlaid with the text,[83] "Has it occurred to anyone that if you're able to organize this many people for a protest you can organize this many people to clean up your community and get rid of the criminal element causing the problem?"[84] The account tagged the image with #DemThrones, the only use of the hashtag by this user, clearly to insert the tweet into a timeline dominated by Black users. Regardless, nonstandard hashtags, usually a Black vernacular–inflected iteration of a TV show's name, continue to be popular with Black Twitter users. There are many variations, often using AAVE iterations of "them," "that," and "they," such as #DeyWalking and #DemDeadz for *The Walking Dead*, #DatStrain for FX's vampire horror show *The Strain*, and #DatArrow for CW's superhero show *Arrow*. During the airing of the 2016 miniseries *The People vs. O.J. Simpson*, participants used the hashtag #DatJuice. Thus, such a strategy seems to have continued utility for insulating fan practices.

#BernieSoBlack: Oscillation under Duress

The response to the 2015 hashtag #BernieSoBlack demonstrates not only how the networked public oscillates, but also how the contingency and fluidity of imagined affordances can allow outside pressure to shape this process. In response to the way that Sanders handled the 2015 protest at Netroots Nation, the network deployed Twitter as a counter-public to critique Sanders. His appearance at the Presidential Town Hall had been disrupted by Black Lives Matter protestors, after which he was heavily criticized for inadequately addressing issues of racial justice. It is common practice for celebrities, politicians, and public figures to be the topic of discussion and criticism on Twitter. Because of its role as a real-time central clearinghouse for information, Twitter was the first platform where many in the network expressed their critiques and where Sanders's supporters initially both encountered and responded to the criticism of their candidate. Often such counter-public engagement becomes the topic of discussion in the network's enclaves, as participants interpret events and produce their own discourse shielded by informal barriers that deter interlopers. But, with #BernieSoBlack, the fervor around the issue generated sufficient motivation for Sanders's more zealous supporters to not only penetrate the enclaves but also force them to oscillate and function temporarily as a counter-public.

Rod initially created the hashtag as a response to the contentious counter-public engagement occurring on Twitter. Often criticism of Sanders was met by assertions of his Civil Rights Movement bona fides, including the fact that Sanders had worked with Congress of Racial Equality (CORE) and was present at Martin Luther King Jr.'s 1963 March on Washington, and proclamations of his devotion to Black communities with statements such as "[He was] literally fighting for black rights before you were born."[85] Some responses went so far as to suggest that Sanders had done more for Black Americans than the Black people critiquing him.[86] Rod explained that comments like these were the impetus for the hashtag: "The reason it started trending at first is that so many Black people had had this experience online with his supporters."[87] His sentiment resonated so deeply within the network, that within a few hours, the hashtag was on Twitter's US trending topics list.

In addition to resonating with the experiences of the network, the #BernieSoBlack hashtag spread easily because it was also compatible with common uses of Twitter and hashtags for verbal games and humor. Black Twitter has long been known for its use of hashtags as loci around which to engage in signifyin', a Black tradition of verbal performance that emphasizes dexterous use of language and the communication of multiple levels of meaning simultaneously.[88] Siginfyin' is often employed for social and cultural critique through the use of humor and requires a plethora of cultural competencies to understand. Thus, the hashtag #BernieSoBlack, which allowed for both critique of the overzealous Sanders's supporters and an opportunity for the display of wit, fit within well-established communicative norms of this predominantly Black network, making it unsurprising that it was taken up and spread.

The critique within the #BernieSoBlack hashtag was packaged in humor and deep cultural references. This was in keeping with the use of the network as a Black communicative space. But it also served as an added layer of critique. The authority to speak on issues of racial justice is often understood as being derived from the lived experience as a racialized subject. Black Americans are the experts on their own racial oppression because they are the ones who live it. Within this understanding, the assertion that Sanders's commitment and authority to speak on Black racial oppression exceeds that of many Black people can be interpreted as a claim to "Blackness." Rod responded to such defenses of Sanders saying, "You won't even let us be like, 'Hey, we would like Bernie to do this.' . . . 'Nope. You don't get to make any demands. He's Black enough. He's too Black. He's Blacker than you. Shut the fuck up.' That's it."[89] The jokes made using the #BernieSoBlack hashtag, about just precisely "how Black" Sanders is, all required substantial Black cultural competencies to create and interpret, highlighting the difference between Sanders (and those who would assert his authority on race) and the Black people critiquing him. This reinforces the experiential distance between Sanders and Black Americans, troubling the ability to claim Sanders's authority on Black social issues.

Many of the tweets required knowledge of Black popular culture, specifically music. One user tweeted "#BernieSoBlack he thought #SayHerName was a hit song by Destiny's Child."[90] The reference to the popular 1990s R&B group, in which Beyoncé got her start, and their iconic song "Say My Name" implies that Sanders's deep level of Blackness created confusion for him at the Netroots Nation protest as he though the hashtag-turned-protest-chant "say her name" was the song. Similarly, @MJGWrites tweeted, "#BernieSoBlack he NEVER forgot about Dre."[91] The joke here references Dr. Dre, member of NWA and Hip-hop icon, and his 2000 track "Forgot about Dre." The song featured Eminem, who delivers the well-known line, "And motherfuckers act like they forgot about Dre." Thus, the tweet plays on the notion of a connection between forgetting Dre and a lack of Black authenticity, asserting that Bernie's, in his profound Blackness, never forgot about Dr. Dre and his iconic status.

Due to the visibility created by the trending topics, attempts were made to silence participants, and especially Rod himself. Because many of Sanders's more zealous followers directly addressed Rod and others critiquing Sanders using the @-reply function and/or inserted themselves into the conversation by using the hashtag, the counter-public function of Twitter came to the forefront. Often these attempts took the form of taking the #BernieSoBlack hashtag and using it in a way that stripped the elements of signifyin' out of it. For example, one user tweeted, "#BernieSoBlack he marched with MLK, was arrested protesting segregation, and has spent 50 years fighting for civil rights. #FeelTheBern,"[92] while another tweeted, "BernieSoBlack he marched on Washington with MLK Jr in 1963 & marched in Selma with Barack Obama in 2015."[93] These responses not only rebut the critiques of Sanders but do so in a way that strips Black linguistics traditions, AAHHR, and Black interpretive frameworks from the exchange, removing any traces of Black epistemologies or practices. These responses, grounded in whiteness, strip the Blackness out of the hashtag at the semiotic level.

Twitter often functions as a point of articulation between the network and mainstream media and establishment politics. The visibility of Black Twitter generally and the micro-celebrity status of Rod, Gandy, and White, who are followed by journalists, pundits, and editors, pushed the #BernieSoBlack conversation into legacy media, where it became part of the media narrative around the Netroots Nation protest put out by Reuters, the *Guardian*, Bloomberg News, MSNBC, CNN, and *Slate*.[94] Rod gave interviews to Vox.com, the *Los Angeles Times*, and the *Daily Beast* and himself became as central part of the story.[95] This, of course, prompted more Sanders supporters to engage Rod on Twitter and even to begin penetrating some of the digital spaces that usually serve as enclaves.

While the discussion, and at times hostility, surrounding these hashtags was publicly available on Twitter, less visible were the digital enclaves where these podcasters and their listeners interpreted discourses and constructed counter-discourses. *TBGWT*, hosted by Rod and Karen, discussed the initial protest, the reactions to the protest, and the ongoing arguments on Twitter. The meanings and discourses constructed in such a digital enclave were then circulated on Twitter as well. Additionally, participants in the network used TBGWT's private Facebook group to discuss events, including the emergence and backlash to the hashtag and the media coverage of both. In fact, the day that Rod created the hashtag, immediately after tweeting his initial jokes, he logged off and went to do a live stream of *TBGWT*, in the midst of which he and Karen learned that the hashtag had hit the US trending topics list,[96] When one user made an announcement in the chatroom, "#bernie so black is trending on Twitter now!"[97] Other listeners indicated they were following the hashtag while they were also in the chat.[98]

TBGWT podcasts were used as an enclave to interpret events through Black frameworks and produce counter-discourses. Rod, Karen, and the listeners participating in the chat highlighted a number of counterarguments to the response to #BernieSoBlack. *TBGWT*'s interpretation of the reaction from Sanders's supporters relates to many of the same issues raised around the Occupy movement, in particular, the adherence to colorblind logics, a reluctance or refusal to deal with issues of race, and a focus on issues of class instead. Rod, Karen, guests, and listeners reiterated the critique of white progressives who believe economics to be the primary cause of racial inequality or its best cure. Rod and Karen elaborated on this point several times over the course of that week's episodes. Rod pointed out that by responding to questions about race with economic considerations, Sanders and many of his supporters were "equating being poor with being Black . . . like 'I'm antipoverty therefore I am pro-Black.' . . . Those are not the same thing."[99] Karen argued, "You can still get shot being Black in the street with a mothafucking job. *Job* is not the problem."[100] This preoccupation with the economy was largely read as an attempt to silence Black voices and maintain the comfort of white progressives. In this context, Rod pointed to the deeply ingrained impulse to avoid discussion of race is in the United States:

> Most white people do not want to be educated on race. They want to lecture you on why you need to stop caring about racism. And that's really what this entire exercise has been for me, is a buncha people tellin' me to stop caring about the racism that affects my community, that affects my people, that is leading to death. . . . When it's time to vote, they just want us to shut the fuck up, get in line, and tell 'em we're gonna support whoever they tell us is the person to support.[101]

TBGWT, their guests, and listeners also went on to assert that this colorblind framework was no longer viable, given the election of President Obama and the growth of social media, which meant that white Democratic and progressive politicians must pay more attention to Black communities. Not only was the election of the first Black president a historic milestone, but, as Rod and Karen argued, the election also increased attention to issues of racial inequality and created a new expectation among Black Americans. Karen pointed to the counter-public function of social media platforms, noting that Black voters had more ways to respond when they were dissatisfied with a politician's engagement with their community:

> If you're a Democrat and you're running, you cannot blow past race. Because every time you do, people are gonna hit you up on Facebook, hit you up on Twitter, hit you up on Google+, Tumblr, all these social medias and let you know that they're not satisfied with these actions. You can't be like "I want the Black vote" but you don't want to talk about the Black issues.[102]

Co-host of *Whiskey, Wine, and Moonshine*, Sojourner Verdad, who was a guest on *TBGWT* that week, reiterated the importance of social media and asserted that it would only grow in influence:

> [Politicians] also underestimate the power of social media in this election. . . . Back in 2012, I mean, people were on Twitter and you know all that. But, not like they are now in 2015 and they're going to be in 2016. So, for [Rod's] hashtag to take off like it did and people had never even heard of Bernie Sanders. Like, this is gonna be something that is unprecedented. You can't just mess up in one area because that is going to be a national issue before you leave, and that is something people are underestimating right now.[103]

Additionally, *TBGWT* podcasts were used to analyze and interpret the media coverage of the hashtag, including articles from Hiphop-wired.com, the *Daily Dot, NewsOne, Raw Story*, MSNBC, PolicyMic. com, Vox.com, the *LA Times*, and the *Daily Beast*.[104] Rod explained that he wanted to cover the articles to see how each one covered the story differently: "I remember what I said in the interviews. And then I saw the process of how it was presented to the people, and I saw the process of how it happened organically on Twitter to how it was written about in different publications."[105] The podcast focused on the news coverage of #BernieSoBlack was intended specifically for the network, not those outside. Rod explained, "I felt like that was an inside thing for the fans. Like, 'This is what I said. Check out how different people wrote about this.'"[106]

Rod noted that the majority of the articles followed the same formula, which relied heavily on embedded tweets.[107] The articles in the *Daily Dot, NewsOne, Raw Story,* MSNBC, *PolicyMic.com,* and the *Daily Beast* all used embedded tweets as the central part of the article, often including more tweets than text written by the reporters. Rod asserted, "The framing behind how you get to the tweets really determines a lot of the response to me. Because people are coming to say to me like, 'You attacked this man.' I'm like, 'That's not what happened.'"[108] Regarding sensationalistic titles such as the *Daily Dot*'s "Twitter Takes Aim at Bernie Sanders's Minority Strategy with #BernieSoBlack," Rod commented, "This is why people were hittin' me up. They read the title to this. They don't read anything that I've said about it."[109] Rod and Karen also used this episode of the podcast to discuss inaccuracies in the reports—such as the many news outlets that referred to Rod as an activist when he asserted in each interview that he is not—and the way journalists foregrounded Rod while minimizing or erasing the Black women who organized the Netroots Nation protest.

The way the #BernieSoBlack hashtag unfolded demonstrates how the network oscillates from addressing those outside the community to addressing the community directly in a digital enclave and vice versa. While under normal circumstances *TBGWT* and its various channels for listener feedback would be limited to those within the network, the attention garnered by the hashtag brought in outsiders who turned that digital enclave into a space for debate. In addition to being flooded on Twitter with responses from Sanders supporters, the channels for listener feedback—comments on the webpage, emails, voicemails— and even more closed spaces like the live chatroom and the private Facebook community were used by Sanders supporters for responses that ranged from attempts to persuade to outright harassment.

Initially, Rod and Karen attempted to block such interlopers and preserve the enclaves for themselves and their listeners. Several Sanders supporters attempted to join TBGWT's private Facebook group to use it as a platform to tout the positive characteristics of their candidate. Rod and Karen responded by banning these individuals from the group

and addressing them on other platforms.[110] Similarly, on July 19, during
the live stream, a user who joined the chatroom and began defending
Sanders had to be banned. These are not the only instances in which
users were banned from TBGWT's digital spaces; it happens periodically around other issues, but usually to people attached to the network
in some way. #BernieSoBlack attracted people from unrelated digital
networks. In all cases, Rod and Karen have been very clear that the space
they have created is to exclude exactly the kind of instrusive behavior
displayed by the Sanders supporters.

Both email and voicemail were deployed by Sanders's supporters to
challenge and persuade Rod and Karen. For example, during "Episode
999: Bernie Marched Way in the Back," Rod played a voicemail message he received from a woman who wanted to discuss some issues with
them. In her message, she said,

> Hey, Rod. Hey, Karen. I'd actually like to have a conversation with you
> off, whattya call it, not off camera, off audio or whatever. But, I'd like to
> have a straight conversation with you guys, if you're up to it. I took the
> challenge, a friend of mine who posted your audio podcast and I am
> listening to it. Aaaand, uh, I'd like to hash it out a little bit with you and
> unpack it 'cause I'm on both sides. But, I wanna disagree about a few
> things, points you made. So, please don't air this because my number is
> going to be on it. But you can call me any time after like 11 a.m., if you
> choose, at 408—

At this point, Rod stopped the audio before the remainder of her phone
number could be heard. Reiterating his longstanding refusal to orient
conversation to outsiders, Rod responded, "Yeah. Don't call up here anymore. Next time I will play your number on the air. I. do not. want. to
debate you."[111] Pointing to the deluge of tweets and attempts to inform
and persuade him, he argued,

> Every single one of these mu'fuckas that wanna explain something to me.
> You're the seventeenth hundred motherfucker to try to explain it. It ain't
> gonna happen. You already talked about it. I've already talked about it.
> Everyone on Twitter's already talked about it. Your candidate just gotta
> step up on his own and talk to Black people about these Black issues and

not pivot to muthafuckin' jobs and then you get my vote. It's easy. It's easy. You're making it way more difficult than it has to be.[112]

Despite their efforts to maintain their podcast and its related social media and feedback channels strictly for intragroup discussion, the pressure of Sanders's supporters eventually forced the oscillation of the podcast, as it began to function as counter-public because it had drawn so many people wishing to debate. Though the affordances of podcasts engender the creation of enclaves, there is still no formal barrier to those outside the network. In general, they are deterred by inconvenience. But, #BernieSoBlack was high profile and dealt with a controversial enough issue to motivate users from other networks to devote the necessary time and energy to gain entry. Yielding to the pressure to shift from enclave to counter-public, Rod and Karen devoted a forty-five minute segment on one of their shows to play and respond to all the information sent to them by Sanders's supporters. Rod explained,

> I've heard Bernie Sanders talk about race before. You know, matter a fact, lemme do you all a favor. 'Cause I know this is the shit that you all keep sending me. Y'all keep sending me the same fuckin' videos over and over. . . . "Have you seen this video? That you seen that?" I've seen that shit. Um-kay. Cool. Y'all wanna hear it on the show? Y'all wanna hear my reaction to it on the show? That's cool. We can do that. I don't mind. But, you know, I feel like if we gonna do that, I'm gonna need y'all to leave me alone after this.[113]

This episode represents a moment when what is usually an enclave oscillated, somewhat under duress and out of frustration, to address members outside the group. Rod explicitly reaffirmed that the episode was out of the ordinary, saying, "This is probably the only time we're gonna do a podcast that ever has addressed a white audience, in general. Because I just typically don't do that."[114] Throughout the episode, Rod and Karen directly address the Sanders supporters attempting to debate them, moving systematically through the material and arguments they had been repeatedly sent. Speaking directly to white Americans, Rod explained the way that white Americans' refusal to deal with race makes political alliances difficult.

You have to face the sum totality to what you have done, what you have wrought, what you have done to other people. And since you can't do that, we become victimized further and further, because you refuse to take a look. You don't want to take any history courses. You wanna take Black history outta school. You don't wanna think about what you've done. And the fact that you're a liberal doesn't mean shit to me. Because you don't even know your own history.[115]

He later explained that the behavior directed at him by some Sanders's supporters in response to #BernieSoBlack exemplified the reason for the tense relationship between white liberals and progressives and Black Americans.

One of the reasons Bernie So Black was trendin' was 'cause your fans tried to take up the mantle of tryin' to control the narrative and ended up *embarrassing* yourselves in white privilege. Embarrassing yourselves. It really is a shame. It's a shame that you can't listen. You're not my allies. You're not my friends. You can't be with this type of attitude toward what I'm saying. . . . I don' give a fuck if you've been to Occupy Wall Street. Or you went to a Black Lives Matter march. You still don't know shit about being Black in America. You don't know what it's like. So, since you do not, I suggest you shut the fuck up and listen if you can't be constructive.[116]

He explained, that the reaction he was getting from some Sanders's supporters felt like attempts to silence him. "I'd love to chalk it up to something else. But what else could it be? What else would drive someone to think you know better? 'Cause it's really, 'Shut up and vote, niggers. We know better than you.' That's really what y'all tellin' us, and you don't."[117]

In addition to providing Black counter-discourses in response to each video and article they were sent, Rod and Karen expressed the profound anger and pain many Black Americans carry daily. Here again, these sentiments were not aimed at their usual audience but at possible interlopers. Rod explained, "I said, 'I'm angry.' But, we should be angry. Anger is the only thing that's ever gotten Black people progress in the United States of America. And they said, 'Well, people should be learning from Martin Luther King's example.' Nigga, he was *angry.*" Karen continued:

> Your co-workers, your mailman, all these people that you speak to and interact with, . . . they may not have hate in their heart. But they're, underlying, always angry. A lotta people are. And just because it don't show, just because they have a smile on their face, just because they're always chipper to you, just because they always speak to you. . . . Most black people you meet are underlyin' angry. They're really angry and they're upset and they're *hurt.* A lotta Black people are.[118]

Thus the #BernieSoBlack hashtag shows how the network was able to intervene in the dominant discourse. But it also exemplifies the ways that digital media can create channels for unwanted attention, in effect forcing the network to oscillate under duress. Users on Black Twitter shared heavily not only because of the cultural resonances of the tweets organized under the hashtag, which drew on Black history, culture, and media references, but also because, as Rod pointed out, the hashtag spoke to a shared experience interacting with some of Sanders's supporters. Hence, the hashtag moved from the network at the center of this book into the larger Black Twitter network, where the traffic was picked up by Twitter's algorithm, making it visible to Twitter users more broadly, including the Sanders supporters who responded in defense of their candidate. Additionally, Twitter's @-reply function allowed the Sanders supporters to address specific users, especially Rod, who, as the originator of the hashtag, received a particularly large number of responses. Moreover, because he uses Twitter in conjunction with his podcast, he was easily found by Sanders's supporters wishing to rebut and debate. While technically, these channels of interaction are generally available to those outside the network, they are usually obscured by the "noise" generated by the sheer volume of information online. But, the hashtag gave them visibility and provided Sanders's supporters a motivation to use these channels. In this way, they forced the network's enclave to function as a counter-public and engage in active debate in a way that it does not normally do.

Conclusion

If a networked public is comprised of both a digitally enabled *space* and the *collective* that is formed and maintained in that space, then the distributed and transplatform nature of this *collective* requires that the *space* of the public also be conceived of as transplatform. Deploying an analytical framework that transverses platform boundaries reveals the strategic use of Twitter, Facebook, podcasts, chatrooms and so on, depending on the exigencies of a given moment. This transplatform public operates as both enclave and counter-public, oscillating between them.

The oscillation between enclave and counter-public occurs in two primary ways. First, users move from one platform to another based on the functionality it offers, using one platform to communicate within an enclave and another to engage as a counter-public. Twitter, for example, is an ideal counter-public. As a public, easily searchable platform, which uses algorithms to make content more easily discoverable, Twitter enables multiple publics to encounter one another. Additionally, the general visibility of Black Twitter and the well-established micro-celebrities on the platform often attract other users looking for debate. It is common practice for journalists and commentators, many of whom follow Twitter micro-celebrities, not only to draw topics from Twitter discussion, but also to report directly on the activity on Twitter itself. Thus, insofar as Twitter serves as a gate to legacy media, it enables discourses to move to a larger audience. However, at times, these same features make Twitter a hostile and undesirable space. In such moments, participants in this network will shift to other platforms that offer affordances that allow for greater privacy.

In addition to moving between platforms, this networked public will oscillate through creative work-arounds that mitigate the undesirable characteristics of a platform, reimagining affordances in ways that differ from normative understandings. The use of AAVE-inflected hashtags to live-tweet television shows is one example. Twitter is optimal for synchronous co-viewing, yet makes activities potentially highly visible to outsiders. AAVE hashtags allow users to continue live-tweeting while sequestering their fan practice from the official fan timeline on Twitter. This technique is fairly effective, provided that the hashtag does not grow popular enough to appear in the trending topics. Recently, some participants have begun using the closed Facebook community groups of several of the independent Black podcasts to create live threads for new episodes of TV programs in lieu of live-tweeting on Twitter. This allows both synchronous and asynchronous discussion of the show, but has not been as popular as Twitter.

Finally, oscillation is not always a deliberate choice. There are few formal barriers to these digital enclaves. They remain largely sequestered spaces simply because it is inconvenient for outsiders to penetrate them. However, as demonstrated with #BernieSoBlack, given the right set of circumstance, motivated users will put in that time and energy, inserting themselves into these enclaved Black social spaces and disrupting their normal function. This can force what was previously an enclave to shift to behave like a counter-public.

Indeed, in recent years, the penetration of Black digital spaces by those outside has dramatically increased. At times the interlopers are well meaning, but unwilling or unsure how to embrace the epistemes and interpretative frameworks of the AAHHR that often characterizes such spaces. Such intrusion can be disruptive because it reinscribes the dominant epistemologies and discourses the Black participants were seeking refuge from and often leads to conflict as the Black users' resistance to this shift is read as hostility and exclusion. However, oftentimes, such intruders are there to deliberately harass Black participants. As of the time of this writing, the phenomenon of outsiders entering and disrupting Black digital enclaves has become a major concern in Black digital networks, which are beginning to alter their digital practices to more aggressively keep interlopers out.

3

"MLK, I Choose You!"

Using the Past to Understand the Present

In January 2011, TWiB!'s Elon James White introduced a segment on the *Blacking It Up!* podcast by saying, "I'm gonna call someone that I think is responsible and very smart. I'm calling my good friend Dr. Blair Lynn Murphy Kelley. I'm calling the historian." To which co-host Aaron Rand Freeman responded, "Wooooow. That's like calling the police. That's awesome."[1] This call to the "history police" was prompted by a segment on Tea Party–media personality Glenn Beck's show. A few days prior, Beck had the defended then Congresswoman Michelle Bachmann's assertions that the founding fathers of the United States actively tried to eliminate slavery. Beck claimed Frederick Douglass's writings supported Bachmann's assertion, quoting Douglass as saying, "I defy the presentation of a single pro-slavery clause in the Constitution." Beck chided Bachmann's critics, "Why do you hate Frederick Douglass so much? Why do you hate Black people so much?" Kelley, who was in her car driving when White called, contextualized Douglass's words, undermining Beck's claim. She explained, "Indeed, Frederick Douglass did say, if strictly construed, according to its reading, the Constitution is not a pro-slavery instrument." She then pointed out that the quotation Beck used is part of a larger statement.

> But, Douglass continued, "I now hold, as I've ever done, that the original intent and meaning of the Constitution, the one given to it by the men who framed it and those who adopted, and the one given to it by the Supreme Court of the United States, makes it a pro-slavery instrument. . . . one that I cannot bring myself to vote under or swear to support."

In her discussion, Kelley referred to Douglass as "one of the most important African Americans to live"—which, White highlighted, was exactly the reason Beck had invoked him: "That's why Glenn Beck is pulling him out there. 'Cause if he can somehow be on the side of Frederick Douglass, he feels like he's bulletproof. That's why he's makin' that argument."[2]

This seventeen-minute segment on *Blacking It Up!* exemplifies several common themes. Beck demonstrates two key issues around racial uses of history. First, the past is frequently marshaled to obscure the significance of US racism, prioritizing the preservation of contemporary notions of the country's fundamental goodness and justness. Second, Black American historical figures are deployed to claim moral high ground and deflect criticism, particularly criticism coming from Black people. *Blacking It Up!* and its on-call historian worked against these goals to simultaneously make visible and undermine the strategies used to achieve them.

Remembering is site of contention where the discourse of colorblindness can be reified or undermined. Dominant discourses of the US past construct structural racism as a historic, rather than contemporary, phenomenon, acknowledging past wrongdoings while rendering the present blameless. This casts racism as a nonissue for the twenty-first century United States and provides the foundation upon which colorblindness rests. Participants in the network at the center of this project are acutely aware that understandings of the past deeply shape our interpretation of the present. Digital networks and platforms provide resources with which to challenge the strategic amnesia of dominant US cultural memory in ways that destabilize colorblindness and undermine the racial status quo.

Participants utilize their transplatform network to engage in memory work that undermines dominant accounts of history through a vernacular pedagogy. As in the situations discussed in the previous chapter, Twitter functions largely as a counter-public, creating a place to directly engage people outside the network, while podcasts facilitate the creation of a more insulated environment that enables nuanced discussion. Like other distributed discussions in the network, these conversations tend to be multimedia and move across platforms. Technological capabilities allow for dialogic engagement with discourses though the use of audio and video recordings and of retweet and tweet quoting functions. Finally, this memory work also makes use of the connection some participants, like White, Imani Gandy, Feminista Jones, and others, have to larger mainstream media outlets, to push counter-discourses out of the network and make them more visible to a larger public.

This chapter focuses on the kinds of discursive work that can be accomplished in this transplatform environment. I begin with an explication of the function and importance of remembering and its relation to contemporary power structures and identities and demonstrate not only the ongoing importance of history to the network, but also how an understanding of the power of remembering runs through its content and interactions. I then focus specifically on how the Civil Rights Movement and Martin Luther King Jr., who serves as a contemporary avatar for the movement as a whole, are deployed in dominant discourses to obscure and silence assertions of contemporary racism. I explore how King is remembered in sanitized form, devoid of radicalism, and invoked to chastise and silence Black Americans and their critiques. I conclude with an examination of how the network strategically re-remembers King to turn his legacy into a critique against the very people who would claim King's authority to silence them.

The Social Functions of Remembering

Scholarship of cultural memory and history is fraught with debate over the meaning and boundaries of memory and history.[3] Pierre Nora, in his foundational work on *lieux de mémoire* (sites of memory) makes a stark distinction between memory and history, arguing that the former is traditional, premodern, and social, while the latter is "is how our hopelessly forgetful modern societies, propelled by change, organize the past."[4] Astrid Erll, on the other hand, advocates for the dissolution of the distinction that renders history rigid and memory "flexible and alive" and asserts history and memory are two intertwined modes of remembering.[5] This approach is particularly warranted when discussing Black Americans' engagement with the past because, as Melvin Dixon points out, distinctions such as the one made by Nora possess a strong Eurocentric bias.[6]

Remembering is a potent strategy for resisting the racial discourses that undergird colorblind racism. Because race is a fundamentally sociohistorical concept, its construction is deeply imbricated with processes of remembering. Stuart Hall explicitly theorizes identities as positions or points of identification within historical narratives, making them deeply connected to our relationship with the past. A full understanding of racial politics must recognize the centrality of the past in defining race and racism and maintaining racial hierarchies.[7]

But the past is neither stable nor objectively knowable. Remembering is not a process of simple recall, but one of reconstructing and reshaping the past. Our individual and collective recollections of the past do not exist fully formed in our minds; rather, they are fragments, which must be transformed into memories through social processes that are continuously unfolding and changing.[8] These contingent processes are deeply imbricated with present needs and concerns. Remembering the past occurs in the context of present discursive frameworks; it "colonizes the past by obliging it to conform to present configurations."[9] As Michael Schudson points out, "If every society's symbols form a vast cultural system whose job is that of telling stories that represent and reproduce the existing society, then for good or ill . . . culture constrains how we tell the tale."[10]

Further, it is through our understandings of the past that we then "perceive and comprehend current events"[11] Our understanding of the past is both shaped by and shapes our understanding of the present. Debates about the nature of the past do not take place in a vacuum; they occur within a larger sociocultural framework. Thus, remembering is never an end in its own right, but a means of asserting power and legitimizing social relations. Both *what* is remembered and *how* it is remembered involve selection and perspective.[12] Silences are "as important as inclusions in historical production."[13] Barbie Zelizer argues that any "effort to determine what is known and remembered about the past . . . is an effort to claim and exert power."[14] Appeals to the past can be seen as powerful strategies for validating political traditions. Groups draw on and create versions of the past, which, in turn, enable frameworks for self-interpretation that are legitimized by the past.[15] However, the cohesion and stability one group may derive from the past often comes at the expense of marginalized groups. "One group's political glue becomes the unraveling of another. In studies of repression, for instance, memory silences the voices of those who seek to interpret the past in contradictory ways."[16]

When it comes to race and racism, how one understands the past drastically impacts one's understanding of the present. Colorblindness depends on a belief that structural racism has ended and been replaced with an individualist meritocracy—thus on a belief grounded in extensive erasures. Strategic amnesia has allowed for structural racism to be relegated to the past and given the discourse of colorblindness traction in the dominant culture.

The dominant historical accounts of US history frame racism as a relic of the past and obscure contemporary racial injustice. These accounts are often characterized by the themes of reconciliation and the redemption of the United States from past wrongs, reinforcing the meta-narrative of US exceptionalism and the inevitability of its progress toward ever-greater freedom and justice. Perhaps no chapter of US history is more called upon to interpret the nation's racial present than the Civil Rights Movement, which is cast as the final chapter in the struggle to rid the United States of structural racial oppression. Peniel Joseph argues that the dominant account of Civil Rights Movement history is focused primarily on the "heroic" period between *Brown v. Board of Education* (1954), the Supreme Court case that desegregated publicly funded schools, and the Voting Rights Act (1965), which ensured equal access to the polls.[17] These legislative successes, along with the nonviolent direct action of Martin Luther King Jr. and his supporters, have become enshrined as the moments of national triumph over the forms of institutional and structural racism that have plagued the United States since its founding. Such a narrative allows Americans to declare structural racism a historic, rather than contemporary, phenomenon, preserving the United States' national self-image as a bastion of liberty and equality, while simultaneously obscuring, and thereby protecting, the nation's systems of race-based privilege and oppression.[18]

By painting the heroic Civil Rights Movement era as the final chapter in structural and institutional racism, the dominant history effectively relegates such racism to the past, thereby neutralizing it as a contemporary political issue. In US culture, historicizing an event often serves to depoliticize it and allows for the creation of the "illusion of consensus."[19] The themes of reconciliation and redemption that characterize the dominant Civil Rights Movement history combine with the historicization of racism to preserve the turbulence and injustice of the racial past while rendering it "ideologically safe."[20] This strategy allows for a narrative that maximizes temporal distance between the present and the racism of the past and encourages Americans to believe that systemic racism has ended in the mid-twentieth century and that the US nation-state was ultimately on the moral right side of the struggle.[21]

Within this context, counter-histories can make visible contemporary systemic racial oppression.[22] Manning Marable argues that narratives we construct about the past "have the potential capacity to reshape contemporary civic outcomes." Central to the efforts to achieve greater justice is "the contestation of the 'master narrative,' and the construction of an alternative history."[23] For this reason, Marable advocates active engagement with the past in ways that "obliterate the boundaries that appear to divide the past from the present, and from the future."[24] By undermining historic amnesia, counter-histories can reduce the temporal distance between the pre– and post–Civil Rights era in United States, suturing past and present together to highlight a continuum of injustice. By making visible that which was erased, such histories unsettle the illusion of consensus created by the "master narrative."

"Old Takes" and the Vernacular Pedagogy of *Historical Blackness*

The network at the center of this project has always placed importance on remembering the past. This is particularly true of TWiB!. In the first full year of its existence, *Blacking It Up!* had many episodes engaging directly with history. TWiB! has an annual MLK Day show that discussed King's legacy, the first of which, on January 17, 2011, began with King's Drum Major speech in its entirety and then featured White's mother, known a "Mama White" to the TWiB! audience, as a guest to talk about King's legacy, the Civil Rights Movement, and her own experiences with racism as a child. Additionally, the *Blacking It Up!* hosts and their audience read Manning Marable's biography of Malcolm X when it was released and had the historian Blair L. M. Kelley on the show to discuss the book.[25] History is of such importance to TWiB!, that in early 2014, it began a new podcast, *Historical Blackness*, which was hosted by Kelley and ran for twenty-six episodes. The show was part of the freemium service, the TWiBUlarity, meaning that it was available for free when it streamed at scheduled times and for download with a subscription to TWiB's premium content.

Kelley is Associate Professor of History and Assistant Dean of Interdisciplinary Studies and International Programs at North Carolina State University. Throughout her career she has produced both deep interventions into established Black American histories and a wide range of public-facing scholarship, both of which are reflected in her work on *Historical Blackness*. Her first book, *Right to Ride: Street Car Boycotts and African American Citizenship in the Era of Plessy v. Ferguson (2010)*, won the Letitia Woods Brown Best Book Award from the Association of Black Women Historians and is a critical corrective to well-established historiography of the Black Freedom Struggle at the turn of the twentieth century.[26] Kelley demonstrates that this period, which canonical academic histories have deemed accommodationist, was rife with resistance. Exploring the complicated tensions between gender, class, and colorism, Kelley also highlights the vital importance of Black women in this period of protest. Further, Kelley has engaged extensively in public scholarship, including writing for the *New York Times*, the *Washington Post*, the *Root*, the *Grio*, and *Ebony*, and often draws on historical contexts to explicate contemporary events. *Historical Blackness*, an iteration of this investment in public historical pedagogy, was groundbreaking, anticipating the popularity of history podcasts that emerged in the years following.

Historical Blackness served a multilayered pedagogical function. First, Kelley demonstrated the need for deeper historical knowledge, persuading listeners of the necessity of a historical perspective. Second, she provided historical education, exposing erasures and elisions in the dominant accounts of the past. Finally, she demonstrated how, once obtained, complex historical accounts can be used to produce alternative interpretations of present events. Predicated on a recognition that the US educational system limits most people's historical knowledge, the podcast offered lesser-known and more complex accounts of history. It highlighted how discourses and practices of race and racism from the past are still operative today. This resists the rupture between past and present that undergirds colorblind discourse and instead recontextualizes contemporary events as the most recent iterations in an unbroken continuum of white supremacy, which began with chattel slavery.

Kelley explicated how dominant historical narratives, as taught and perpetuated by US institutions such as the public school system, are reductive in ways that limit our understanding of the past. In one episode Freeman commented on today's media culture, saying, "Everyone's got the hottest take" on recent events. To which Kelley replied, "My take is gonna be old, an old take. And it's going to be a history take."[27] She explained her belief in the value of history, speaking of the "misshapen way that most of us learn history from the very beginning." She went on to explain the deficiencies of contemporary understandings of history that have resulted from the priorities of the US educational system, which she argued does not convey the "messy background" of history:

> Most of what we get is the sense that there were extraordinary men who guided our past and thank goodness that we had them there to guide our paths and to lead when times were tough. So, the way we learn [and] teach US history is centered around US presidents as exceptional people who were about to achieve great things, who marched us on toward progress through the years. That's really how most of us see our history. . . . And so you're not really gettin' a sort of a social history sense. Right? Looking at the way people interrelated with one another and thinking that everyday lives are important.[28]

She identified the deficit in the dominant historical narrative, pointing to patterns of what is remembered and what is erased. *Historical Blackness* filled the gaps left by accounts of these "extraordinary men" and created more complicated contextualized accounts of the past.

Kelley's show reduced the temporal distance between past and present that is necessary to sustain neoliberal colorblindness, suturing past and present together through a number of strategies. She often spoke of the historical "residue" in which we live our lives. For example, after recounting the origins of blackface minstrelsy, Kelley noted that

> minstrel shows became popular as music. And so, the sheet music of minstrelsy was sold all over the country. They became the most popular songs of the day, and many of those songs are still with us as children songs and folk songs. And many people don't even know that the, you know, "Camptown Races," "Someone's in the Kitchen with Dinah," "Di-

xie," "Carry me Back to Old Virginy," all of these were "coon songs" that were part of minstrelsy.[29]

She explains that these songs, laden with racist tropes, spread throughout the United States and served a pedagogical function for white Americans, particularly in the North, as "real stories about how you should treat free Black people."[30] Kelley offers the example of how these "coon songs" were instrumental in establishing and reinforcing the stereotype that Black people eat chicken. Prior to the popularity of minstrel songs, this stereotype did not exist. As White put it, "If you showed up in the seventeenth century and were like, 'Man, Black people love fried chicken,' everybody'd look around like 'What? What are you talking about?'"[31] To which Kelley responded, "Yes, but if you showed up in 1850 everybody'd be like 'Yuuup, they'll steal your chicken and cook it right up.'" She pointed to "Ain't Nobody Here but Us Chickens," saying, "You've heard that before, right? Coon song. 'Cause it's a . . . minstrel's hidin' in the chicken coop, getting' ready to steal the chickens." She explains how this stereotype, circulated in song, was a twisted understanding of the tactics enslaved people used to survive the brutality of slavery:

> And that's the joke about slavery, right? That the enslaved people, who were hungry, right? That they literally were given tiny rations, and they were hungry after working like eighteen-hour days. That they would steal food. So, that became the joke in minstrelsy, that you were a thief. As if you could steal from the person who stole your labor, who stole your children, who stole your family, literally, day after day by enslaving you. But that's the joke.[32]

She explained that a similar perversion of the behaviors of the enslaved spawned the stereotype that Black people were lazy because enslaved people found creative everyday ways to resist their enslavement:

> Of course they would try to shirk outta work, or say they were sick, or burn down your barn. Sure they would. . . . But, now you're lazy. And so, the very things you could do to resist your circumstances became the stereotypes that your children then had to carry forth into the world.[33]

Thus, Kelley demonstrated that the racism of the past is still with us, not only through the continued presence of the music but also the continuation of the racist beliefs it carried. Further, she highlighted the ways Black people's own tactics of resistance, grounded in humanity and offering some measure of control, were easily perverted to become ways to police and oppress.

Kelley also used history to contextualize contemporary events in ways that emphasize the continuum of racist oppression and violence in the United States. For example, in the second episode, Kelley used the history of lynching to discuss the shooting death of seventeen-year-old Jordan Davis, who was killed by a white man, Michael Dunn, at a gas station. Davis was sitting in the back seat of his friend's parked car with music playing. Dunn demanded they turn the music down and after Davis and his friends refused to do so, opened fire on the car, later claiming he feared for his and his girlfriend's safety. Kelley observed:

> It's the logic of lynching, right? It's the idea that you have to protect white womanhood from scary threatening Black manhood. And that it's indiscernible; it's a mass of people. They're threatening no matter the circumstances unless they're just sort of grinning and skinning and yessir bossin'. And that Black men just can't be minding their own business or doing their own thing.[34]

Kelley draws a straight line from the lynchings of the past to the logic that resulted in Davis's death. Contextualized within the dominant racial discourse, Davis's murder is an anomaly, at worst the actions of an individual racist. However, recontextualized within a history of lynching, it becomes the most recent iteration in generations of racist violence and terror, undermining notions that such violence is a thing of the past.

Kelley also uses her historical expertise to contextualize contemporary efforts by Black Americans to resist oppression. For example, after Michael Eric Dyson wrote a critical essay about fellow Black academic Cornel West, many criticized him for having public conflict, or beef, at that time, citing it as damaging to the movement to battle police violence. Kelley pointed out that such conflicts are neither new nor do they mean the movements in which they occur will not be effective. She recounted the very public and intense conflict between W. E. B. DuBois and Booker T. Washington in the early twentieth century and concluded:

> Beef's not new. And see how that's a terrible time period in American history, right? So, you know, this whole notion of like, "We're goin' through hard things, so get along." That's the height of lynching. That's the height of the passage of segregation laws. It's the height of disfranchisement, literacy tests, and poll taxes. Never is there a worse time than this time in which DuBois is battling Booker T. Washington.[35]

Thus, not only do lionized figures of Black American history become humanized. The knowledge that this conflict between these figures did not derail the Black liberation movement reduces the urgency to suppress conflict.

Podcasts are ideal for the vernacular pedagogy of *Historical Blackness*. Their extended and nuanced discussion allowed Kelley to demonstrate the importance of history and call attention to nonhegemonic interpretations of the present. This undermines the discourse of colorblindness by destabilizing the historical narratives on which it is built. Kelley demonstrated that structural racism is not a relic of a past age; it is a present reality, somewhat obscured but little changed. She sutures together past and present and illustrates how different accounts of the past can be used to reinterpret the present through a color-conscious, rather than colorblind, lens.

Sanitizing the Civil Rights Movement and Martin Luther King Jr.

Perhaps no period of US history is more called upon by neoliberal colorblindness than the mid-twentieth century Civil Rights Movement. Strategic amnesia and the reliance on the "great man" trope are clearly visible in the dominant history of the Civil Rights Movement and the contemporary public image of Martin Luther King, Jr. The dominant narrative of the Civil Rights Movement positions it as the successful end of white supremacy in the United States and the beginning of a new era of equality. These accounts depict the movement as centered on tolerance and individual achievement. Any controversial or contradictory messages or accounts of the past are erased or marginalized. Further, the dominant versions of the past allow Americans to distance themselves from racism by denying federal responsibility and structural support for racism and to focus instead on individual bigots and extremist organizations such as the Ku Klux Klan, which are portrayed as a regional problem confined to the South.[36] Additionally, Civil Rights Movement remembrances focus predominantly on spectacular and violent forms of racism while ignoring its subtle and day-to-day manifestations. Defining racism as a localized and spectacularly overt problem enables the conflation of the *de jure* eradication of Jim Crow laws and lynching with the eradication of racism itself. Evidence of ongoing racism, such as police brutality, is routinely excluded from Civil Rights Movement memorials, and controversial elements that might disrupt the narrative of reconciliation and redemption are routinely excluded from memorializing practices. For example, the site where Fred Hampton, Mark Clark, and other members of the Black Panther Party were killed, originally included in an early edition of the official Illinois African American heritage guidebook, was later omitted because it was deemed "too controversial."[37]

The dominant narrative celebrates the activities of the heroic Civil Rights era and asserts that a "decline" characterized by urban protests and rebellions ensued.[38] Accordingly, the "good" movement is exemplified by Martin Luther King Jr.'s nonviolent direct action during the "heroic" period, whereas the "bad" expressions of the movement are represented by more rhetorically militant activists such as Malcolm X and the emergent Black Power Movement.[39] As Jacquelyn Hall argues, "In the dominant narrative, the decline of the movement follows hard on the heels of the Civil Rights and Voting Rights acts, and the popular struggles of the 1970s become nothing more than identity politics, divisive squabbles that promoted tribalism, alienated white workers, and swelled the ranks of the New Right."[40]

This narrative obscures the post-1965 gains of the movement, such as desegregation of schools and the workplace and the establishment of equal hiring practices.[41] The heroic Civil Rights Movement is confined to "the South, to bowdlerized heroes, to a single halcyon decade, and to limited, noneconomic objectives."[42] This enshrines it as a triumph, while casting it as no longer relevant. Thus, the dominant account of the Civil

Rights Movement obscures structural injustice in ways that are apparent in how its most lionized figure has come to be remembered.

Martin Luther King Jr., in particular, has become a central figure in the remembering of past racial justice movements. King's legacy looms large in a "civic mythology of racial progress in late twentieth-century America."[43] Marable argues, "Few Americans will ever forget 'I Have a Dream,' uttered by Martin on the steps of the Lincoln Memorial that hot August afternoon in 1963. Stamped deeply on public memory, it is now central to our understanding of what American democracy should be."[44] Moreover, as Fred Powledge observes, "In the minds of untold numbers of Americans . . . the Reverend Dr. Martin Luther King, Jr. *was* the civil rights movement. Thought it up, led it, produced its victories, became its sole martyr. Schoolchildren—including Black schoolchildren—are taught this."[45] Thus, King has come to embody the entirety of the moral authority and legitimacy of the movement itself. To claim King's legacy is to claim the moral authority and legitimacy of the entire Civil Rights Movement.

In the process King has been sanitized, purged of his radicalness, and reconstructed in an image that serves to mute contemporary racial turmoil. The man who is memorialized with monuments and street names and celebrated with public holidays is representative of "good" Civil Rights Movement and associated with nonviolent direct action. This memory of King obscures the radical and revolutionary aspects of King's beliefs and actions. Representations of the man who praised Malcolm X on the occasion of his death, who took his antiracist efforts to Chicago in 1966 and asserted that he found the "worst racism" he had ever experienced there, who called the United States the "greatest purveyor of violence in the world" when condemning the Vietnam War in 1967, and who argued that capitalism was the root cause of inequality as he organized a Poor People's Campaign in 1968, has largely disappeared from media retrospectives and mainstream historical accounts.[46]

Instead, the image of King has been fixed at the moment of his 1963 speech. As Vince Harding put it, "Brother Martin spent a fair amount of time in jail, but his worst imprisonment may be how his own nation has frozen him in that moment in 1963."[47] Through public memory and annual MLK Day celebrations, King's legacy was brought in line with dominant racial discourses. By the end of the 1980s, "King had been sufficiently domesticated," and the "racial conflict" surrounding him had been "subsumed in the broader dream of national harmony—something that can presumably be achieved if we are 'all our best.'"[48]

Beginning in the 1970s, the Right began reconfiguring King's legacy to strategically support an agenda of deregulation and an emphasis on individual rather than collective racism. "The Right reworked the discourse of colorblindness," redefining it as the erasure of racial distinctions.[49] It recast the policies intended to remedy racism as the source of inequalities and refocused efforts on the impact of individual acts of discrimination, ignoring historical and institutionalized injustice oppressing Black Americans as a group.[50]

Despite Reagan's opposition to both the 1965 Voting Rights Act and the institution of the MLK holiday, Reagan regularly invoked King in his speeches. He used King's words to imply equality had been achieved and that individuals "now had to take responsibility for any additional progress that was needed."[51] Reagan once argued, "The Voting Rights Act of 1965 had made certain that from then on black Americans would get to vote. But most important, there was not just a change of law; there was a change of heart. The conscience of America had been touched. Across the land, people had begun to treat each other not as blacks and whites, but as fellow Americans."[52] This shift of conscience presumably negated the necessity of any further legal protections. The Right has made much of King's dream that "children will one day live in a nation where they will not be judged by the color of their skin but by the content of their character.[53] To Reagan "equality" meant that people should be treated solely as individuals with no regard to the advantages or disadvantages suffered by a particular group.[54] Appealing to the discourse of colorblindness, Reagan supported dismantling of Federal Civil Rights Law, asserting it was inconsistent with King's beliefs.[55] Reagan's attorney general, Edwin Meese, argued that the administration's opposition to affirmative action was "very consistent with what Dr. King had in mind" when he envisioned a "colorblind society."[56] By the mid-1980s, King began making regular appearances in speeches to justify the Reagan administration's opposition to affirmative action laws.[57] And by the twenty-first century, King's legacy had been so profoundly recrafted that it could be claimed to support almost any political position.[58]

In the contemporary moment, King's legacy is often called upon to bolster the racial status quo. Between 2010 and early 2016, King was frequently invoked to silence Black Americans' attempts to highlight and critique racism, and his public image was often marshaled to support a wide array of sometimes contradictory political positions. In response, participants in the network have engaged in discussions that both interpret invocations of King and create counter-discourses that contest such rememberings. The struggle over King's public image intensified after the emergence of the Movement for Black Lives, as King was persistently deployed by the movement's critics.

MLK Fan Fic: Re-Remembering King

King's legacy is frequently invoked to criticize Black Americans and to provide cover for any number of positions across the political spectrum. King has been used by the Tea Party to justify their policy positions and delegitimize accusations of racism and by the Right more generally to condemn unions and labor protests. Liberals and progressives have made appeals to King's legacy to counter criticism for their handling of racial issues and legitimize political positions. Regardless of politics or topic, King is often deployed to further two related goals. The first is to bolster one's argument or position by aligning it with King and thereby claiming his moral authority. The second is to police Black people's behaviors and to deflect criticism, a move White has dubbed "throwing your Negro shields up," by positioning them in opposition to King.[59] The network at the center of this project has long addressed and challenged such appropriations of King.

The sanitized colorblind individualist King whom Reagan had constructed was used to support the discourses and policy agendas of the Tea Party. The Tea Party, a movement often criticized for its tolerance for the racist language of some of its proponents, positioned itself as the inheritors of King's legacy while placing the vast majority of Black Americans who were opposed to the Tea Party's political agenda as betrayers of that legacy. For example, when right-wing commentator Glenn Beck held his "Restoring Honor" rally at the Lincoln Memorial on August 28, 2010, the forty-second anniversary of the March on Washington, he described members of the Tea Party as "people of the Civil Rights Movement. We are the ones that must stand for civil and equal rights, justice, equal justice. Not special justice, not social justice. We are the inheritors and protectors of the Civil Rights Movement. They are perverting it".[60] Similarly, after the National Association for the Advancement of Colored People (NAACP) voted for a resolution that called upon the Tea Party to denounce racism and those bringing racist signs to Tea Party rallies, the Tea Party Patriots, an umbrella organization for thousands of local groups across the country, posted a petition on its website demanding that the NAACP revoke the resolution. The petition claimed, "It is nothing less than 'hate speech' for the N.A.A.C.P. to be smearing us as 'racists' and 'bigots,'" adding that "we believe, like Dr. Martin Luther King Jr., in a colorblind, postracial society. And we believe that when an organization lies and resorts to desperate tactics of racial division and hatred, they should be publicly called on it."[61] Additionally, Alveda King has become a frequent guest on right-wing media and at Tea Party rallies, often proclaiming her uncle would support Tea Party politics and policies. Of Alveda King's role in Beck's rally, conservative blogger Kathleen McKinley once asserted, "Don't u love it? Even the left can't bear to criticize MLK's niece. She's bulletproof."[62] From the recreation of King's most iconic moment (with Beck symbolically and physically substituting himself for King), to the use of Civil Rights–era rhetoric, to the exploitation of King's family relations, the Tea Party laid claim to King and his legacy.

TWiB! often took aim at such assertions by right-wing figures using less-known and more complex accounts of King to undermine their shallow, reductive version of him. For example, on an early episode of *Blacking It Up!*, White, co-host Bassey Ikpi, and guest Kriss, from the Movie Trailer Reviews (MTR) Network, discussed the ways the Right and the labor movement were struggling over the legacy of King in the midst of the 2011 labor protests in Wisconsin in response to proposed state laws that would damage collective bargaining rights.[63] With the focus on labor rights and unions at the center of national attention, the American Federation of Labor and Congress of Industrial Organizations (AFL-CIO) organized rallies across the United States under the moniker "We Are One" on the forty-third anniversary of King's assassination.[64] The AFL-CIO noted that King often connected the rights of Black Americans to labor rights and that at the time of his death in Memphis, he was standing with Black sanitation workers who were demanding recognition of their union. Beck, on both his radio program and on his *Fox News* show, rejected and derided this image of King, arguing that the association of King with labor rights was "absurd." He echoed the colorblind framing of King's legacy, asserting that he "gave his life fighting for civil rights, the right for all men to be judged by the content of their character, not the color of the skin or their union label."[65] *Blacking It Up!* addressed the connection of King to unions and Beck's claims to the contrary by playing a clip of from Beck's radio show in which Beck said derisively, "Wait, wait, hold it, just a second. Dr. King lost his life for collective bargaining for the public unions, really? Did you know that? 'Cause—that—we have to update our history books, because I didn't know that. Did you know that?"[66] In response, Ipki turned the tables on Beck:

> Yes, we fucking do need to adjust our history books because what's in there is a lie. *Lies My Teacher Told Me*, clearly. Martin Luther King didn't become an enemy of the state until he started backing unions and telling people they needed to fight for their rights and he started going after big name corporations. That's why he got killed. Not because he had a dream.[67]

In the same segment, White, Ipki, and Kriss expanded their criticism to address the Tea Party more generally and its ongoing attempts to claim King. They played audio of commentary from Tea Party activist Lisa Fritsch, who said on *Fox News* that the comparison between labor rights and King's work was an "ugly comparison" that was "completely invalid" and outright "immoral."[68] White pointed to the irony of a Tea Party member criticizing the corruption of King's legacy when

> they have specifically been corrupting Martin Luther King's ideas, talking about how they're fighting for quote-unquote civil rights as well. . . . They continue to talk all this bullshit about how Martin Luther King wasn't fighting for unions and things like that. . . . But then all of a sudden you start to hear things like, quote, "Negroes are almost entirely a working people. They are pitifully few Negro millionaires and few Negro employers. Our needs are identical with labor's needs. Decent wages, fair

working conditions, livable housing, old age security, health and welfare measures, conditions in which families can grow . . . That is why Negroes support labor's demands and fight laws that curb labor. That is why labor-hater and labor-baiter is virtually always a twin headed creature spewing anti-Negro epithets from one mouth and anti-labor propaganda from another mouth." Martin. Luther. King.[69]

In addition to being coopted by the Right for their political aims, King is also often deployed by liberals and progressives, particularly as a "shield" against Black critique. This was exemplified by an exchange between White and *Salon*'s David Sirota. White had challenged Sirota's attempts to use the acquittal of George Zimmerman to bring attention to US military drone strikes in the Middle East. White asserted that doing so hindered important discussion about US racial oppression by diverting attention away from the specific ways oppression functions in Black American lives and communities. Many criticized Sirota for the timing of his critique and for what were perceived as his attempts to use the visability of Martin's death to highlight his own political priorities. Sirota responded by tweeting Martin Luther King Jr. quotations at White, Gandy, and many of his other critics with his added commentary, including "tell that to Dr. King," and "Dr. King disagrees with you."[70] White used Twitter to express his dismay at Sirota's attempts to shift the discourse, and Sirota responded that White was suffering from "willful ignorance."[71] When White continued to challenge him, Sirota retweeted an earlier tweet of his that said, "ICYMI: Dr. King's rejoinder to those who say fight for civ rights at home has nothing to do w/military policy abroad" and included a screen capture of the following remark by King:

Over the past two years, as I have moved to break the betrayal of my own silences and to speak from the burnings of my own heart, as I have called for radical departures from the destruction of Vietnam, many persons have questioned me about the wisdom of my path. At the heart of their concerns this query has often loomed large and loud: "Why are you speaking about the war, Dr. King?" "Why are you joining the voices of dissent?" "Peace and civil rights don't mix," they say. "Aren't you hurting the cause of your people?" they ask. And when I hear them, though I often understand the source of their concern, I am nevertheless greatly saddened, for such questions mean that the inquirers have not really known me, my commitment or my calling. Indeed, their questions suggest that they do not know the world in which they live.[72]

To this, Sirota added a message addressed directly to White: "@elon-james you sound like the kind of critic Dr. King decried."[73] Sirota had tweeted this King quote out to a number of critics that day on Twitter. White responded, saying,

The idea that in the midst of an issue concerning civil rights @david-sirota, that you would throw an MLK quote at me? To deflect? Really?

My critique was with your methods sir. @davidsirota To speak against injustice is fine—to misappropriate and then condescend is assholic.

And the idea that all you have to do is post an MLK quote and then hit your #BBoystance is ridiculous. Answer the critique. @davidsirota.[74]

When a others within the network responded to Sirota by suggesting he had gone too far in his instance of claiming King, Sirota responded with tweets like, "agreed—it is outta hand to ignore Dr. King," adding the link to the same quotation again.[75] The exchange between White, Sirota, and other members of the network continued for almost three hours, during which Sirota repreatedly deployed King to meet criticism directed at him.

After the network's encounter with Sirota on Twitter, White, Gandy, and Freeman used a *TWiB! Prime* podcast to unpack and interpret Sirota's tactics at length. White and Gandy outlined Sirota's position, affirmed their opposition to drone strikes, and proceeded to explain their issue with Sirota's framing. White read the exchange he had with Sirota on Twitter, interjecting commentary and discussion as he went, in much the same way as they do with video and audio clips. While he initially highlighted on Twitter why sending the quote was problematic, White went more in depth on the podcast:

At first when he sent me the quote, my response was, "This mutherfucker did not just quote Martin Luther King at me!" That was my response out loud. I was like, "What? Wait. What?" Because there has been a lot of discussion about spaces within progressivism, the progressive movement, using Martin Luther King and conservatives, in all honesty, using Martin Luther King to fit their own needs at that moment when they want to make an argument. Especially, to quell Black voices. It's like, "Oh, look. Martin Luther King said this. What? b-boy stance." And you're supposed to all of a sudden calm to hell out.[76]

Gandy noted, "It's a silencing tactic." She went on to point out that the practice of quoting King to defend against critique is "a logical fallacy that instead of answering to critique you throw out other people who agree with you, that's an appeal to authority. That doesn't end the argument. That doesn't mean you win. It actually means that you know that you've lost because you can't answer the critique. You cannot make an argument to defend your position."[77] A similar appeal to authority was made by some Bernie Sanders supporters to rebut critiques of him by the Movement for Black Lives and others during his 2016 primary run. This tactic was particularly visible in the wake of the disruption of the presidential town hall meeting at Netroots Nation in 2015, when protestors demanded that Sanders address the deaths of Black women in police custody. When Gandy tweeted a post by Eclecta Blog, a progressive blog site, titled "White progressives get a taste of anger and frustration as #BlackLivesMatter activists upstage Bernie Sanders,"[78] she received responses such as "Bernie marched with MLK and was arrested fighting for civil rts. What has she done except 'Look at me.' Pathetic."[79] Gandy was not the only target of such tweets. White, the Media Director of Netroots Nation at the time, was directly blamed by some for staging the protest.[80] As he took to Twitter to defend the protest and assert that all candidates should be pushed on the issues, he received tweets informing him that "Bernie Sanders had participated in the historic March on Washington in 1963"[81] and arguing that "Bernie is the ONLY one who has supported black lives for 50 years. . . . disrupt foes not friends!!!!"[82] These tweets were not isolated events. Iterations of Sanders's civil rights bona fides featuring King proliferated in the discussion online. When Civic Action Executive Director of MoveON.org, Ann Galland, tweeted, "The presidential candidates need to do better," with a link to the official MoveOn response, she received replies like "Bernie Sanders has been fighting for civil rights for decades & marched w/ MLK. I don't think he needs to be lectured."[83] Writer and poet Hanif Abdurraqib, who works with *MTV News* and *Muzzle Magazine*, summed up his exasperation, tweeting, "You tweet out one joke about Bernie Sanders, and the Bernie Sanders supporters summon MLK within literal minutes. Sheeeeeeesh."[84]

The use of King as a means of silencing or undermining Black voices has become so prevalent that participants in the network have developed terminology to discuss the phenomenon. In January 2013, Freeman coined the term "MLK fan fiction" to describe how so many people, of virtually any political stripe, seem to claim King would have supported their position if he were alive today. At the time, White, Freeman, and then-co-host Dacia Mitchell were on *TWiB! Prime* discussing an article that Barbara Arnwine, the Executive Director of the Lawyers' Committee for Civil Rights Under Law, had written,[85] arguing that King would have opposed allowing the nation to go over the "fiscal cliff," the term that was being used to describe the combination of the expiration of the Bush Tax cuts and the automatic implementation of draconian spending cuts through budget sequestration. Arnwine was emphasizing King's focus on economic inequality and used this to ground her argument that the fiscal cliff would have had a disproportionate impact on Black Americans. As Mitchell introduced the story, White interjected, "Stop, stop, stop, stop. Stop. Stop. I don't care about this story. And here's why. I am getting sick and tired of people telling me what MLK would think of something or what MLK would do with something." To which Freeman responded, "You mean you don't like MLK fan fiction?" White asserted. "MLK fan fiction is possibly one of the most annoying types of fan fiction in the world. Because, guess what? We have no clue what MLK would have done if he did not get shot."

The network has also created two different metaphors to describe the way people often invoke King—the Big Joker and Pokémon. The former is a reference to the game Spades, in which the Big Joker trumps, or beats, all other cards. It emerged in the aftermath of the Zimmerman acquittal in 2013, when Rod from TBGWT called in to *TWiB! Radio* as it was live-streaming. Observing that many white Americans were responding to the event by delegitimizing Black critique and pain, Rod also referred to White's conflict with Sirota, which had occurred the previous evening:

> I think when it comes to Black commentary, it's just like Spades, . . . and, of course, Martin Luther King is the Big Joker. . . . White people are playin' Spades. White people are playin' Spades with our commentary. And that's why, last night, you lost, man. . . . He pulled out Martin Luther King, and we all know there's no recourse for the Big Joker in Spades. So, you have to back down. That's the rule.[86]

The second metaphor describes King and his frequent rhetorical function by way of the popular Japanese franchise Pokémon (a contraction of the Japanese words for "pocket monster"). In the cartoon series based on these creatures, the Pokémon are captured in "Poké Balls," about the size of a baseball, after which they become the property of their "trainer" and must obey the trainer's commands. The Poké Balls are deployed in battle, as the trainer throws the ball while yelling "[name of the Pokémon], I choose you!" The Pokémon then emerges and fights on behalf of its trainer. King as Pokémon frames King as an on-call easily deployable fictitious figure that is thrown out to fight one's battle.

Rod and Karen used both analogies—Big Joker and Pokémon—in their interrogation of legacy media during the 2015 uprising in Baltimore following the death of Freddie Gray. Gray was a twenty-five-year-old Black man who suffered fatal injuries to his spinal cord while being arrested and then transported alone in the back of a police van. The officers involved were accused of excessive use of force, and the ensuing protests resulted in property damage. During the unrest, activist Deray McKessen, who rose to prominence during the 2014 protests in Ferguson, appeared on Wolff Blitzer's CNN show to talk about the events in Baltimore. Blitzer repeatedly asked McKessen questions attempting to lead him to condemn the property damage caused by the unrest and to legitimize "peaceful protest." In reply, McKesson distinguished between "violence," which he asserted had been perpetrated by the police on the bodies of citizens, and property damage, refusing to fit his comments in the narrative offered by Blitzer. After a few moments, Blitzer said, "I just want to hear you say that there should be peaceful protest, not violent protest, in the tradition of Dr. Martin Luther King."[87] When TBGWT played the audio from this interview on its podcast, Rod observed,

> He played the Martin Luther King Big Joker. White people's go-to card. Favorite card in the deck. The Martin Luther King Big Joker ain't even got no print left on it form all d' thumb grease that has been used on that muthafucka. . . . You can only tell it's the Martin Luther King Big Joker now because it's still got the bullet holes in it form when they killed that muthafucker.

He continued by making reference to Picachu, one of the most popular Pokémon in the franchise, and playing with the fact that Pokémon only say their own names. "But, they keep playin it. Like it's the Pokémon in the deck. It's Picachu. It's like 'MLK! MLK!'" Karen asked, "That the only muthafuckin' card you got? Know there's some other cards in the deck, right?" To which Rod replied, "Not to mention he got other quotes. But, but we gonna keep goin' to the same, you know, non-violence shit. Oh, we gotta pull out the MLK Pokémon. 'MLK, I choose you!'"[88] Blitzer's interview with McKesson not only demonstrates the use of King as Big Joker and/or Pokémon, it also illustrates how the dominant public image of King has been used to delegitimize the protest and political strategies of the Movement for Black Lives.

The Movement for Black Lives and the Struggle to Reclaim King

While King has long been deployed as a means of disciplining Black resistance, this strategy intensified with the emergence of the Movement for Black Lives in 2014. Its critics called upon the dominant sanitized construction of King to condemn the movement as wholly un-Kinglike and therefore illegitimate. Accordingly, the Movement for Black Lives was situated in the lineage of unruly and dangerous Black movements and the narrative of declension that frames the post–Civil Rights era. In response, the network at the center of this project has become an arena in which to disrupt such dominant constructions of King and work to rearticulate his vision and reclaim his legacy, thereby legitimizing the work of contemporary activists and protestors.

Because King functions as a symbol for the entirety of the Civil Rights Movement in the dominant historical narrative, claims to King are claims the romanticized and venerated movement writ large. Marable argues that the movement for Black liberation, beginning from the Great Migration of the early twentieth century, has become a template for resistance to oppression, not just in the United States, but worldwide. As such, it has become the yardstick against which all movements for liberation are measured, but especially those by Black Americans.[89] Thus, claims to King function as claims to the correct and proper way to protest and produce change. Critics of the Movement for Black Lives invoke King as a means of distancing the movement from this "appropriate" form of protest, framing it as illegitimate and even dangerous.

King's memory is often mobilized to condemn the contemporary movement, particularly its use of disruptive tactics such as blocking intersections and interstate highways to impede the flow of traffic. In January 2015, McKesson tweeted a Vine of one such protest.[90] In response, conservative blogger Kathleen McKinley tweeted, "I mean seriously, this isn't the protests of MLK. He would hate this."[91] When criticized because she was a white woman using King to chastise Black people for how they chose to fight injustice, McKinley replied, "What does it matter what color I am. MLK never used profanities or screaming & insisted everyone stay dignified."[92] McKinley has frequently been playing the MLK "Big Joker" since she first joined Twitter in 2008. A prolific author of 140-character MLK fanfic, McKinley has deployed King to condemn a range of Black individuals and their behaviors—chastising protestors for property destruction during protests, admonishing Roland Martin that "MLK wouldn't like [him] bragging about" fund raising, bemoaning the "entitlement" in the "inner city" that "was NOT MLK's dream" but rather his "nightmare," and claiming that "no doubt MLK would be embarrased [sic] by [Jesse] Jackson and [Al] Sharpton today."[93]

In early 2016, former member of the House of Representatives, Joe Walsh, fired off the following series of tweets invoking King to condemn the Movement for Black Lives.

> MLK Jr was all about "the content of our character, not the color of our skin." #BLM is only about skin color.

If MLK were w us 2day he'd say: "Quit whining. We've made amazing racial process. You'll never know the racism that I knew. Celebrate that!"

MLK Jr would tell young blacks today to quit blaming racism for everything. He'd tell em they are in charge of their own lives & futures.[94]

Again, just like McKinley, Walsh has a long history of MLK fanfic, with posts about King coinciding with moments of high-profile racial tension and protests. In August 2013, on the anniversary of the March on Washington and shortly after the acquittal of Zimmerman, Walsh posted a series of tweets beginning with King's famous, "I have a dream" and completed with statements that represent Walsh's own views, such as "I have a dream that young black men will stop shooting other young black men" and "I have a dream that black America will take responsibility for improving their own lives."[95] Walsh put forth an image of King mirroring the one pioneered by Reagan. Walsh's King is an ardent individualist who believes Black Americans should pull themselves up by their bootstraps—which, coincidentally, are the same political views held by Walsh.

In response to attempts to use King to delegitimize the Movement for Black Lives, efforts to reframe and reclaim him as radical are common in the both network and the movement, and they also serve to legitimize the Movement for Black Lives. One key component of this effort has been the #ReclaimMLK movement, which was started in December 2014, after the unrest in Ferguson and continues each year on the weekend of Martin Luther King Day. For activists, this holiday has become a day of action rather than a day of service, as it has traditionally been considered. As Ferguson Action website posted, "On MLK day, do as Martin Luther King would have done and resist the war on Black Lives with civil disobedience and direct action. Take the streets, shut it down, walk, march, and whatever you do, take action."[96]

On the weekend of MLK Day 2015, activists across the country engaged in four days of action. The Coalition Against Police Violence (CAPV), consisting of individuals and organizations working together to "eradicate systemic injustice and state sanctioned violence" through the use of "relentless activism, economic sanctions, and pragmatic strategies of reform," organized the 4 Mile March, which included various forms of protest, in cities across the country , including San Diego, Salt Lake City, Atlanta, Charlotte, Philadephia, Oakland, Chicago, Boston, Minneapolis, New York, St. Louis, and Washington, DC.[97] Other actions were organized around the hashtag #ReclaimMLK. In Oakland, where activists undertook ninety-six hours of protest beginning on January 16, actions included shutting down transit stations and protesters from a variety of racial, ethnic, and national backgrounds chaining themselves to Oakland's Ronald V. Dellums Federal Building holding signs reading "Third World for Black Power." The San Mateo–Hayward Bridge was shut down on January 19 by protesters who physically blocked traffic in both lanes with their bodies. Protesters blocked streets in DC, Seattle, Cincinnati, Minneapolis, Atlanta, and many other cities. Protesters also went into Wal-Mart stores and placed "warning" labels on toy and pellet guns; these had an image of John Crawford, a twenty-two-year-old Black man who was shot and killed by police while holding a BB gun sold by Wal-Mart, and stated: "Persons of color picking up this object may be subject to serious injury or death at the hands of Wal-Mart and police," accompanied by the hashtags #ReclaimMLK and #36seconds, a reference to the time between the officer entering the store and firing. Protesters in Oakland went to Mayor Libby Schaaf's house and projected an image of King on her garage door with the quotation "A riot is the language of the unheard" and the hashtag #IfWeCantBreatheYouCantDream, a reference to the last words of Eric Garner, before dying as a New York police officer held him in a headlock.[98]

Social media, particularly Twitter and Instagram, were central in circulating images of and information about the actions as they took place. Many of the actions were small, performed by only a handful of participants. But, when publicized by social media, these smaller actions filled people's timelines, effectively creating a sense of a nationwide effort.[99] The strategies of agitation and disruption, as expressed by the saying, "Shut shit down," were performed and contextualized with the images of King the radical. As an activist going by the handle WyzeChef tweeted, "No justice, no peace. We are out here indefinitely. Get comfortable with being uncomfortable. #ReclaimMLK."[100]

Such activist efforts were discussed throughout the network, which interpreted the dominant discourse about King, deconstructed it, and offered a different vision. Just as *Historical Blackness* sutured together past and present to address the ongoing reality of structural racism, participants in the network re-remembered King as opposing the same injustice, sharing the same politics and tactics, and receiving much the same criticism as the Movement for Black Lives.

On the August 19, 2015, episode of *TWiB! Prime*, Freeman described the unrealistic way King is often remembered and highlighted the absurdity that this superhuman vision is proffered as a model for Black resistance:

Martin Luther King, from hearing people talk about it, he deflected punches and bullets. Not only was he nonviolent, but nothing actually affected him emotionally. He would walk into the river like a terminator and out the other side like a terminator. He actually felt nothing but compassion for everyone. Nothing. He didn't eat. He didn't drink. He didn't sleep. It was all compassion, 100 percent of the time from Martin Luther King. So, why don't Black people act like that?[101]

Participants in the network often acknowledge that this popular image of King—the nonviolent compassion-filled terminator—is made possible only through strategic amnesia that erases similarities between King and the contemporary movement. For example, on the fourth episode of the *Ferguson Response Network* podcast, Leslie Mac, who is active in the movement and also hosts podcast called *Interraical Jawn* with her white husband, discussed the upcoming MLK Day events with Ricky Hinds, of Americans United Again, and attorney, activist, and artist Esther Baldwin. Mac asserted, "There are so many parallels between the Civil Rights Movement and MLK and the work that he did and was trying to do at the time of his death and what we are all trying to accomplish now."[102] Baldwin further pointed out that

obviously, it is not convenient . . . to remember that he was the target of FBI investigations. That his message was often manipulated against him by the government, in the same way that they are trying to change the narrative about our movement. They're trying to cast us as terrorists when our movement has always been about non-violence. I think there are a lotta correlations to today's movement.

They played clips of King's speeches and read excerpts of "Letter from a Birmingham Jail," drawing parallels between King's own words and the current movement.

After playing a clip from King's 1967 sermon in which he denounced the Vietnam War and referred to the "triple evils of racism, economic exploitation, and militarism,"[103] Mac noted that

> he could have been making this speech today. . . . We need his legacy and his message. Badly, you know? You talk about the dead end that the country is leading on, and it ends on a street outside Canfield Apartments in Ferguson, Missouri. Militarization. Racism. Economic exploitation. This is everything that is going on and that this movement is fighting against still 'til today.[104]

Here Mac made a direct connection between the sociopolitical issues being addressed by King and the contemporary issues at the heart of Movement for Black Lives. Canfield Apartments is the apartment complex where Mike Brown was shot and killed by Ferguson police office Darren Wilson, the event that set in motion the unrest in Ferguson in August 2014 and is largely considered to be the beginning of the Movement for Black Lives. Rather than asserting a historical break between past and present, she constructs a continuum that allows the Movement for Black Lives to position themselves as the inheritors of King's struggle.

In addition to framing King as responding to similar oppressions, *The Ferguson Response Network* also pointed out that King employed tactics similar to those of the contemporary movement. In response to criticisms like those from McKinley about the movement's disruption of traffic and people's daily routines, something she maintained King would "hate," Mac and her guests argued that King was nothing if not an agitator and that the concept of King's nonviolent direct action "seems to have evolved into a passivity that really was not anything that MLK was about. . . . He was about confronting issues."[105] She read the excerpt from "Letter from a Birmingham Jail":

Nonviolent direct action seeks to create such a crisis and foster such a tension that a community which has constantly refused to negotiate is forced to confront the issue. It seeks so to dramatize the issue that it can no longer be ignored. My citing the creation of tension as part of the work of the nonviolent resister may sound rather shocking. But I must confess that I am not afraid of the word "tension." I have earnestly opposed violent tension, but there is a type of constructive, nonviolent tension which is necessary for growth.

Mac then added:

I love that piece because I think that is what we're trying to do. And part of the sanitization of him is this idea, like, "Oh, he was this passive dude. He didn't want to upset anybody. He wasn't tryin' to get in people's face." And it's like, no. He was always in someone's face. . . . That's what he was calling everybody else to do.[106]

Much of the discursive work performed around King's memory in the network focuses on the similarities between King's public reception and that of the Movement for Black Lives. For example, White and Freeman discussed King's 1960 appearance on *Meet the Press* on one episode of *TWiB! Prime*. White played part of the interview in which Lawrence Spivak criticized tactics such as lunch-counter sit-ins, and asked King if he thought those tactics were hurting the cause, and then White paused:

Let's have that moment. They just asked Martin Luther King, . . . the man who gets quoted at us all the time, all the fuckin' time—"If you were just like King, if you would just do things like King, if you just acted like King." But then at the same time, when Martin Luther King was being, I don't know, *King*, white folks were like "Listen, I feel like you're hurting your cause. . . . What's *your* problem, Negro?"

Freeman summarized the argument, "They asked Martin Luther King if he could sit less aggressively. . . . 'You're making us uncomfortable.'" White then continued, "That is what just happened. With all of the bullshit that people talk about the movement, about how things work and all that stuff. Literally, Dr. King had the exact same things being said to him as the movement had said about them. But, *we* should act like King. Literally, that's what they're saying."[107]

King's position as agitator has often been emphasized by the circulation of images of King being arrested and of his mugshot. For example, a few days prior to the 2015 #ReclaimMLK actions, one user tweeted, "What is your position? #blacklivesmatter #reclaimthedream #reclaimmlk," accompanied by the image of MLK in a suit and hat being arrested at a lunch counter with the text, "There comes a time when one must take a position that is neither safe nor politic, nor popular, but he must take it because conscience tells him it is right.—Dr. Martin Luther King, Jr."[108] Participants in the network often point out that King was considered a dangerous radical when alive. As White put it, white people "have been throwing MLK in our faces for yrs but when MLK was saying that real shit they called him a Nigger."[109]

In addition to foregrounding the controversy surrounding King in his day, the network drew a parallel between the "white moderates" criticized by King and the twenty-first century "allies" of the Movement for Black Lives who object to its tactics or politics. On Twitter, while mentions of problematic white moderates as obstacles to justice go back to at least 2010, they became more commonplace after the uprisings in Ferguson and Baltimore. The following passage from King's "Letter from a Birmingham Jail," along with an image of King, circulated widely:

> I must confess that over the past few years I have been gravely disappointed with the white moderate. I have almost reached the regrettable conclusion that the Negro's great stumbling block in his stride toward freedom is not the White Citizen's Counciler or the Ku Klux Klanner, but the white moderate, who is more devoted to "order" than to justice; who prefers a negative peace which is the absence of tension to a positive peace which is the presence of justice; who constantly says: "I agree with you in the goal you seek, but I cannot agree with your methods of direct action." . . . Shallow understanding from people of good will is more frustrating than absolute misunderstanding from people of ill will. Lukewarm acceptance is much more bewildering than outright rejection.[110]

This passage has appeared in various social media incarnations in response to the criticisms levied at Black activists and protestors for failing to advocate for change in more acceptable and less "aggressive" ways.

In August 2015, Gandy published an essay titled, "Dr. King and the White Progressive™," which aggregates and summarizes much of the discourse that had been circulating in the network regarding the shortcoming of white supporters of racial justice, specifically those who evoke King. In it she reads contemporary events through King's criticisms of white moderates in the 1960s. Gandy's use of the "TM" in her title reflects a rhetorical move employed to mark generalizations that apply to a critical mass, but not the entirety of, a particular group. As she once explained on *TWiB! Prime*, "It's about the brand. It's not about individual people. . . . [If] it doesn't apply to you, then it doesn't apply to you. Don't worry about it." To which White added, "If you are not actively part of the brand, then it's not really a critique on you."[111] Though its exact origin is uncertain, the users and content creators at the center of this project have appropriated the language of the trademark to demarcate between the discursive formations and individual white people. It has been applied to a variety of categories—White People™, White Progressives™, White Feminism™—to indicate that the speaker was referring to a configuration of hegemonic discourses that produce each category and the power relations involved in their formation. The intent was to ameliorate conflict that might arise from the impression that critiques of whiteness are attacks on individual white people.

Gandy tweeted a link to the post of her article with the message "I wrote this for ppl who use MLK as their Pokémon."[112] In the article itself she argued,

In the wake of the white progressive think pieces decrying the Black Lives Matter activists as rude, stupid, immature, idiots, bullies, participating in a circular firing squad, or alienating allies—as well as similar sentiments expressed on Facebook, Twitter, and in the comments of my previous articles . . . the parallels between the white moderates whom Dr. Martin Luther King criticized in 1963 and certain white progressives whom many Black activists are criticizing in 2015 are clear.[113]

She set up this parallel by outlining criticisms of King by white moderates and progressives of his day as well as King's response to these critiques. To do so, she cited an open letter titled "A Call for Unity," written by a group of white clergy in the wake of King's arrest during nonviolent protests in Birmingham in April 1963, who suggested that King was too confrontational. Noting that while the protests themselves were nonviolent, they incited hate and violence, the authors of the letter called the protests "unwise and untimely" and suggested that matters of racial justice are best pursued in the courts. To illustrate King's response to these criticisms, Gandy offered quotes from King's famous "Letter from a Birmingham Jail," in which he argued that freedom would come only if demanded by the oppressed and criticized white moderates for prioritizing order over justice and then went on to quote King further:

> **Actually, we who engage in nonviolent direct action are not the creators of tension. We merely bring to the surface the hidden tension that is already alive.** We bring it out in the open, where it can be seen and dealt with.

After setting up the historic conflict, Gandy went on to argue that the critiques of King by the white moderates of his day are mirrored in those of contemporary white progressives™ in response of the Movement for Black Lives. She pointed to Marissa Johnson and Mara Williford, the two women who were accused of being outside agitators after they disrupted a Bernie Sanders rally in Seattle in summer of 2015, and the progressives who said that such protests were poorly timed because it was an election season. Pointing out that "white progressives who are behaving more like the white clergymen who opposed King than the white allies who supported King are the first to criticize the Black Lives Matter activists for not being more like King," Gandy argued that their vision of King erased the reality that he was a disruptor and lawbreaker who "was not beholden to protesting the right thing, at the right time, in the right space according to white moderates' timetable."[114]

Finally, in the dominant narrative of King was often deployed, as it was by Blitzer, as a means of condemning property damage that occurred during periods of unrest. In response, participants in the network often relied on King's words, "Riots are the language of the unheard" not to condone such behavior, but to position it as a symptom of the larger problem. That is how L. Joy Williams, co-host of *TWiB! in the Morning* at the time, framed the disturbance that occurred during a vigil for sixteen-year-old Kimani Gray, who had been killed by police in Brooklyn in March 2013:

> I don't think that people ever plan to riot. . . . I don't know very many riots that were planned. It was, you know, an immediate response that, you know, boiled over. . . . When you have a community that has pent up anger and already feels mistreated, you are going to have sometimes unreasonable responses.[115]

White, who had seen reports of the unrest on social media and went down to the vigil to report, interviewed Jumaane Williams, a New York City Council member who was on the scene and who also invoked King:

> It was a peaceful vigil for the young man Kimani Gray, Kiki, who was shot and killed. By the time I got to the vigil, a group of people had broken off. . . . Dr. Martin Luther King said, "Riots are the language of the unheard," and I think this community has been unheard for quite some time.[116]

The gravitas of King's words is used to reframe the situation—to understand the unrest as an expression of pain and anger, rather than an unruly outburst of criminality. Here King's status as a Civil Rights icon is used to humanize the individuals who destroyed property, framing them within a history of oppression.

Conclusion

Remembering the past has always been of importance in the network at the center of this project. Because how we understand the past has such impact on interpretation of the present, historical accounts become key sites of struggle. Dominant racial ideologies, which construct the present moment as free from structural and systemic racism, rely on an account of the twentieth century in which the Civil Rights Movement stands as the final chapter in the struggle for racial justice. Thus, to make contemporary racism visible as more than individual bad behaviors, the network often challenges the dominant and most widely circulated accounts of the era.

Martin Luther King Jr., in particular, has become a locus of contention in this struggle. Idolized and sanitized of his radicalism, King has come to stand as the avatar for the entire mid-twentieth century movement. In this way King has also become a means of delegitimizing efforts to address racial politics outside of the paradigm of colorblindness. King's image as a proponent of nonviolent direct action and his famous speech at the 1963 March on Washington are frequently used to silence Black critiques of contemporary racism. King's legacy has been used to justify everything from dismantling affirmative action laws to condemning modern-day activists.

The struggle over the past, and particularly King's legacy, has intensified since the emergence of the Movement for Black Lives. Just as King was presented as the "good" Civil Rights leader in juxtaposition to the "bad" and dangerous radicals of the Black Power Movement, King is used as a contrast to the contemporary movement in order to delegitimize it. Simultaneously, the Movement for Black Lives and those aligned with them politically have begun to reclaim King and his legacy, challenging assertions that he would condemn their tactics and, instead, reviving King as a radical very much in line with their movement.

4

"This Is the Resource Our Community Needed Right Now"

Moments of Trauma and Crisis

In video of an interview with the *New York Times* on the one year anniversary of the death of Mike Brown, activist Deray McKesson observed, "The death of Mike Brown and the protests that immediately followed set a precedent for how our generation would react to and . . . challenge systems and structures that oppress people."[1] His statement was immediately followed by a series of hashtags connected to deaths of Black people in police custody in the year after Ferguson—#EricGarner, #ICantBreathe, #JohnCrawford, #WalterScott, #TamirRice, #FreddieGray, #SamuelDubose, #IfTheyGunnedMeDown, #SayHerName, #SandraBland. With the uprising in Ferguson in 2014, the practices and possibilities of Black digital networks garnered the attention of journalist, academics, and the broader public in an unprecedented way. Subsequently, much has been learned from research devoted to the social, cultural, and political importance of Black Twitter, with particular attention to the role of hashtags. My aim here is to broaden the focus and examine how Twitter and the political use of hashtags fit into larger transplatform networks and strategies.

Black digital networks have been crucial in the efforts for racial justice during and since Ferguson. But they did not coalesce at that moment. They already existed, having been created and maintained over years through daily, often mundane, interactions. They migrated from earlier websites and platforms—Black Planet, message boards, Live Journal—and were cultivated around popular culture, political commentary, linguistic games, and the sharing of day-to-day experiences. These processes created Black digital networks that were then able to galvanize and mobilize people together in moments of crisis, such as the deaths of Trayvon Martin and Mike Brown. The network at the center of this project is part of larger Black digital networks that have been a resource in these moments.

The flexible, multimedia, transplatform nature of this network allowed for a variety of responses to the exigencies of any given moment. Its dual nature—broadcast-style and social network—facilitated both journalistic and word-of-mouth practices of information circulation while its transplatform nature provided a range of affordances that could be used in tandem for a variety of goals. At times of racial turmoil, the network was deployed for five intertwined functions—the circulation of information, the interpretation of events, the production and circulation of counter-discourse, the construction and maintenance of solidarity and community, and mobilization for specific actions. These functions often occurred concurrently, though some emerge as more prominent at different moments. This chapter explores how the network was utilized in response to the cases of Martin and Brown, when the Movement for Black Lives emerged and became a national force.

The accounts here present a partial sketch of the ways emerging media functioned in the two pivotal cases. While the political narrative of Black Twitter often starts with its influence in bringing the Trayvon Martin case to broader awareness, the strategies the network deployed around the Martin case began to crystalize well before 2012, with the cases of Oscar Grant and Aiyanna Jones, both of whom were killed during interactions with law enforcement. Before devling into these cases and the digitial responses, I consider how the network is utilized for news and commentary.

News and Commentary in the Transplatform Network

In 2011, the Wisconsin labor protests, Occupy Wall Street, and the Arab Spring solidified Twitter's role as a source of information and a means of mobilization for social movements. Twitter's always-on flow of information has made it an important resource through which users both receive and circulate information in several ways. First, Twitter's constant stream of ambient information, to which users can tune in and out, creates a "monitorial" relationship to information that allows Twitter to serve as an alert system for events of interest. Second, the immediate and synchronous nature of Twitter makes it an ideal platform for improvisational reporting and eye-witness accounts. Finally, this same immediacy makes Twitter an excellent platform for instant reactions, evaluations, and commentary on information and unfolding events.

Twitter is a central component in "an ambient media system where users receive a flow of information from both established media and from each other."[2] This stream of information—a series of digital fragments—can be accessed from a variety of devices.[3] Alfred Hermida argues that this allows Twitter to function as an "awareness system" that is "always-on and moves from the background to the foreground as and when a user feels the need to communicate."[4]

Twitter's immediacy and accessibility make it ideal for eye-witness reporting in real time. According to Alex Bruns and Jean Burgess, "Live tweeting [is] a more important practice on Twitter than comparable live activities have been for previous platforms."[5] As early as 2008 and 2009, journalists were using Twitter as a source for unverified eye witness accounts during Iran election protests and the Mumbai bombings.[6] Live accounts may come from professional journalists on the scene, from citizen journalists, or from ordinary people engaging in "random acts of journalism" in improvisational and contingent ways.[7]

These affordances make Twitter a valuable tool for contemporary citizenship practices. Michael Schudson argues that citizens have developed a "monitorial" attitude toward information, "scanning all kinds of news and other media sources . . . for topics that matter to them personally."[8] Bruns calls this "gatewatching." Building on the longstanding concept of "gatekeeping" in journalism, in which official entities function to select what information is reported and circulated, he argues that users observe "the output of gates of news publications and other sources, in order to identify important material as it becomes available."[9] However, because Twitter's information stream is comprised of heterogeneous information fragments, the news stories amplified by gatewatching exist next to eye-witness accounts, commentary, and interpretive processes. People are not just watching news publications for relevant information, but also watching micro-celebrities in their Twitter networks—including activists, online personalities, and independent media producers—as well as monitoring for hashtags that might signal an important topic and for repetitions of information, a phenomenon often described as "my timeline is talking about X." John Zaller has argued that journalism functions as a "burglar alarm," which sounds loudly to indicate that a problem needs urgent attention.[10] On Twitter, official news, citizen jour-nalism, hashtags, and network chatter can all serve to "raise the alarm" and attract the attention of the monitorial citizen.

However, Twitter is only one component of the network I discuss here. Twitter is able to serve as such an awareness system for its users in large part because it functions as a central clearinghouse for informa-tion posted on other platforms, such as Facebook, Tumblr, Instagram, and Vine, and can provide links to live streams on Ustream, Periscope, and Facebook Live. Thus, people reporting from events can make use of whatever platform has the appropriate affordances—Instagram for images and videos or Ustream for long-form streaming video—and ex-ploit Twitter's function as an alert system, without being confined by its limitations.

Additionally, podcasts and other long-form media provide arenas in which to aggregate, synthesize, and interpret the fragmented stream of information available on Twitter and generate more cohesive linear narratives about events. As Hermida notes of the fragments of infor-mation that comprise the ambient information stream on Twitter, "The value does not lie in each individual fragment of news and informa-tion, but rather in the mental portrait created by a number of mes-sages over a period of time."[11] These fragments—official news reports, citizen journalism, random acts of journalism, commentary, reactions, interpretations—work together to form an overall impression and in-terpretation of an event. The podcasts in the network create a space in which participants in the network, including podcasts host, guests, and listeners, can aggregate, evaluate, synthesize, and interpret these frag-mented streams, collectively generating a narrative of a given event. This process often includes the generation of color-conscious interpre-tations of events and critiques of dominant discourses circulated by leg-acy media. At times the "alarm" to which they are responding is not an event, but a discourse around an event that participants in the network see as problematic or inaccurate.

While Hermida suggests that even though "tweets are atomic in na-ture, they are part of a distributed conversation through a social network of interconnected users,"[12] I would argue that they are actually only one component in a conversation that is distributed across platforms. Pod-casts allow not only for greater depth than Twitter, but also for linearity.

They also enable these conversations to take place in network enclaves, relatively secluded from others and shielded from harassment. In fact, participants in the network have often remarked of the hostility that surfaces on social media around moments of trauma. The podcasts can thus become a space to discuss this phenomenon, in addition to offering refuge from it. The evolution of these practices can be seen in the digital responses to the deaths of Oscar Grant and Aiyanna Jones.

Early Responses to Racial Injustice

Prior bringing attention to the death of Trayvon Martin, users of Black Twitter made connections through everyday talk, jokes, and live-tweeting television. As early as 2009, when Twitter only had about 18 million users, compared to the 140 million it had by Martin's death in 2012, Black users were live-tweeting television shows together, long before it became the norm on the platform. During the 2009 BET Awards, Elon James White and Bassey Ikpi, then co-hosts of TWiB!'s podcast *Blacking It Up!*, live-tweeted the award show using the hashtag #TWiBET09 and offered live blog commentary hosted on TWiB!'s website. Many TWiB! listeners and other podcasters also live-tweeted the show. In 2009 and 2010, Black Twitter could also be found watching shows like *The Boondocks* and *To Catch a Predator* in real time together on Twitter. Such networked co-viewing practices relied not so much on hashtags as on the homophily of the Black Twitter network and would often dominate the trending topics with related words and phrases on these nights.

Sometimes Black Twitter's activity was organized around a specific hashtag, but often it was not. It is important to remember that early Twitter, circa 2008–2010, had significantly fewer features than its later incarnations. The platform did not yet have an automatic retweet function. Users "retweeted" by manually cutting and pasting and adding the prefix "RT." Twitter also lacked any mechanism for connecting replies to the tweet to which they were responding. Tweets could be addressed to specific user with the @-reply function, but were not tethered as a reply to a specific tweet. This made it difficult to follow conversations one was not involved in. Hashtags ameliorated this by organizing tweets by topic, and the approach of Black Twitter users aided further.

Black users developed a homophilic approach to the platform that differed from the microblog status updates intended by its developers. Brendan Meeder's analysis of Twitter data during this period found dense clusters of users who followed one another and noted that such clusters were predominantly Black. This arrangement helped create the network density that allowed Black Twitter to have a pronounced presence on the trending topics.[13] It also aided in creating a sense of collectivity steeped in ongoing group conversation and shared communicative and cultural practices. It was extremely common for members of the Black Twitter network to contribute to conversations with no hashtag or other marker indicating what they were responding to. Pronouns and references would go undefined. A tweet might indicate "she" is doing something or "this" is hilarious or problematic, and so on, without ever defining what the user was referencing. The meaning could be inferred only from the broader context of what was being discussed that day. In-group references, to both Black American culture and to Black Twitter in-group knowledge, functioned similarly. These practices reproduced longstanding Black American modes of communication practices that rely on opacity and misdirection and require cultural competencies and contextual awareness to decode—hence the importance of cultural specificity to scholarly analyses and the dangers of over-reliance on hashtags in analysis of Twitter.

Early on, Twitter was used to circulate and discuss instances of police violence. Among the first was the death of Oscar Grant at the hands of an Oakland, California, transit police officer, Johannes Mehserle, on New Year's Day 2009. Grant's case was the first to be caught on cell phone video, posted on YouTube, and have the link circulated via social media platforms. Twitter was used to share the links to news coverage of the incident, at first from local news like Fox affiliate KTUV and independent Bay Area publications such as *Topix San Francisco* and *Oakland Focus* and eventually from major national outlets like CNN.[14] This early reporting also came from This Week in Blackness, which posted the story on its website and tweeted the link from both its account and White's own with the statement: "From This Week in Blackness Twitter: New From TWiB: UNACCEPTABLE: Shooting of Oscar Grant."[15] Actions such as the January 7 vigil for Grant at Fruitvale Station were also announced on Twitter.

From late 2009 to mid-2010, YouTube and Twitter formed avenues for information about the Mehserle trial.[16] This was before videos could be posted directly to Twitter and instead had to be uploaded elsewhere. In particular, Youth Radio, a nonprofit founded in 1993 to train youth as journalists, had reporters at the trial and tweeted information on the hashtag #MehserleTrial. They also posted video interviews from eye witnesses and protestors as well as coverage of the protests and unrest following the verdict.[17] Freelance journalist Thandisizwe Chimurenga, who describes herself as practicing "emancipatory journalism," created a Twitter account @OscarGrantTrial (now @OscarGrantCoverage) and attended the trail and tweeted as it unfolded.[18] Davey D, Hip-hop DJ, songwriter, producer and journalist, who is politically active in the Bay Area, also disseminated information via his Twitter account, in addition to his work in radio and other broadcast mediums. When unrest broke out in Oakland following the verdict, information from freelance journalists, citizen journalists, and everyday participants was circulated by YouTube and social media in conjunction.

Between the 2009 death of Grant and the 2012 death of Trayvon Martin, information about a handful of police-involved shootings of Black people circulated in Black digital networks. In 2010, the death of seven-year-old Aiyana Jones, who was killed by a bullet from an officer's gun during a SWAT raid on her home, was discussed heavily on Twitter. Jones's death was first reported on Twitter by white Israeli-born gender-nonconforming Hip-hop MC and activist, Invincible, who posted: "Justice for Ayanna Jones! Tonight 6pm News Conference 8pm Candle Light Vigil 4054 Lillibridge by Canfield on Detroit's east side."[19] As in Grant's case, Twitter users shared links to local reporting in the days immediately following and then from larger sites like CNN.com as they picked up the story. As the case unfolded, Twitter users also circulated a petition demanding that footage of Jones's death be released, marked the day of her funeral with remembrances, and mourned on what would have been her 8th birthday. They followed and shared allegations of a cover-up by Detroit police, the indictment of Joseph Weekley on involuntary manslaughter and reckless endangerment charges, and the subsequent trails (which occurred between 2013 and 2015 and ended in mistrials).

These early cases are instructive because although Twitter was not yet a widely used platform, it was beginning to take shape as a place for information circulation and mobilization. The use of Twitter for citizen journalism was also developing, although because of Twitter's technical limitations—140 characters and no capability for images or video—information circulated mostly through links to content on other platforms, such as YouTube or TwitPic.

During the years 2009–2011, TWiB! and the Chitlin' Circuit podcasts were also in their formative stages. TWiB!'s video series began in 2008, while *Blacking it Up!*, which had a brief run in 2009, returned permanently in 2011. In 2010, there were only a handful of Black podcasts, with *The Black Guy Who Tips*, *Insanity Check*, and *Where's my 40 Acres?* being key among them. It was not until a few years later that podcasts developed into a robust element in the network's distributed discussions.

Trayvon Martin

The death of Trayvon Martin and the subsequent trial and acquittal of his killer were watershed moments for the network, when the strategies that were deployed during the uprising in Ferguson and that have become central to the Movement for Black Lives coalesced. In the immediate aftermath of Martin's death, Twitter served as alert system and tool for mobilization, while during Zimmerman's trial it was primarily a channel for information obtained through gatewatching. Twitter, TWiB!, and the extant Chitlin' Circuit podcasts all covered the story, with Twitter being the primary space for public engagement. The acquittal of George Zimmerman in 2013, was a key moment when the network as an oscillating networked public fully coalesced, with a clear strategy for creating enclaves for solidarity, community, and catharsis.

Martin was shot and killed on February 26, 2012, and while local news media covered his death immediately, it took nearly two weeks for the story to gain prominence on Twitter, where mentions early on amounted to personal reactions and remembrances. It was through gatewatching and the use of Twitter as a central clearinghouse for information posted elsewhere that the case first gained traction on Twitter. Benjamin Crump, who represented Martin's family, brought on board a public relations professional, Ryan Julison, who in turn was able to obtain significant national news coverage for the story, including coverage by Reuters and *CBS This Morning*. By March 8, Martin's death was being covered by both legacy and independent media sources and a Change. org petition to bring charges against Zimmerman had been created and was quickly gaining signatures.[20] Links to these news stories and to the petition served as "alarms" on Twitter. Almost immediately, Black users were sharing the story—both links to reporting and their own 140 character summaries—and the petition.

Bringing the Trayvon Martin case to national attention was a dialogic process between legacy media and social media. Once Black Twitter was alerted to the story, it was instrumental in circulating it and helping to maintain pressure to bring charges. By 2012, Black Twitter itself had been covered by many news outlets, including *Slate*, National Public Radio, *NewsOne*, and *Forbes*, and had enough visibility to affect how the case was taken up in the news cycle.[21] Furthermore, while Twitter was instrumental in organizing and publicizing protests such as the Million Hoodie March in New York City in March 2012, it also became a terrain for protest, with users posting images of themselves in hoodies with hashtags like #WeAreTrayvonMartin. Twitter was also the medium where outrage and calls for justice were expressed. Whereas cable news and talk radio focused on gun control and legal analysis and blogs focused largely on racial politics, Twitter traffic leaned more toward humanizing Martin, sympathizing with his family, and demanding justice.[22]

Throughout the trial, the network participated heavily in gatewatching, following, aggregating, and circulating news about the case as it emerged primarily from legacy media outlets. After the initial protests following Martin's death, most of the information circulated within the network was from professional news outlets. Users on Twitter, Chitlin' Circuit podcasts, and TWiB! all followed the story and discussed it when there were notable developments. The "gates" were watched not only for valuable information, but also for problematic information and media narratives in need of rebuttal.

Much of the discussion of the case involved creating counter-discourses that offered alternative interpretations and critiqued much of the legacy media reporting. It was not uncommon for members of the network to watch the televised trial, tweeting summaries and commentary that others could follow online. White watched and live-tweeted much of the trial, occasionally receiving inquiries from people at work who were unable to watch and wanted clarification and elaboration.[23] There were also a number of hashtags associated with the case, with #Justice4Trayvon being key among them. However, other more specific hashtags were created to discuss or critique elements of the trial as it progressed. Hashtags served as vehicles for both information and catharsis. The hashtag #zimmermantrial was used to share and comment on developments in the trial. Other hashtags were more humorous. Because of his direct and forceful tone, the testimony of the medical examiner, Dr. Shiping Bao, was tweeted under the hashtag #BaoDown, a reference to a recently released Beyoncé song containing the lyrics "Bow down, bitches." After the prosecutors rebutted Zimmerman's account of Martin's death, asserting "I guess the victim has 2 or 3 hands," White created the hashtag #ThatThirdHand:

> White: #ThatThirdHand is why Zimmerman needed to kill #TrayvonMartin. Y'all didn't know that Negroes have a secret 3rd hand to deal w/ crackas?

> L. Joy Williams: #ThatThirdHand is what my Grandma would threaten to use to slap the Black off of me

> Tracey Clayton: #ThatThirdHand helped black people vote for Obama an extra time in the booths this last election

> Dacia Mitchell: We got #ThatThirdHand because of affirmative action. #zimmermantrial[24]

Many of the podcasters discussed the case as it unfolded, as well as engaging listeners in its interpretation. For example, in March 2012, TWiB! did several shows that analyzed not only his death but also the reactions to it. The latter was taken up by *Single Simulcast*, which discussed the social media meme of "Trayvoning," in which white people were mimicking Trayvon Martin lying dead with Arizona Iced Tea and Skittles next to him, and the "Angry Trayvon" game that was pulled from both the iTunes and Google Play stores. On July 11, just days before the Zimmerman verdict was handed down, *Straight Outta LoCash* brought on Defense Attorney Jasmine Crockett to discuss the trail and the possible outcomes.

Catharsis, Solidarity, and Community

On night of July 13, 2013, when news media reported Zimmerman's acquittal, many Black Americans took to their social media networks to express their thoughts and feelings about the verdict and its implications for Black Americans in the contemporary United States. Within thirty minutes of the announcement, the US trending topics were dominated by the verdict. Many network participants tweeted about their grief, anger, and disgust, frequently expressing a sense of being treated as second-class citizens, noncitizens, or generally disposable by the broader society. Many of these users experienced harassment, including White, who, minutes after expressing his outrage over the verdict on Twitter, received responses calling him a "hateful race-monger" and comments such as "awwww you need a tissue? You gonna make it? :(JUSTICE SERVED!"[25] Aaron Rand Freeman, co-host of *TWiB! Radio*, said, "Social media is a war zone."[26] TWiB! quickly began an unscheduled live stream, accompanied by a chatroom, to shift the discussion from the counter-public space of Twitter to the more secluded space of the podcasts. These podcasts were initially used to process the impact of the verdict. As days went on, they took on a greater interpretive function, with participants collectively working to understand the event and seeking to challenge the dominant discourses surrounding the acquittal. The night of the verdict, White and Dacia Mitchell, then co-host of *TWiB! Radio*, began live-streaming at about midnight EST. The unexpected show was announced via White's personal Twitter account to his roughly 20,000 followers as well his Facebook and Google+ profiles. White's tweets included both the link to the live stream and its accompanying chatroom and the number to call in to the show. He quite literally shifted his audience from his Twitter timeline to the live stream, gathering and insulating participating members of the network from the attacks they were experiencing on Twitter. Within thirty minutes, as heavy traffic kept crashing the TWiB! website, White tweeted to direct the audience to listen through the mobile apps TuneIn and Stitcher Radio. After taking phone calls until well after three in the morning, *TWiB! Radio* was back on air by noon the following day, using the same social media mechanisms to alert listeners. White, this time with Imani Gandy, co-host at the time of *TWiB! in the Morning*, again took listener phone calls for over three hours. Despite being on an extended hiatus at the time, *TWiB! Radio* broadcast for several hours a day, every day for the next ten days.

TWiB!'s response to the Zimmerman acquittal closely mirrored Black radio's well-documented function of informing and unifying Black communities in times of turmoil.[27] Black radio DJs were key political and community actors during the tumultuous years of the 1960s and 1970s. In the wake of the assassination of Martin Luther King Jr., Black DJs across the country suspended their regularly scheduled broadcasts and "gathered people around the microphone to ponder and probe the unfolding American tragedy with the listeners."[28] In 1992, in the chaos that followed the acquittal of two Los Angeles police officers in the beating of Rodney King, LA's Black-owned and operated radio station KJLH responded with an unscheduled broadcast of *Front Page*, its news and current events program. *Front Page* went on air and broadcast nonstop for days, taking phone calls from listeners and providing the community with a forum to discuss events as well as with vital information as civil unrest unfolded in the city.[29]

Many saw the Zimmerman acquittal not only as a failure of the legal system, but as an affirmation of Black Americans' exclusion from the fundamental rights and protections of US citizenship. The verdict also laid bare the oppression and devaluation of Black life that contemporary postracial colorblind discourses worked to obscure. Here, the work of Ghasson Hage is helpful to understanding the dynamics.[30] Hage draws on Louis Althusser's theory of interpellation, the process though which individuals come to occupy certain subect positions throught the "hail" of social interactions, to explore the complex processes that constitute racialized subjects. "Mis-interpellation" occurs when a racialized subject who seems to be hailed as part of a collective is suddenly made aware of being excluded. This individual "believes that the hailing is for 'everyone' and answers the call thinking that there is a place for him or her awaiting to be occupied," writes Hage. "Yet, no sooner do they answer the call and claim their spot than the symbolic order brutally reminds them that they are not part of everyone."[31] Hage argues that mis-interpellation is particularly traumatic because it is so unexpected—the "subject is ambushed." He explains, "Just as [the subject] is led to believe that there is every reason to be hopeful, its hope is killed before its very eyes. The subject shatters and its effort to pull itself together following that moment becomes Herculean."[32]

It is precisely "hope" that made the Zimmerman acquittal so traumatic for many Black Americans. The language of colorblindness and its denial of contemporary racism had come to saturate US political culture. Barack Obama, who was often praised for his ability to "transcend" race, became the first person of color to be elected to the office of the president. Many saw the event as proof that Martin Luther King Jr.'s dream had come to fruition. However, on the night of July 13, Black Americans found that rather than living in King's Dream, they were instead still living behind of DuBois's veil.

One hundred and ten years prior to the Zimmerman trial, W. E. B. DuBois wrote of the color line as a veil that separated the Black and white worlds.[33] While it is unlikely that the majority of Black Americans ever believed the veil had completely vanished, it had become easy to see Obama's election as an indication that the veil had at least become thinner, more permeable, and less determinative of Black Americans' life chances. In seeking, and to some degree expecting, justice for Trayvon Martin and his family, Black Americans ran smack into the color line, finding that it was still much stronger than many had allowed themselves believe. White expressed this sentiment on *TWiB! Radio* the night of the verdict:

> There is an extra amount of, I guess, bitterness that comes with this, because at the moment we are being served up that America is this meritocracy, racism is over, and all you have to do is pull yourself up and you'll be fine. And we're learning, day by day, night by night, that this is consistently not true.[34]

Or as Blair L. M. Kelley put it succinctly, "I just want a time in which we are all citizens and respected as such. And I thought we were there, and we are not."[35]

As the symbolic order expelled Black Americans from full citizenship, their Herculean effort to reassemble their shattered subjectivity unfolded in part online. On Saturday July 13 and Sunday July 14, in the immediate aftermath of the verdict, TWiB! staff and fans called into the TWiB! live stream and took to social media to express their grief, fear, and anger. Digital networks provided an instantly available, widely accessible means of connecting to others and enabling a collective expression of emotion. As Vince from Charlotte, who called in Saturday night, put it, "I think we are just looking for someplace to go. For someplace, for somebody else to feel the same way that I'm feeling right now. . . . just to understand that I'm not alone in this."[36]

Whether it was the TWiB! hosts, the callers, the people in the chatroom, or the people on social media, all expressed a sense of alienation from the American body politic. As White tweeted shortly before the Saturday night broadcast, "Next time you hear someone ask 'Why do you have to be "black," why can't you just be American?' remember this moment."[37] Or as Monica Roberts responded to White and two other users, "This nation only wants us when they need soldiers to fight a war."[38]

The sudden expulsion from citizenship, as the American symbolic order rebuked Black Americans' sense of belonging, was made all the more traumatic as Black parents had to grapple with the pain and helplessness of watching as this moment of mis-interpellation devastated their children as well. To many Trayvon Martin became an avatar for Black youth in the United States, a symbol for the way that the broader culture regarded Black lives. During the two *TWiB! Radio* broadcasts the weekend of the verdict, callers expressed despair at watching their children face the harsh reality of the institutionalized devaluation of their lives.[39] One caller, Sunny from Birmingham, AL, encapsulated this experience, "My son asked me, 'Mom, why don't I matter?'"[40] Another TWiB! listener tweeted, "I'm having a baby girl in two weeks . . . & I've gone from elated to terrified."[41]

Such expressions of individual subjective experiences of mis-interpellation transformed the Zimmerman acquittal into a collective trauma. Sociologists have argued that trauma is not simply the result of a painful experience, but a social process through which symbolic representations of that event define it as an injury to the collective, thereby allowing that pain to enter "into the core of the collectivity's sense of its own identity."[42] It is through processes of representation that an event is constructed as a collective trauma, which implicitly involves a shift in collective identity.[43] It was in digital media spaces that many Black Americans represented their experiences of mis-interpellation and, feeling stripped of their identity as Americans, worked to reify their Black identity.

A few days after the acquittal White explained to me in a personal exchange that he believed a "Digital Black Nation" was emerging in response to the verdict and providing an alternative citizenship for Black Americans. He argued that TWiB! was "like a city" within a Black imagined community and that, though fraught with internal tensions and conflicts, it came together in solidarity in times of crisis. Black Americans have long existed in imagined communities connected by transportation, music, Black-owned newspapers, and the like, and it is not uncommon in certain strains of Black thought to construct Blackness as having the status of nationhood. White pointed to the unprecedented availability of real-time, geographically unfettered interactive media as solidifying those existing bonds.[44]

TWiB!'s live stream the night of the verdict provided the kind of synchronous listening experience that has traditionally made radio a powerful medium for the constitution of imagined communities. Like radio, the podcast provided the experience of "liveness," the feeling of being part of a group listening simultaneously in real-time, which can create a powerful sense of connection.[45] Further, TWiB!'s use of the call-in format allowed the audience to participate in meaning-making processes around the acquittal. Though it is not uncommon for TWiB! to take phone calls for portions of shows, it rarely used the call-in format for an entire broadcast until that night. The decisions to take back-to-back phone calls from twenty-one listeners made the broadcast a collective effort. In addition, audience participation not only demonstrated to listeners who the members of this community were but also served as performances of Black collective identity.

Throughout the broadcast, White and Mitchell also interjected comments from the chatroom into the discussion, allowing those who could not, or did not wish to, call in to be part of the conversation. Beyond this, the chatroom allowed the listeners to interact not just with the show, but with each other. The chatroom simulated the way a group of people might have listened to KJLH during the unrest of 1992, gathering around and commenting and discussing among themselves.

Similarly, Twitter provided an additional channel for synchronous participation, allowing listeners to interact with the show and with each other. For listeners using Twitter, TWiB!'s longtime hashtag #TWiB-nation and White's personal Twitter account served as focal points for these interactions. The addressivity enabled by the @-reply feature of Twitter and conversational coherence created via the use of hashtags allowed TWiB! listeners to converse on Twitter about events and comment on the show.[46]

The resulting discursive space allowed both hosts and listeners to engage in collective meaning-making about Black racial identity and the nature of TWiB! itself. The comments of TWiB! hosts and listeners revealed a clear conceptualization of TWiB! as a space of community, rather than a network of individuals. Early in the broadcast, White explained to listeners his rationale for going live that night, saying, "[W]e need to talk about it. Because I was just sitting there angry and I didn't know what to do either. But we figured we'd allow for an outlet for people, kind of, to weigh in."[47] Mitchell spoke to the sense of collective experience, saying that she hoped that listening to the broadcast lets "people know they aren't alone." Just days after the Zimmerman acquittal, White explained to me that he felt that TWiB! had "an obligation to be there" for the community.[48] TWiB!'s response—ten days of unscheduled coverage of the event—was a clear manifestation of that sense of responsibility.

TWiB!'s listeners indicated a shared vision of TWiB!'s function as space for the community. Callers expressed gratitude to TWiB! for broadcasting that night, and many listeners echoed these sentiments on Twitter. Long time listener @AwakeBlackWoman tweeted during the broadcast that it was "truly lifesaving to have #TWiBNation on the air, taking calls: Here For Us."[49] Another longtime listener, @CoquiNegra tweeted to the hosts of *TWiB! Radio* the following day that TWiB! was "the resource our community needed right now. Thank you."[50]

Additionally, hosts, callers, chatroom participants, and Twitter users, with few exceptions, interpreted Zimmerman's acquittal through the lens of a Black collective identity. Many that night spoke of Black Americans' shared status as marginalized second-class citizens, which they tied to the history of Black oppression in the United States. Expressing the feeling that Black lives were simply not valued, hosts and listeners articulated the shared experience of living in as racialized subjects in the US in the era of supposed colorblindness.

The show also addressed the sense of isolation many listeners felt, seeing many of their fellow Americans seemingly untouched by this event. White asked, "The question is who is feeling the pain? This feels like a dark night in America for us. There are tons of people who are paying no mind to this." He continued, "There are two different countries under one umbrella here. And sometimes when you see stuff like this, it highlights it. You clearly see the two different spaces we live in."[51]

TWiB's collective meaning-making process unfolded synchronously across TWiB!'s multilayered digital structure. Perhaps the most striking example of this was an exchange between White and two other listeners who were participating from Korea and Germany. At about 2:20 a.m. EST a listener named Jack called in from Seoul, South Korea, saying, "No matter where you go in the world, any Black person who sees this case relates to it, relates to, you know, the injustice."[52] He continued that people often ask him why he does not want to return to the United States, and stated pointedly, "This is an example of why I'm not in a hurry to go back home." Minutes later, another listener, @HaggBoson, tweeted from Germany using the #TWiBNation hashtag, "Re: the caller from Korea. I'm in Germany and feel no desire to go 'home,' for the same reason."[53] Approximately thirty minutes later, White said on air that he was "scanning the feed," looking through the hashtag on Twitter. He came across and read the tweet from @HaggsBoson on air, which in turn prompted those in the chatroom to discuss their experiences and feelings regarding international travel and living abroad.

The pain of mis-interpellation echoed across the podcast Chitlin' Circuit as well. Several of its podcasters participated in TWiB!'s live streams and were present in the chatroom or part of the related interactions on Twitter, and many were in dialogue with TWiB!'s live streams, recapping and responding to what TWiB! had discussed on their shows. The same sense of grief and the experience of alienation from the US citizenry were in the foreground. However, the Chitlin' Circuit podcasts varied in how, and even whether, they covered the verdict.

Many of them echoed the same sentiments as TWiB!, emphasizing how Obama's election and the discourses of "postracial" America merely temporarily obscured racial oppression. The day following the verdict, *TBGWT* addressed the issue. Although the podcast has become increasingly political over time, at that point, Rod and Karen were largely avoiding topics that they considered too heavy because they wanted the podcast to be funny and entertaining. But as Rod said of the verdict, "As funny as I want the show to be, if I just avoid talkin' about it then that's probably not good. . . . I don't have any jokes for it really, because it's not funny to me." He asked Karen and their guest Amber P., who hosted her own podcasts *Black, Sexy, Geeky, and Mental* and *Black Chick Watching*, their reactions. Karen pointed to the sense of mis-interpellation saying, "Black issues in our country are not considered American issues. Our children dying are not considered American children dying. We're considered a subculture, a subsection, Other, less than."[54] Rod echoed this, asserting that even having a trail was a victory of sorts because "just the American right to have our death investigated wasn't even there." Reggie, co-host of the *What's the Tea?* podcast, described the feeling:

> It's like America had this banner like, "Your life isn't worth shit and we really don't give a fuck about you," But, you know, the banner got covered up by Obama 2012. But, now they've rehung the banner, and they're like, "Remember, we don't really give a fuck about your life."[55]

The enclave created by the podcasts also served as space to escape these potent emotions, allowing a brief respite for those who were emotionally weary. After expressing their perspectives, the *TBGWT* hosts quickly moved on to more humorous topics. All three stated that they didn't follow the trial very closely because it was simply too painful. These sentiments were echoed in *TBGWT*'s live chat. Kriss and Kev, then co-hosts of the MTR's *Insanity Check* podcast, mentioned the verdict only to say that they weren't going to discuss it. Kriss explained, "Normally, while I like talking about things even if they make us uncomfortable, this joint hits a lot closer to home." He said that they had wanted to show to be a distraction from the tragedy.

Gatewatching and Counter-Discourse Production

In addition to serving as a haven for those looking for catharsis, solidarity, or distraction, the network served as a tool for collectively gatewatching and challenging the mainstream news media's coverage of the acquittal. This was no small task, given that the expression of

a uniquely Black social and historical experience was in direct violation of the edicts of colorblindness. The conversations taking place
in many Black digital media spaces asserted race as a central organizing structure of the United States and a major locus of inequality. The
recognition of race as something more than a trivial individual characteristic quickly elicited attempts to silence the Black voices making
these claims, as many white Americans on social media platforms and
in mainstream media and politics set about to dismiss or coopt those
expressions of Black experiences. The network functioned as a preex-
isting infrastructure for alerting participants to problematic reporting,
directly challenging its authors, and producing alterative interpretations
of events.

In legacy media, commentators and pundits attempted to reassert
neoliberal racial logics and label those discussing race as the true racists. People such as Newt Gingrich, who continued the practice in which
proponents of colorblind racial logics coopt Civil Rights Movement language, condemned the people protesting in the days following the verdict as a misinformed "lynch mob." When President Obama validated
Black collective experiences of racism by saying that thirty-five years
ago he could have been Trayvon Martin, several pundits responded by
calling him the "race-baiter in chief" and accusing him of "tearing the
country apart" by foregrounding race. Conservatives like Bill O'Reilly
tried to reassert the primacy of individual characteristics rather than social structures in sustaining racial inequality by deploying paternalistic
discourses of personal responsibility, asserting "the deterioration of the
Black family" due to "poor individual life choices" on the part of Black
Americans. CNN anchor Don Lemon echoed O'Reilly's sentiments but
said they did not "go far enough" and, reinforcing the emphasis on individual behavior, invoked the politics of respectability, telling Black
Americans to pull up their pants, stop littering, and stop using the word
"n-word." Freeman described the general discursive climate saying,
"These last ten days has been America collectively explaining in various
ways and forms about how the Black experience isn't really important,
and it really shouldn't be that important to you as a Black person."[56]

TWiB! functioned as a space in which to resist the reinterpretation
of events in ways that eliminated Black experience and downplayed the
severity and institutionalization of contemporary racism. Beginning the

Monday after the verdict, TWiB! shifted from providing a space for collective grieving to being a center for counter-discourse production that addressed and rebutted attempts to reframe events. White explained:

> The first couple of days we broadcasted, it was—it was just this *pain*, and just like horror about what is actually happening. And then all of a sudden we've been going into this space of dealing with the fuckery that people are throwing out there and like batting it down, going "No, that's bullshit."[57]

TWiB! podcasts systematically analyzed, deconstructed, and rebutted each attempt to dismiss or reframe.

Both TWiB! staff and listeners engaged in this practice on both Twitter and on-air during the TWiB! podcasts. In response to the sheer volume of problematic commentary circulating after the acquittal, White created a hashtag, #TMFRH, an abbreviation of the phrase "this motherfucker right here," to allow the TWiB! network (both the organization proper and the social network in which it is embedded) to crowdsource and tag problematic commentary for discussion on TWiB! shows. On July 21, after the hashtag had been in circulation a few days, White tweeted, "The folks at @WEEKinBLACKNESS and I are going to be scanning that hashtag regularly. If you see something, say something. #TMFRH."[58] Many listeners used the hashtag to flag commentary for *TWiB! Radio* hosts. The hashtag was given two related *TWiB! Radio* episodes—Episode 451: The This Motherf*cker Right Here Hour and Episode 452: The #TMRH Hour 2.

Thus, when *Salon*'s David Sirota moved to recenter the discussion of Trayvon Martin tragedy to one of his primary political issues—US drone strikes—both Gandy and White engaged Sirota on Twitter, making use of the platform's counter-public enabling affordances to challenge his attempts to redirect public attention in a way that they felt was coopting the pain of Black Americans and foreclosing discussions of domestic structural racism.[59] White challenges to Sirota (which were Storified by another user[60]) included the following tweets, among others:

> I'm genuinely confused as to why @davidsirota keeps trying to connect the #ZimmermanTrial to Obama and drone strikes. Sir . . .[61]

There isn't an equivalency to #TrayvonMartin and Drone strikes. To do so erases the circumstances that leads to both.[62]

To use the pain & grieving of a community to make a nonsensical political argument is not only cheap—it's insulting. @davidsirota.[63]

White, Gandy, and Freeman discussed Sirota's tactics at length on *TWiB! Radio*. During the conversation, Gandy expressed her frustration:

Can we just talk about what Black people right now need to talk about right now at this moment, for like a week at least? We can't even go a week? Until some white liberal is coming along . . . saying, "Oh no. We need to talk about this now. Y'all had your moment."[64]

In addition to responding to the minimization and erasure of Black Americans' feelings and experiences, *TWiB! Radio* podcasts also served as a means for preserving these responses. TWiB! came to be an alternative archive of sorts, or, as White put it,

almost like an audio record of the fuckery that's occurring. . . . Because the fact is, after a couple of weeks, a month or two, people will pretend like nothing happened. Nothing fucking happened. And I—I will not. I will point it out. . . . And there's going to be a record. You can' pretend like it didn't happen. But, there's a record, where it was literally collected. Like Pokémon. Racist-ass Pokémon. I wanna collect them all.[65]

Because remembering is so central to identity, how the moment of the George Zimmerman verdict was, and is, remembered has dramatic consequences for the possibilities of Black collective identity in the future. Remembering the collective expulsion from full citizenship solidifies a Black collective identity grounded in a shared experience of oppression. Defending the memory of this experience is a strategy for defending the collective identity it speaks to. Thus, the nature of this memory is not only a matter of contemporary urgency, but also one that stands to affect the future viability of Black collective identity in the colorblind ideological context.

While TWiB! was deliberately functioning as a counter-public, other podcasts continued to serve as enclaves, where participants could interrogate and interpret discourse. While the Chitlin' Circuit podcasts did discuss the same problematic narratives covered on TWiB!, they tended to do so without any intention of debating or challenging those outside the network.

Humor was a key strategy for processing the dominant discourse about the verdict. Just a few days afterward, *TBGWT*'s hosts asserted that people on cable news networks were debating the verdict "like ESPN treats football." After discussing how many news outlets were anticipating riots, a white woman who rushed the stage and attacked a Black musician after he dedicated a song to Martin, and the reported book deal of Juror B37, Rod summarized his experience of the news: "I really feel like people just fuckin' with us." He went on to explain, "Fuckin' with us, dog. White people just fucking with us. That is theme of today's show. . . . I looked at today's topics and I was just like, damn, white people just fuckin' with us. What is going on? It's like at an all-time high right now."[66] Soon Rod and Karen instituted "Fuckin' with Black People" as a regular segment on the podcast and then developed an introduction that involved gameshow-style music to which they sang, "Fuckin' with those Black people, we're just fuckin' with those Blacks! We're just fuuuuckin' with, fuckin' with Black people." Rod explained the "game," saying, "That's right, it's time for the game that we all hate to play, where we find news stories and rate them from zero to one hundred, in increments of twenty-five, based on how much we feel fucked with." Regular contestants on the game include "everybody" and "Donald Trump."

The case of Trayvon Martin—his death, the activism to bring charges, and the trial and subsequent acquittal of George Zimmerman—was a pivotal moment for the network at the center of this project and for Black digital networks more broadly. It was with this tragedy that the network fully coalesced as a resource for times of turmoil. The strategies deployed became the basis for the complex and multilayered use of digital technologies as unrest gripped Ferguson, Missouri, in the summer of 2014.

Mike Brown and the Ferguson Uprising

On August 9, 2014, Mike Brown, an unarmed Black eighteen-year-old, was shot and killed by a white Ferguson police officer, Darren Wilson. In the immediate aftermath of the shooting, members of the Ferguson community took to the streets to mourn and demand answers. The situation escalated quickly, and within forty-eight hours police armed with military-style vehicles and weapons were deploying tear gas as a local convenience store was being looted. Over the next ten days, protests and unrest continued and were met with overwhelming force by the police, including the repeated use of tear gas and nonlethal rounds on protesters. Functioning as an awareness system, Twitter was instrumental in bringing Brown's death to local, and eventually national, attention. The initial coverage of Brown's death took place through interactions between Ferguson residents, existing social media micro-celebrities, and local news media.

The first alerts came from Ferguson residents and local news media who used Twitter, Instagram, and Vine to both share and seek information. Local news media played an important role in the initial reporting of the story. Brown was shot at approximately noon (Central Time) on August 9. The local Fox affiliate reported the shooting on its website at approximately 1:30, prior to the gathering of the large crowd that prompted police response.[67] Local television station KPLR and the *St. Louis Post Dispatch* both reported the incident between 4:00 and 5:00 p.m. This was after a crowd of local residents had started to gather, and therefore the community reaction was included in this reporting.[68] These local news stories were heavily retweeted. Websites of the *New York Times*, the *Huffington Post*, the *Los Angeles Times*, NewsOne, NBC News, MSNBC, CNN, and the BBC included the story—though as a minor story taken from the news wire.

Alongside these news stories were accounts from local people, who provided local news with information and circulated their own eyewitness contributions. A resident of the Canfield Green Apartments, which face the street where Brown was shot, tweeted within minutes of the shooting that he saw the police shoot and kill someone, and then, within the next hour, he tweeted an image of Brown's body in the street with two officers standing next to him, taken through the slats of his patio. The tweet with this image was retweeted over four thousand times. Minutes later, another user also tweeted and indicated witnessing the police shoot a young Black man. This post included an image of a handful of residents standing near the scene, taken from a different vantage point in the apartment complex.

In the first hours after Brown's death, social media functioned as a channel for such word-of-mouth information-sharing. Early on, before any official information had been released and while the news reports still lacked detail, Twitter in particular allowed people to circulate information they "had heard." This included that Brown was killed after shoplifting cigarillos and the number of shots fired.[69]

Reporters used social media as a resource for getting information for their own reporting. Brittany Noble-Jones, a local news reporter, solicited information from the community via Instagram and Twitter, asking people to send her pictures they were seeing on social media.[70] National news media unfamiliar with the region used Twitter to contact locals. The journalist Wesley Lowery, for one, did so as he was making arrangements to come into Ferguson, telling his contacts, "Will touch base right after I land. Important to tell this story correctly."[71]

Simultaneously, users alerted people who lived locally using Twitter and other social media. For example, Patricia Bynes, then a Ferguson Township Democratic Committeewoman, was @-replied by another Twitter user about the incident. When Bynes responded that she didn't know anything about it, the user supplied her with a link to the *St. Louis Post Dispatch* story. The original tweet to Bynes was at 4:52 p.m., and by 5:40 she was tweeting from the spot where Brown had been shot. Noble-Jones learned of the incident via Instagram, went to Ferguson to report, and at 5:43 p.m. tweeted she had arrived on the scene.[72] She provided coverage, both officially for her station and unofficially through her own social media accounts late into the night and for several days to follow.

Many local residents went to the scene of the shooting and began engaging in "random acts of journalism," reporting as events unfolded. In addition to Bynes, Antonio French, an alderman of a neighboring ward, local Hip-hop artists Tef Poe and T-Dubb-O, local radio personality Tammie Holland, local activists WyzeChef and Ashely Yates, and others went out among the crowd and gave real-time updates via social media. As protests continued the following day, even more people took to the streets, posting as events unfolded; some, such as C. Jay Conrod, @GeekNStereo, Netta Elzie, and others, quickly became trusted sources of information. In addition to posting what they themselves witnessed, many of these users also gathered and posted eye-witness accounts from bystanders and residents.[73] From these fragments of information a narrative of Brown's death began to take shape.

By 2014, Twitter users, particularly those who were part of the Black Twitter network, were well aware of the power Twitter had for raising visibility and impacting mainstream discourse. Many of Black Twitter's most influential moments came in 2013—including the cancelation of the book contract obtained by a juror in the Zimmerman trial, which was as a result of Black Twitter's mobilization. Consequently, many users seeking to increase the visibility of the situation went to Twitter, often including links to local news coverage. People tweeted at news outlets and celebrities or tagged them in the comments of Instagram posts. For example, T-Dubb-O tweeted images of the scene, including one of Brown's body, to Jesse Jackson, Al Sharpton, CNN, and local TV station KSDK.[74] He then continued tweeting at them, making use of Twitter's reply feature, which allows users to connect their tweet to the one they are replying to and create a thread. People also used this feature to reply to their own tweets, to express longer thoughts in a way that would remain intact and linear in the interface. T-Dubb-O used it to offer commentary on the image in the original post, asserting that "we cannot continue to allow this type of treatment from an organization that is funded by tax dollars" and "we should not have to be afraid of those sworn in to protect and serve their community." Users tagged Tef Poe's Instagram post of the same images with the handles for CNN, the local Fox affiliate, *Oprah*, and *Time Magazine*.[75]

Additionally, micro-celebrities on Twitter were instrumental in disseminating information. These users had been having their usual conversations—ranging from serious discussion about the impact of street harassment to jokes about Lifetime's casting decisions for an Aaliyah biopic. Seeing the social media posts coming from Ferguson residents, either because they were addressed directly or because they simply saw the posts moving through the network, prompted many to use their visibility to highlight the story. For example, in response to

Tef Poe's tweeting, "Basically martial law is taking place in Ferguson all perimeters blocked coming and going. . . . National and international friends Help!!!"[76] Feminista Jones asked how she could help.[77] They had a brief exchange about the importance of circulating information and generating visibility, which concluded with Feminista tweeting, "Ok well I'm gonna follow you so if I can use my reach to do anything, I'll do my best."[78] As events in Ferguson unfolded over the next several days, many of the micro-celebrities in the Black Twitter network worked to boost the social media posts coming from Ferguson. For example, Baratunde Thurston tweeted, "Why are you looking at this tweet when you should be diving into @AntonioFrench's feed? #Ferguson #MikeBrown," directing his tens of thousands of followers to Alderman French's Twitter timeline.[79] Others made lists of users on the ground in Ferguson. For example, Tracy Clayton, a Black Twitter micro-celebrity who later became an editor for Buzzfeed, created a list called "Ferguson Locals & Journos" which included Elzie, Zellie Imani, and Noble-Jones.[80]

Because of its image and video capabilities, Instagram was an important tool for posting real-time updates. Instagram allows users to take images and videos in app, meaning that users can open the app, take a picture or record a thirty-second video, and post it immediately to their feed. At the time, when other social media platforms lacked this capability, there was already a large Black network on Instagram. While much has been made of how Black Americans are a larger percentage of users on Twitter than they are of the US population, it is rarely mentioned that they are even more heavily represented on Instagram. As of 2014, 38 percent of Black internet users were on Instagram, compared to 21 percent of white users and 34 percent of Hispanic users.[81]

However, Instagram is not designed to optimize spreadablity within the plaform. It lacks a built-in share feature. In 2014, the only way to repost on Instagram was to take a screen shot or to use a third-party app, such as InstaGetter, to download Instagram images to one's phone and edit them, or various "regram" apps like Repost for Instagram or Regram that allow users to share another Instagram user's post to their account. However, Instagram does facilitate sharing one's posts to other platforms, specifically Facebook, Twitter, and Tumblr. The Instagram app itself has a feature that allows users to link their Instagram accounts to other social media accounts. When they post to Instagram, the post is then pushed out to their other accounts. Thus, images and videos can be taken and posted easily on Instagram, where they are difficult to share, but then simultaneously posted on other platforms that enable greater circulation.

Vine also played a crucial role in the social media coverage of Ferguson. Vine, now a defunct platform owned by Twitter, allowed users to post six-second videos that played in a loop. August 2014 was before Twitter's live-streaming service, Periscope, was created and before Facebook launched its streaming service Facebook Live. Anyone who wanted to live-stream had to use a service such as Livestream or Ustream, which were too complicated for ad hoc and improvisational media creation because they required advance set-up. While there were a number of live-steamers, such as Argus Radio, Rebelutionary Z, and Bassem Masri,[82] many on-the-ground opted instead for video capabilities built into Instagram and Vine.[83] French was one of the heaviest users of Vine during Ferguson. He began tweeting from Ferguson at about 6 p.m. CST and quickly became a trusted source of information via social media. French posted almost four hundred Vines between August 10 and August 30, with his heaviest posting day (99 Vines) being August 12. As of 2014, Vine had 40 million registered users worldwide, not nearly the reach of other social media platforms.[84] Six of French's Vines were shared, or revined, on the platform over one thousand times, and one was even revined 8,600 times, but most were shared fewer than one hundred times, with about half hovering in the twenty-to-forty range. Vine, like Instagram, posed a challenge of spreadability, which was ameliorated by cross-posting links to Vine videos on other social media platforms, particularly Twitter.

Social media was an important resource not only for disseminating information, but also for coordinating on the ground, especially in the first few days of the unrest. In the hours following Brown's death, many used Twitter to discuss where the police were restricting movement and where crowds were gathering to protest. For example, Tef Poe tweeted information he received from family members in the area and then eventually his own updates after he arrived on the scene.[85] When Yates tweeted that she was heading to Ferguson, another user informed her that people were assembling outside the Ferguson Police Department on Florissant Road.[86] Conrod, who lived around the corner from the incident, but was in a different area when the shooting occurred, used Twitter to solicit information about whether he could get through the police lines to his house.[87] Later, after being able to make it home unimpeded, Conrod contributed his update to the Twitter timeline, "For those wondering, traffic on W. Florissant is fine. Just got home. Everything is business as usual."[88] Many of the people who emerged as sources of information clearly had pre-established relationships with one another and were using Twitter to coordinate parking and meeting places. As days passed, people even began using Twitter to organize carpools across the country to Ferguson to participate in the protest. But even as Twitter can be useful for ad hoc planning, it also makes such activity visible, and so protestors eventually stopped using the platform as much for these activities after it became clear that law enforcement was tracking their movements through it.

Additionally, Ferguson locals used social media to contextualize Brown's death in the history of the area. For example, after seeing reports of the fatal shooting, Conrod tweeted about the way local police disproportionately stop and ticket Black residents.[89] He discussed what locals refer to as the police's "curb service," when "police not only pull you over, but sit you on the curb (sometimes in cuffs) while they search your car."[90] He described the practice as "degrading" and putting people "on display for all passing drivers"[91] and concluded, "This is why there's animosity concerning the police."[92] T-Dubb-O made similar statements, such as "it's known that ferguson police department is racist and have always been and it's not the first time they have done this," referring to use use of deadly force on an unarmed Black person.[93] He later posted an image of the looted and burned convenience store on August 11 with the caption, "This is what years of harassment turned into last night."[94] Another resident turned activist, @GeekNStereo, told a similar story: "I moved to the city for a reason. The harassment from county officers has haunted me since my teens."[95] WyzeChef posted on Instagram, and also shared the link to this post on Twitter, an image of statistics showing that Ferguson police disproportionately targeted Black residents in the stops, searches, and arrests they made.[96] He later added on Twitter, "I swear there was a time when the police were shooting the hell out of black kids every week in Stl,"[97] and "They shot those lil cats 20+ times at the Jack n the Box on Hanley and 70,"[98] referring to an incident in which undercover officers shot and killed two men in the parking lot of the fast-food restaurant in 2000.

One of the most important and persistent aspects of social media during the days of unrest in Ferguson was its dialogic relationship to legacy news outlets. From the outset, people monitored the coverage of Ferguson, challenging what they felt was inaccurate and commenting on the racial biases they believed framed it. For example, when the *St. Louis Dispatch* tweeted, "Fatal shooting by Ferguson police prompts mob reaction,"[99] French used the quote function in Twitter to retweet and added, "'Mob'? You could also use the word 'community.'"[100] Similarly, a few outlets, including the *Guardian* and *NBC News*, reported that the crowd was chanting "kill the police."[101] Twitter users rebutted this. Yates tweeted, "A few blocks up from the police station and residents are walking there chanting 'NO JUSTICE NO PEACE' NOT 'kill the police.'"[102] @Vandalyzm tweeted directly at *NBC News* saying, "I was there. Literally. Nobody chanted 'Kill the Police' fuck outta here @NbcNews."[103]

A number of critiques concerned ways in which news reports were sensationalizing the story and portraying Black Americans as violent. After a peaceful day of protest, Elzie asserted, "The media isn't interested in peaceful black people. Very few reporters were out there."[104] Some local Ferguson residents suggested that police allowed property damage so that Black residents could be portrayed negatively in the news media. Conrod, for one, tweeted, "I think police let this happen. This situation could've been contained hours ago. They let it escalate. Now excessive force seems justified,"[105] and "I can't stress that enough. Tension didn't rise until police blocked off streets. Then they did nothing to prevent or contain the looting."[106]

Citizen use of social media networks were also important to provide accounts of the professional reporting taking place on the ground. For example, Yates tweeted an account of the crowd reacting negatively to the crew from local station KSDK, which had reported that Brown was carrying a weapon: "Ppl became angry when they spotted their news crew and started yelling at them to leave. The camera man grew angry and flustered," and "The KSDK camera man said 'You want us gone? You want us to leave?! FINE, WE'RE LEAVING.' He picked up his gear and walked off."[107] While many criticized the news media, some felt that some news outlets were doing a good job, and they publicly thanked and highlighted reporters whom they believed to be trustworthy.[108] In this way, local residents used social media to certify the veracity of reporting to their social networks.

As events unfolded and social media offered fragmented accounts and bits of information, users collectively began constructing a narrative from those fragments. This narrative, which tended to be in opposition to the one being presented by national news media, was seen by many in the network as the more authoritative and honest version. It was this ongoing distrust of legacy media that prompted TWiB! to go to Ferguson and report.

TWiB! Reporting from Ferguson: Independent Media and Citizen Journalism

In August 2014, at the behest of its audience, TWiB! made two trips to Ferguson to report live, the first from August 13 to 16 and the second from August 18 to 23. On Wednesday August 13, 2014, when White, TWiB! sound engineer and TWiB! Prime co-host Aaron Rand Freeman, and White's wife, Emily Epstein-White (who is white), arrived on location in Ferguson, they began using their existing broadcast-style network and social media networks to give voice to local accounts of the events, offering a narrative opposing that of mainstream media outlets. They were able to leverage their existing networks to provide on-the-ground coverage that simultaneously bypassed and intervened into legacy news media coverage.

During TWiB! Prime's regular broadcast the Monday following Brown's death, TWiB! reported on the events taking place in Ferguson. TWiB! was already attempting to make interventions into the coverage of the events. By this time, the unrest in Ferguson was in its third day. The podcast opened with audio from a news report about Ferguson that included Brown's mother saying, "You took my son away from me. You know how hard it was for me to get him to stay in school and graduate? You know how many Black men graduate? Not many!" White recounteds Brown's death noting, "People on the ground and the police department are saying two different things," about how events transpired. From this first coverage of Ferguson, TWiB! was devoted to analyzing how legacy media was framing the story and to producing alternative accounts of events grounded in reports of local residents.

To this end, TWiB! had invited a local Ferguson woman, Jeanina Jenkins, onto the show to give her account of events. The shooting occurred directly across from her job while she was at work. White asked, "The reports that were coming out of there, out of Ferguson, apparently, you guys are in the middle of some sort of apocalyptic nightmare with people just freaking out. Is that's what's happening on the ground?" Jenkins responded, "Basically, we're just doing chants. We peacefully chant, saying 'No justice, no peace.' And we were just walkin' back and forth with our signs, saying 'I am a man, I am a woman.'" Jenkins continued:

> The rally was peaceful. The police was out with their machine guns. They had their dogs barking at us. . . . They had their batons out like they were ready to beat us. And we were, like, doing it so peacefully. And, yes, there was a riot. But, it was a few people. It wasn't a lot. It was a few people who were going off of their emotions. It wasn't, like, everyone . . . It was just a few individuals that made it look like it was everyone, but it wasn't. It was peaceful. We were all comin' together as a Black community. Because we're tired. We're saying enough is enough.[109]

White inquired about the history of the relationship between the people of Ferguson and the police department, in response, Jenkins recounted the ongoing issues with profiling and stops that had been described by other locals.

During this first coverage, and throughout the weeks that followed, TWiB! highlighted the disparity between legacy media coverage and the accounts circulating on social media. Mid-show, as White and Gandy continued to discuss the contentious issues surrounding the coverage of Ferguson, White commented, "I think we might end up going down to Ferguson to talk to people on the ground." Explaining that people like Jenkins should have their stories heard, he argued that " as opposed to the narrative crafted by media, the narrative should be crafted by the people on the ground. And media should be used to thereby highlight that story." Gandy elaborated on the ways that social media provided resources for countering legacy media, which were complicit in furthering racist interpretations of events:

We're living in this new digital age where basically citizen journalism is on the rise. And I think that it's an important way for communities to shine a light on what's really going on. Because the mainstream media is basically useless, in a lot of instances. I mean, they craft a narrative. The narrative says that Black people are violent. The narrative says that "oh look at these Black people looting." Irrespective of the fact . . . that white people love themselves a riot too. I mean, anytime the Red Sox lose, anytime the Red Sox win.[110]

It was during this conversation that TWiB! began receiving messages via social media from listeners who felt distrustful of the news coverage and who were eager to see TWiB! travel to Ferguson. One longtime listener, a white woman using the handle @tealdeer, tweeted to White, "I don't know if it's something you're considering, but I would totally kick in $ for you guys to go cover #Ferguson."[111] White responded, on Twitter, that they were working on determining if it was financially feasible.[112] Shortly after, White announced on the show that during the next forty-eight hours first-time donations would go to funding their trip to Ferguson. Donations started immediately, before the show had even ended, and soon thereafter, when White announced that TWiB! would be traveling to Ferguson, he noted that enough money to cover airfare and hotel costs had been raised in just twelve hours because "that's how much people don't trust the news."[113]

TWiB! used its usual broadcast-style audio podcast to report, as well as producing five live-stream "dispatches" from Ferguson between August 13 and 16. During the second trip, while *TWiB! Prime* co-hosts Freeman and Gandy resumed regular shows, White called in with updates, as well as continuing to release dispatches from Ferguson. Listeners were notified of live streams via social media and could listen live via TWiB!'s website, Stitcher Radio, and TuneIn Radio. All of this content was then available later, streaming through the same services and for download via iTunes, Stitcher and RSS feed. Some of the Ferguson dispatches were also posted to YouTube as audio accompanied by a TWiB! logo as the visual.

TWiB! also circulated these dispatches through their social media channels, which funneled them directly to Black Twitter, who, in turn, retweeted and posted the material from other platforms. At the time, TWiB! was using a now-defunct service called "Donate your account," which allowed users to give an entity access to post one tweet a day to their account; in this way, TWiB! was able to extend its coverage via other users' accounts and further expand its reach.

Social media also served for broadcast-style reporting of information. The TWiB! team, and especially White, posted a constant flow of information on social media. While Twitter served as a real-time central clearinghouse for information, Instagram housed images and videos, with links posted to Twitter. Exemplifying the blurry boundary between TWiB! the podcast network and TWiB! the social network, all social media updates the TWiB! team posted were on their personal accounts. The official TWiB! account, @TWiBnation, had only the autogenerated updates created when they posted audio files to Libsyn, their podcast hosting service. The imbrication of TWiB's content creation with the social network it anchors was evident throughout TWiB's reporting. For example, when White used his personal Instagram account for quick video dispatches, mundane pictures of his garden, his dog, and brunch were next to them on his feed.

Social media was also a resource for connecting with Ferguson locals and crowdsourcing information, both before and during TWiB!'s time there. For instance, the day before heading for Ferguson, White tweeted, "#ICYMI: #TWIBnation will be in #Ferguson tomorrow afternoon. Any tips or orgs you think we should talk with let us know—ferguson@twib.me."[114] Meanwhile, Ferguson locals tweeted at White about connecting with the TWiB! team when they arrived. Brittany Packnett, for one, tweeted "@elonjames dope. Hope to see you out in these streets in solidarity. Glad #TWiBNation will hear from our young ppl. #DONTSHOOT #MikeBrown."[115] They then had a brief Twitter exchange in which White solicited advice about organizations TWiB! should connect with. For his part, @GeekNStereo tweeted to White, "Hey @elonjames, hit us up when you land we're in Ferguson cleaning up!,"[116] referring to community efforts to clean up the debris and damage that resulted from previous nights of property damage and looting. Longtime listener Monika Brooks tweeted White a list of on-the ground journalists that had been compiled by the Breaking News Twitter account and suggested he contact Noble-Jones.[117]

By the evening of August 13, the TWiB! team was on location, with White tweeting their movements: "#Ferguson is locked down hard.

We're parking and going in on foot."[118] From the time they landed at the airport until he went to bed for the night, White tweeted fifty-seven times.[119] The tweets detailed what they were witnessing and adding editorial interpretation. There were five images, three of which were posted on Instagram, and one video. Epstein-White also used Twitter and Instagram similarly, while Freeman focused on sharing commentary about the emotional toll of the situation. Social media also served an ad hoc broadcast function. For emergent situations, White used Instagram's video capability to record a series of fifteen-second dispatches, which he posted to other social media sites. Epstein-White also made use of her Instagram account in conjunction with Twitter, posting images of the police presence.[120]

The following day, TWiB! posted a two-minute video to the *Root* from footage taken the previous day.[121] The team also posted a twenty-seven-minute audio dispatch to YouTube, in which they described their experience the previous day, contextualized their social media reporting in a more detailed account, and constructed a linear narrative out of the previous day's brief ad hoc updates.[122] That evening, they streamed live from the National Moment of Silence (NMOS14) protest in St. Louis. The live stream was available through TWiB!'s website, Stitcher, and TuneIn Radio. They went live at 7:18 p.m. EST with White notifying people with a tweet containing the link to the website.[123] Unfortunately, they were able to stream only for forty minutes before losing their signal. The forty minutes were posted as "Ferguson Dispatch #2" the following day. TWiB! also interviewed people at NMOS14, but due to technical difficulties these interviews were lost.

In the late night of August 15 and the early morning hours of August 16, in the wake of the press conference in which Wilson's name was announced and footage of Brown stealing cigarillos was released, there was a more property damage in Ferguson. The TWiB! team was eating a late dinner and received a call about the unrest and quickly returned to the area. White posted several images to Instagram, which were also shared via Twitter, and then live-streamed for about forty minutes, starting at 2:45 a.m. EST, with the notification also going out via Twitter.[124] In a deviation from the norms of legacy media news coverage, rather than filling the stream with talk, White indicated to listeners that they were going to "go silent," and would just leave the stream live and the listeners would hear only background noise. Sometimes there was silence, sometimes noise from cars and bystanders, and White and Freeman could be heard discussing their escape route if necessary.

White returned to Ferguson alone to report from August 18 to August 23. He employed the same methods that he, Epstein-White, and Freeman used on their first trip—a combination of live streams, uploaded dispatches, and social media posts—but since he was alone, his reporting was even more improvisational and ad hoc. It relied heavily on Instagram, which can be understood as a form of witnessing, according to Michael Koliska and Jessica Roberts. Observing that the selfie can facilitate practices of citizen journalism, they note that selfies create a relationship between "space and self [that] is not only a claim that 'I'm here!' in a particular time and space but also a claim that 'I witnessed this event,' which is elementary to any form of journalism." In this way, selfies resemble broadcasting practices, in which a reporter is shown telling a story on location. Thus, selfies can be used in "a form of digital storytelling that embeds personal autobiographical elements (self-portraits) about members of a particular community and displays them in semipublic spaces such as social media."[125] White's use of Instagram to report on Ferguson often drew upon these characteristics of selfies, combining them with video to heighten the impact of witnessing.

The imbrication of broadcast and social network functions were central to the efficacy of TWiB!'s reporting. White used Instagram to provide fifteen-second video dispatches on emergent situations. The videos were shot as selfies, but showed only half of his face.[126] This allowed White to show more of the surrounding location than if he was fully in frame, while still positioning himself as present at a given location. He both mediated and witnessed, showing both the scene and himself as being present in it. This video thus combined a characteristic feature of broadcasting-style reporting with the social media genre of the selfie and became part of what Koliska and Roberts refer to as the overall flow of "personally witnessed history" that emerged from Ferguson. The video, unlike the still selfies discussed by Koliska and Roberts, adds audio to the process of witnessing, creating another channel for information and closely resembling live television reporting. White was very clear that he was reporting from Ferguson because of an obligation he felt TWiB! had as a media company. Yet, throughout the events of Ferguson, White eschewed the label of "journalist," placing himself in a liminal space between professional news reporting and citizen journalism.

TWiB! provided an alternative view of the situation than mainstream news media and was often in direct dialogue with it. White explained the importance of legacy media, "I'm putting a lot of weight on the media, because the media is reason . . . people are hearing these stories. The media has a responsibility to make sure there is a clear understanding of what the hell is happening."[127] Because of this, TWiB! often functioned as a media watchdog, reporting on press activities on the ground, complicating and nuancing legacy media reporting, and providing fact-checking in real time.

TWiB!'s reporting often included information regarding the presence (or absence) of news media and its actions in relation to protestors and police. White repeatedly noted the number of cameras he saw and what the reporters were doing.[128] On August 15, Epstein-White posted an image to Instagram of a cluster of professional media with the caption, "One major difference tonight in #Ferguson? A lot more media here now."[129]

TWiB!'s coverage also functioned to contradict, complicate, or nuance legacy media reporting. One sentiment that was echoed repeatedly throughout the network and by people on the ground in Ferguson was concern that the residents of Ferguson were being represented as dangerous and violent. TWiB!, in contrast, painted a picture of a community that was antagonized, dehumanized, and terrorized by police. Freeman argued that the entire situation stemmed from this treatment:

> The reason why anything happened is because from the very moment they had planned the very first vigil—this is something just people on the ground are telling me—from the very day they planned the first vigil, they've been getting shoved around by SWAT-dressed police officers. From the very moment they decided they were going to do anything in memory of Mike Brown, they've been getting pushed around like criminals.[130]

For their part, White and Epstein-White described a caring and supportive community:

EPSTEIN-WHITE: It was crazy out there . . . There was a line of cars a mile long, honking horns. People standing out, sitting on top of cars. . . . We're trying to figure out how to get across the street, and there were dudes directing traffic from the neighborhood, who were like, "Oh, you want to get across the street? Hold on, one second." Helped us get across the street. . . . People were passing out water and food to make sure that everybody had what they needed. Other people were going around picking up trash. This is a community.

WHITE: They were cleaning up. They were frickin' cleaning up.

EPSTEIN-WHITE: This is a community where people care about each other, and they care about their community. If you just let people be, this is what happens.[131]

In the late-night hours of August 15 and the early morning of August 16, TWiB! live- streamed from outside a liquor store that was being looted. Complicating cable news narratives about looting and violence, TWiB! reported that while drunk teens appeared to have been looting and damaging property, there were also residents out trying to calm the teens and get them to stop.[132] TWiB! also reported that some of the chaos was escalated by white "masked agitators" from outside the community, making a distinction between these masked individuals and the community members attempting to intervene and protect the store.[133] On Twitter, Freeman reiterated the idea that police were allowing property destruction to create a news spectacle of Black violence: "I think the police watched. I think the few unruly people were very clearly causing problems. Citizens very clearly tried to stop it,"[134] and "the police declined to assist. They watched. Nothing. Watched us eat ourselves. By am the narrative will be SEE? Told ya! Niggers!'"[135]

TWiB! also fact-checked reports in real time, which helped prevent early inaccurate accounts from calcifying into the accepted narrative of events. For example, on August 14, there were reports of what were either gun shots or firecrackers. Rumors of the former were spreading rapidly on Twitter. White immediately went to the area in question to investigate and confirmed no shots were fired. In a dispatch, White explained his rationale,

Someone was like, "You should be checking this, because someone else just said there was five gunshots." I said, "No, it was fireworks." That's why I did it. . . . I don't want to run toward the gunfire. [But] if it's not gunfire, someone has to be there to be able to quickly say, "This is not gunfire," especially with no cops there.

He made clear that such verification was necessary not only to keep media accounts accurate, but also to protect the community from further escalation of tensions with law enforcement, arguing that if the noise was assumed to be gunfire, "Then something happens? They would have sent the goddamn National Guard in. There would have been Marines there or some shit if . . . someone got shot in the middle of that. You know it."[136]

Finally, TWiB! in general, and White in particular, became a point of articulation between Ferguson residents and protestors, Black digital networks, and legacy media. This is in part because of the associations TWiB! staff has with established media spaces—White, for one, has made appearances on MSNBC, CNN, and Al Jazeera and written for the *Huffington Post*, *Salon*, the *Root*, and the *Grio*—and in part because of the visibility of Black Twitter, which has prompted journalists and editors to follow key participants, including White. Having cultivated close relationships with local community leaders and activists, White became highly visible and credible as an on-the-ground source of information not only for the network, but also for professional journalists. For example, the *Washington Post* asked in the comments of one of his Instagram posts if his photo could be used in their reporting. He was also invited to do interviews on legacy media outlets, including *All In with Chris Hayes* (though he was bumped) and Al Jazeera (on August 20). Perhaps one of the most notable instances of White serving as a gate between digital networks and legacy media was his appearance on the *Melissa Harris-Perry Show* on August 24 to talk about being part of a group that was tear-gassed in a residential area.

That group consisted of White, Elzie, activist Cherrell Brown, and a handful of Ferguson residents, and as the incident unfolded in the early hours of August 19, White used streaming audio, Instagram, and Twitter simultaneously to report it, as well as recording a copy of the audio stream that he later circulated.[137] On that audio stream, White and his companions could be heard running and yelling, with the popping sound of tear-gas canisters being fired in the background. At first he reported that "it doesn't even look like they're aiming at protestors. They're just gassing areas now."[138] But as the stream went on, White exclaimed, "Shit, they're coming back!"; others yelled "Go! Go now!"; and sounds of the group running and calls to "lie down" became audible, along with the popping sound of tear-gas canisters. White and a couple of othes were able to run back to their car, and once in the car, White described the scene on the audio stream, comparing the tear gassing to pest control pratices, "It's clear that they are trying to exterminate folks." He can then be heard mumbling, "I'm going to say that right now," followed by a pause and him saying:

> Alright, we got back to the car. We got from behind the backyard and we got to the car. Outside, they're just gassing everyone. If they see a human being, they throw a gas canister at it. People are getting rubber bulleted and just getting smacked directly in the face. This is not okay.[139]

White had recorded that statement as an Instagram video dispatch while still live streaming. The pause was him opening the app. Thus, his report went out via both live stream and social media.[140] On the Instagram video, his face was only slightly visible in the dark as he narrated the scene. He also gave a clearer account of the situation on Twitter shortly after the incident:

> We turned a corner to park. We saw 6 dudes turn the corner and an armored van came flying down the street shooting tear gas. This is a fact.[141]

> You can argue "riot" if there's a crowd of folks being rowdy. It was 6 people. Then they gassed us. An entire group of 8. #Ferguson.[142]

> You can't tell me I'm lying. We were fucking broadcasting through it. I have the audio. This shit happened. #Ferguson.[143]

Within a few hours, White had posted a twenty-minute excerpt of the recording of the live stream,[144] which circulated through social media, where it exemplified not only the use of excessive force by the Ferguson police department, but also the problematic reporting of legacy media. The night White and his companions were tear gassed in the residential neighborhood, they had been returning to Ferguson because of conflicting accounts about gunfire and Molotov cocktails. Late on the night of August 18, the police had announced at a press conference that there had been "shootings, looting, vandalism, and other acts of violence that clearly appear not to have been spontaneous [but] premeditated criminal acts."[145] Captain Ron Johnson of the Missouri State Highway Patrol asserted that "multiple Molotov cocktails were thrown at police," causing the police to need tear gas to control and disperse the crowd. However, social media accounts, including those by many who had come to be known as reliable sources, asserted this was untrue. Many pointed out there was no footage or images of these Molotov cocktails or of any resultant fire or fire damage.

On August 24, 2014, White was invited on *The Melissa Harris-Perry Show* to talk about the experience. The segment opened with a clip from the audio of that night and White observing that "the people that I was with thought that they were going to die, and it wasn't the story that we've being told."[146] White went on to explain that while news reports had heavily emphasized rioting and looting, the story on the ground was quite different:

> As we're talking about this, and they're framing it, and the story keeps coming out—the rioters and the looters. And the rioters and the looters. . . . It's not the story. And at this point, you have to question, why would the media even go along with this narrative, as people are actively explaining to you, "Do you understand what's happening on the ground?" . . . Yes, there are some folks who are doing that. But what about everybody else? What about the vast majority of people out there who are not doing that? But you feel that is . . . reasonable, because of police safety. . . . So, basically, your safety overrides my own humanity. You can't do this to people. If this is how police have to be safe, our system is broken completely. We have to rebuild it.[147]

With his appearance on *The Melissa Harris-Perry Show*, White effectively intervened in dominant mass media coverage of the events in Ferguson to paint a more complicated story, which was broadcasted on one of the three major cable news networks and taken up by other outlets.

The Chitlin' Circuit Podcast during Ferguson

The Chiltin' Circuit podcasts provided another arena for addressing events in Ferguson. As information came in a stream of fragmented social media posts and mainstream news reporting that many distrusted, they served an interpretive function. They created a safe space in which hosts and listeners could discuss events and provide one another support while avoiding hostilities they faced on social media or in their daily life as they navigated white spaces.

The information about Ferguson came from two primary sources, citizen journalists and professional news reporting, each posing their own interpretive challenges. Citizen journalists, ranging from local Ferguson residents to independent media like TWiB!, employed a contingent and improvisational mode of reporting that relied heavily on social media and other existing platforms like YouTube and UStream. This fragmented stream of information required an investment of time and attention to aggregate, interpret, and arrange into a narrative. Simultaneously, professional news reports presented clearer, more cohesive narratives, but Chitlin' Circuit participants viewed them with suspicion, seeing them as untrustworthy or as being manipulated by the police. Synthesizing information from both sources for listeners, the podcasts also noted contradictions and controversies around the reporting and provided a space within which to evaluate and critique information as it emerged.

The podcasts drew heavily on citizen journalism, and many of the podcasters spoke explicitly about the role of digital and social media in providing information about Ferguson. For example, on August 15, De Ana, co-host of *Nerdgasm Noire Network*, began a podcast saying:

> So much has gone on over the weekend . . . If you don't know, which you probably don't if you're not on Twitter, is that over the weekend in Ferguson, St. Louis, a young man by the name of Mike Brown was shot and killed by the police. . . . Things escalated extremely quickly in the city of Ferguson. No major news media was covering it. The only way people were getting information about it was via Twitter from people who were there.[148]

On the *Whiskey, Wine, and Moonshine* podcast, co-host Sojourner Verdad explained, "The attention on Ferguson would not have taken place without social media. When Mike Brown was shot . . . people live-tweeted it. You know and so that's how it actually got out and then the crowds and everything that went from there."[149] Kriss, hosting the *Insanity Check* podcast with guest Kylanol, explained the role that mobile technologies and social media played in fact-checking the official statements,

> We now have social media. We now have people on the ground. Everybody has a camera phone now. So, we are now able to document what's going on. So, when they tell us a lie, we can go, "Well, no." "We put Michael Brown's body into an ambulance." No, you didn't. We have video of you putting his body into an unmarked van.[150]

The podcasters drew information from these fragmented streams of citizen journalism and synthesized it with professional news reporting, producing a narrative about both the events in Ferguson and the media coverage of those events. These podcasts focused on interpretation, rather than primarily information circulation. This process was not marked as official reporting, but took the form of the conversational commentary that is standard for these podcasts. Podcasters varied on the specificity with which they cited the sources of their information, often mirroring the informality of casual conversation with statements like, "I saw that . . . ," "Someone on Twitter said . . . ," or "They reported that . . ." There was often an assumption that both hosts and listeners were pulling from the same reservoir of information. For example, a discussion on *Where's My 40 Acres?* gestured toward information that had been on social media and in mainstream reporting without specifically citing or, at times, even fully explaining it:

> MIKE: Apparently, Elon James got a gun pointed into his face for asking for directions. 'Cause he's there right now . . .
> DEIRDRE: There are people who are eating at McDonalds that have gotten harassed.
> MIKE: Those reporters got arrested from being at McDonalds.[151]

Here you have a reference to White from TWiB! and his account of having an officer point a gun at him, which he described on Ferguson Dispatch 1 and on Twitter, as well as to the *Washington Post* reporter

Wesley Lowery and *Huffington Post* reporter Ryan J. Reilly who were detained by police on August 13 after failing to vacate a MacDonald's quickly enough as the officers were trying to clear it. None of these events was discussed in detail or with any specificity but were presented in the way one would in casual conversation, with an assumption that all the hosts and listeners were operating within the same information environment.

However, the podcasters were often very specific when they were rebutting statements and reporting. For example, on *Insanity Check*, Kriss and Kylanol created a dialogic engagement with a press conference given by Ferguson Mayor James Knowles III by playing audio from it and pausing periodically to add their commentary. In the conference audio, a reporter could be heard asking why police had not released the name of the officer who shot Brown and noting that this was very unusual. The mayor responded, "Well, actually that's up to the St. Louis County Prosecutor's Office, and actually it is standard protocol, in St. Louis at least, that we do not release the information related to subjects who have not been charged with a crime and right now, there is an ongoing—" at which point, the recording was paused and Kriss interjected, "That's bullshit because, you know what? They were floating around the name of somebody they were looking for in St. Louis County. It was a Black kid they were looking for in connection to a robbery or something like that."[152]

The podcasts also provided people with a protected space in which to discuss the events, a necessity given the nature of the interactions participants were experiencing on social media and in their workplaces. *Whiskey, Wine, and Moonshine* co-host Sojourner Verdad explained that she has been avoiding conversations about race and Ferguson in public:

> I know we're on a public podcast. But you guys are like my family, so I can have that conversation. I can't have that conversation at work. Because there's gonna be somebody that's gonna say something that's gonna let me know that they have that exact same mentality and if given the right tools they would behave in the exact same manner. . . . That's the part where I don't know what to do with the feelings that I have. 'Cause, it's hard for me to process, it's hard for me—you know I'm a happy go lucky, easy goin', you know, person. But for the last few weeks, I found I'm in

just this, in an enraged state. That I'm having to suppress so that I'm able to go to work.[153]

Other podcasters also expressed similar sentiments about the hostility on social media. Rod explained the response he got after using the hashtag #IGotTheTalk to tell a story of being racially profiled and pulled over by the police while he was in college, saying, "I woke up this morning, and there was all kinds of racist trolls in my mentions and all this stuff, man. 'Cause you know, I said a few things that kind of like got retweeted or whatever, and all of a sudden, just you know, racist people are all up in my mentions."[154]

Many of the podcasters highlighted that their shows were not usually about politics or racial justice, but that they felt compelled to discuss Ferguson anyway. This highlights the flexibility of the network and the ways it is deployed depending on the exigencies of the situation. For example, Kahlief Adams, co-host of *Spawn on Me*, a gaming podcast, explained, "You know we do a . . . gaming podcast. We are Black men first." His co-host, Shareef Jackson, continued, "It definitely affects us, because these people who get killed are gamers, scientists, and engineers, comic book people. . . . There's no filter for being profiled if you're Black, right? Being successful, not successful. Rich, poor, whatever. So, I think it does affect, you know, all content creators."[155] The hosts of *In Deep Show* ended a discussion of the dangers faced by Black children by noting that they don't "want to preach to you all" and that they "don't do it often," but, as co-host Big B said, "I just wanted to put a spotlight on a situation we all are dealing with."[156]

While the network is comprised of individuals from a diverse array of backgrounds and with differing opinions on Ferguson, there was near unanimous recognition of a shared experience as a Black subject, of the impact of this event on every Black American. Jackson of *Spawn on Me* described the experience:

> It's been tough. It's been a really hard week for me. I've been pretty unproductive at work. That's been really stressful because I don't feel like I can talk to anyone at work about it. Kinda just been doin' a lotta tweeting. . . . It's just been tough, man. Like, you know, just being a Black man, y'know. It's just, you just constantly get reminded that you are always a suspect.

No matter what you did, what you're doin', where you're walkin', it's just what is the situation. It's definitely been a very stark reminder of that. Very very tough.[157]

As they did in response to to the turmoil in the wake of the Zimmerman acquittal, some of the podcasters attempted to provide a respite from the trauma. As a guest on *Fiyastarter*, Rod of TBGWT explained:

we talk about it, and then we have fun, because that's what we do. That's our job. I'd much rather you say we party for two hours. We had a ton of people here this week that's just, "I didn't think it was capable for me to laugh, because I was so affected by this. But your show brought me that entertainment and that joy," and it means a fucking ton to me.[158]

In addition to demonstrating the flexibility of these spaces, comments like these highlight their collective nature.

Conclusion

It has become clear to even the most casual observer that digital technologies now play a central role in struggles for racial justice. Research into moments of turmoil—such as Trayvon Martin's death, the Zimmerman acquittal, the uprisings in Ferguson and Baltimore, and the ongoing Movement for Black Lives—routinely discusses the importance of digital and social media. However, this analysis is often limited by its heavy focus on Twitter. While Twitter is of great importance, it is only one element of a larger transplatform networked environment.

Twitter serves as an important "alert system," bringing events and information to users' attention. But in addition to being a source of information and real-time reaction and interpretation, Twitter also serves as a central clearinghouse for links and posts housed on other platforms, such as Instagram, Vine, YouTube, and Ustream. While these have features for the creation and storage of video and images, which are not available on Twitter, they lack the immediacy and brevity of Twitter. By housing content on these platforms and disseminating links or cross-posting via Twitter, users combine the strengths of multiple platforms and are able to customize network affordances in ways that best achieve their communicative goals.

Podcasts serve as a crucial and often unrecognized component of this transplatform ecosystem. Because they lend themselves to the creation of enclaves, podcast and audio streams enable participants to reaffirm community and collectivity, engage in catharsis, and, at times, even find a brief reprieve. Additionally, podcasters aggregate, evaluate, and synthesize the fragmented and nonstop stream of information emerging from social media and legacy media reporting, engaging in a process of collective framing and interpretation and producing narratives and counter-discourses about events as they unfold.

The multimedia transplatform network at the center of this project is vital at moments of racial crisis and turmoil. Built and maintained over several years of mundane and everyday interactions, the network became a flexible resource, able to meet a range of communicative needs, often simultaneously, as events unfolded. This complex interplay of platforms and their respective affordances is a crucial resource for many Black Americans.

Conclusion

Race, Culture, and Digital Studies

This book only scratches the surface of the rich and robust digital assemblage that is its focus. After mapping the transplatform nature of this oscillating networked public, my primary focus was how it was used by racialized subjects as a resource for navigating a white supremacist society, whether that be for memory work that challenges the historic foundations upon which colorblindness rests or to interpret, respond to, and actively agitate against racial violence by the state. The flexible and malleable character of the network makes it a resource for a broad range of practices. However, since the time that I completed my research in mid-2016, several of the fundamental aspects of this network and the context in which it operates have shifted.

The concept of digital publics is well-worn among the disciplines that study digital technologies. However, if we are to take seriously the assertion that digitally networked publics are both *a group of people* and *a technological space* in which that group is constituted, then we must devote more sustained attention to the transplatform technological space in which the collection of people operate. While it often makes sense to limit studies by platform, sustained attention to the interlocking uses of multiple platforms yields additional insights, particularly into the complicated ways that distributed discourse production occurs across platforms and employs a range of media. This approach is particularly urgent given the increasing platformization of the web.[1]

Cultural Specificity and Critical Digital Studies

Throughout, I have heavily emphasized cultural specificity, grounding my analysis in histories of Black communication, media production, and thought and attending to the particularities of the experiences of

Black subjectivities. Given that affordances are imagined through the interaction of the designers' intent, the materiality and functionality of the technology, and the perceptions, beliefs, and expectations of the user, then changing one of these components can yield radically different outcomes. Don Norman argues that affordances must be perceived by the user to exist and be utilized.[2] Users from marginalized cultural backgrounds and subject positions are likely to perceive affordances in ways that differ from their normative hegemonic applications and to see different ways to use technology.

But the utility of a culturally specific approach goes far beyond highlighting the differences in use patterns between groups. If the sum total of the insight offered was, "White people tweet like this. Black people tweet like that," that would be relatively narrow contribution. What is most valuable about this approach is how these differences can help us imagine different possibilities for technologies beyond hegemonic frameworks and thereby allow us to better anticipate and grapple with the social shifts that shape and are shaped by technology.

Marginalized users are often required to be innovators, as Twitter clearly shows. From its inception, white tech professionals on the platform suggested that Black users were using Twitter differently or even "wrong."[3] Black Twitter, as it came be known, was more homophilic and conversational than normative conceptualization of Twitter held by white, mostly male, early adopters from the tech field. This difference was so pronounced that even as late as 2013, when Twitter added the conversations feature that linked a reply to the tweet it was responding to, discussions of the new feature revealed a difference in the Black imagined affordances and the normative imagined affordances of Twitter. White-presenting technology reporter Will Oremus wrote that while he had expected the new feature to be annoying, he found the change to be almost unnoticeable, "because hardly anyone holds actual conversations on Twitter." He described his timeline as full of "techies, academics, journalists, politicians, and comedians," who were all "too busy barking into their own megaphones to respond to anyone else" or "lurking passively in the faceless crowd, piping up only via the occasional timid retweet or favorite." He also noted that the earlier versions of Twitter discouraged replies: "Under the old system, the fact that only the latest reply showed up in your timeline made conversations appear exclusive even when you were following both parties. It felt like you were constantly showing up late to an A/B conversation, and the polite thing to do was to C yourself out."[4] Yet, Black Twitter connected and flourished under these conditions. Black users often saw such A/B conversations as an invitation to collective communication. For this network, hashtags served not only as organizational tools aggregating topics, but as a "call" to participation in the Black American traditions of signifyin' and call-and-response.[5] Though those in tech might have seen these as nonnormative, even uncommon, uses, these use patterns became prominent enough on Twitter to prompt the platform to add a feature to facilitate it.

Because people from marginalized populations are often forced to make do with technologies that were not designed with them in mind, they have become adept at imagining affordances that subvert the social and cultural norms technologies would otherwise enforce. The Chilin' Circuit podcasts clearly demonstrate how changing the users in the triad of users, designers, and materiality and functionality produces affordances can result in starkly different approaches. Through an imbrication of the broadcast-style network and the social network, these podcasts, podcasters have produced a collective space that manages to serve as a digital iteration of traditions of both mass media production and sociality. The podcasts and their listeners, through their collaborative communitarian approach, make these podcasts into nodes in the larger distributed conversation of the network. They serve not only as a means of distributing information and circulating discourse, but also as enclaves that insulate participants from those seeking to disrupt and harass them. Their highly interactive sonic simulations of Black social enclaves are then heard through headphones by listeners who consume the podcasts while in predominantly white spaces. Thus headphones, which are normatively conceived of as technologies of neoliberal individuation, can instead be used to reinforce a sense of connection and collectivity.

This argument about the broad value of culturally specificity comes with two important caveats. First, it is certainly not only Black users who offer valuable insights into the possibilities of technologies. Not only do various marginalized groups have distinct subject positions and epistemologies that generate different perspectives on technology—the ability to perceive a different set of affordances, but they have also long been forced to be creative and savvy in using technologies to suit needs and desires not envisioned by the designers. For example, Lori Kido Lopez has demonstrated how Hmong living in the United States have developed what she calls "teleconference radio," the use of conference-call software and mobile phones to create radio-style programming.[6] Here a marginalized group of users, bringing their own perspectives and expectations, transform technologies designed for one-on-one and small group communication into a broadcast-style medium. They use the mobile phone—a technology that both emerges from and reinforces individualist neoliberal impulses—to cultivate collectivity.[7]

My second caveat is that learning from the practices of marginalized people must be done with humility and a deep commitment to ethics. We cannot treat marginalized users as objects of study from whom we extract knowledge, as has too often been the case. We must conceive of them as interlocutors in the production of knowledge, a sentiment often heard in the academy but less frequently put into practice. How one does this will vary by context and can include greater engagement with the work of marginalized scholars about their communities, taking the time to establish trust and build relationships to work collaboratively, allowing the people you are writing about to have continued and real input into shaping the final results (including allowing them to set the boundaries for what knowledge will be made accessible and what should remain off limits), or making space and providing financial support for the participation nonacademic experts in academic settings. Fortunately, we have generations of ethnographers who have grappled with these challenges and whose work can guide us in finding the line between taking marginalized users' knowledge seriously and just simply taking it.

I do not think it is far-fetched to say that centering marginalized users and what they have to tell us about technology will benefit not only researchers of digital technologies, but also society as a whole. Many white Americans were caught off guard by the hard-right shift and the reemergence of overt white supremacy that accompanied the ascendency of Donald Trump. But there is a direct line from trolls harassing Black feminists on Twitter in 2012 to the emergence of the "Alt-Right." Had we heeded the warnings, rather than writing such incidents off as trivial internet conflicts, we would have seen the ways that digital networks were empowering racism and misogyny as much as marginalized voices. We would have seen the radicalization of young men by the Men's Rights Movement and the emergence of the "incel" (involuntarily celibate) sub-culture thriving on 4Chan, 8Chan, and Reddit. We would have taken seriously their rhetoric and beliefs, which have led to more than one mass shooting—in 2014 in Isla Vista near University of California at Santa Barbara and in 2015 at Umpqua Community College in Oregon.[8]

Racial Regimes in Flux

In the time between concluding my research for this book and its publication, the shift in the US landscape has radically altered US racial discourses and how the network discussed here functions as an oscillating networked public. First, the status of colorblindness as the dominant US racial ideology is now unclear. Key to colorblindness is the conflation of equality with the erasure of difference. By defini-tion, it mandates that race is not to be perceived and requires racism be obscured in coded language and seemingly nonracial policies and discourses. In this way, it preserves, while denying, racial hierarchies. But, increasingly, with Trump's ascendancy, there seems to be no need to camouflage or disguise racist language or policies. In fact, it is often the opposite, with willingness to express overt racism often praised as "telling it like it is." Colorblindness's prohibition on acknowledg-ing race, while remaining intact for those advocating *against* white supremacy, has all but vanished for those advocating *for* oppressive and discriminatory policies.

Trump embodies this shift, tapping into white fear and racism (along with xenophobia, sexism, and anti-LBGTQ sentiment). He has consis-tently employed inflammatory rhetoric that has both unmasked and in-tensified white supremacist values—conflating immigrants and asylum seekers from Central and South America with violent criminal gang MS-13; referring to Haiti and African nations as "shithole" countries; calling for a "a total and complete shutdown of Muslims entering the United States," to name but a few instances.[9] Trump's cabinet appointments and policies have followed a similar trajectory. His Attorney General Jeff Sessions failed to be confirmed as a Federal Judge in 1987 because of questions about his attitudes toward race. Several of his top advisers—

Steve Bannon, Sebastian Gorka, and Steven Miller—have ties to white supremacist organizations and espouse white nationalist ideologies.[10]

Rhetoric and behavior that would have been solidly out of bounds within traditional norms of colorblindness have themselves become normalized. Several studies have shown that Trump supporters were consistently motivated by racial hostility, rather than economic anxiety, as many editorials and think pieces have proclaimed.[11] Membership in hate groups has been steadily climbing, with neo-Nazi groups seeing the greatest surge, and hate crimes steadily rose between 2016 and 2018.[12] There has also been a surge in the construction of Confederate monuments on private land, and the 2018 mid-term elections featured eight openly white nationalist candidates running for national office, including a Holocaust denier who argued Black people have IQs on average 20 points below those of whites.[13] In one of the largest displays of overt white supremacy in recent memory, in August 2017, Charlottesville, Virginia was swarmed by hundreds of white supremacists, rebranded as the "Alt-Right," who carried tiki torches and chanted "Jews will not replace us" and the Nazi slogan "Blood and soil." The rally became chaotic and violent as skirmishes broke out between white supremacists and counter-protestors, escalating into the severe the beating of DeAndre Harris and culminating in a white supremacist driving a car into a crowd and killing Heather Heyer.[14] Trump famously said of the tragedy that there were "very fine people on both sides."[15]

With public displays of blatant white supremacy on the rise, it is possible that we are witnessing the waning of colorblindness and the emergence of a new racial paradigm. Eduardo Bonilla-Silva has cautioned against this assumption, highlighting the parallels between the contemporary moment and the resurgence of more overt racism that occurred during the Reagan administration. The 1980s saw economic hardship—increased foreclosures, personal bankruptcies, and failed small businesses—as well anti-Black rhetoric from the president and an increase in both law enforcement and civilian violence toward people of color. He notes that even with the increase in overt racism, Trump and his supporters still must "genuflect to the color-blind norms of the period." Colorblindness still requires Trump to maintain he is not racist, and he does indeed make frequent claims that he is "the least racist person," as well as courting voters of color, despite ultimately ignoring them on policy issues.[16] Similarly, the stars of the seemingly never-ending stream of viral videos showing white Americans on tirades against people of color inevitably, when identified, also feel compelled to deny that they are in any way racist.[17] Even white supremacists have rebranded themselves as "white nationalists," "Western chauvinists," "identitarians," and the "Alt-Right," advocating the inferiority of people of color and the need for a white ethno-state in one breath while denying they are racists with the other.

Thus, while colorblindness may not be dying, it certainly seems as if we are seeing a new iteration that differs from that of the last twenty-five years. Initially, colorblindness entailed a semantic move that disarticulated the signifier "racism" from any structural or systemic processes of oppression and rearticulated it to a set of individual beliefs, attitudes, and behaviors. The price for this obscuring of structural white supremacy was acquiescence to some modicum of racial progress. Overt displays of racism, such as hate groups, the use of racial slurs, or open discrimination were stigmatized because their normalization would render it impossible to claim race was irrelevant as a social category. It's difficult to claim that United States triumphed over racism if open white supremacy is accepted as part of the normal range of political positions. Or, at least, it used to be.

In the contemporary moment, "racism" seems to have become a floating signifier, articulated to nothing beyond a generally agreed-upon stigma. We all agree racism is bad, with some going so far as to claim "racist" is the worst thing a person can be called.[18] But we increasingly seem unable to identify anything as *being* racism. Previously, only the most overt displays of racism would be labeled as such—for example a fully hooded Klansman burning a cross and yelling racial slurs. Now it seems as if that Klansman could just pull of his hood and proclaim, with little cognitive dissonance and broad acceptance, that he "doesn't have a racist bone in his body" and that he is offended at the accusation. It is this incarnation of colorblindness, one untethered to fact or reality, that allows Richard Spencer—a man who advocates for the forcible sterilization of people of color and the construction of an imperial white ethno-state—to tweet, "What's wrong with loving being white? I am not a supremacist, by the way. I just love my people."[19] The shift in color-blind discourse may just be one of degree, not necessarily in kind. But it certainly seems as if we are witnessing a new incarnation of colorblindness, one to fit our "post-truth" moment. This new sociocultural terrain will require new strategies—discursive and technological—to move forward in the fight against white supremacy.

Listen to Black Women (but for Real This Time)

Much of this book focuses on Twitter as serving a counter-public function, allowing participants to engage other publics, to push counter-discourses into the broader public conversation, and to make interventions in corporate media through dialogic engagement. This strategy seemed to reach peak efficacy between 2013 and 2015. During that time the strength of Twitter as a platform for Black counter-discourses elicited similarly strong attempts to undermine its efficacy as a counter-public. Harassment, abuse, and even Russian bots have increasingly made Twitter less effective for political engagement and much more unpleasant to use. As Imani Gandy explained of the harassment on the platform, "Often, the best solution is to reduce Twitter activity or to quit the platform entirely. I know many women who have already done that."[20]

Since Twitter's trending topics make Black Twitter visible to those outside the network, there have been efforts to harass and abuse Black users, particularly Black users who are also women and/or LGBTQ. I choose here to avoid the word commonly used to describe this behavior—namely, "troll." As Kishonna Gray and Whitney Phillips have both argued, the term works to minimize harassment and its impact.[21] This minimization has helped these behaviors to flourish and to deeply impact not just internet culture, but US culture and politics writ large.

Harassment always occurred on Twitter. But it intensified and coalesced as a coordinated political effort in 2014 and continued to do so through the 2016 presidential election. Harassment was clearly evident during the 2012 advocacy for justice for Trayvon Martin, and it was such behavior that drove participants from social media to the audio enclave provided by TWiB! on the night of the verdict. Both Gandy and Terrell Starr wrote pieces in 2014 detailing years of harassment and abuse that women, particularly Black women, endured online and Twitter's steadfast unwillingness to curb the hostility.[22] Gandy was stalked online, across platforms and under multiple user names, by one user who went primarily by the online pseudonym "Assholster." She describes her tormentor as "an anonymous Twitter asshole who, on most days, creates up to ten different Twitter accounts just so he can hurl racist slurs at me: I'm a 'nigger,' I look 'niggery,' I haven't earned my 'nigger card,' I'm a 'pseudonigger,' 'fucking niggster,' or 'scab nigger.'" He also often tagged others in the network I write about here—Feminista Jones, Elon James White, L. Joy Williams, and Jamie Nesbitt Golden, co-host of the *Nerdgasm Noire Network* podcast, writer, and feminist commentator. Gandy endured his abuse for three years, cataloging and reporting his interactions with her to no avail, before identifying and doxing (releasing personal identifying information) him herself in 2015.[23] Her story is not an outlier.

Moreover, attacks became more coordinated and sustained, starting in 2013, when users from message boards such as 4Chan and Reddit began creating fake accounts in attempts to impersonate, infiltrate, and sow discord among what they termed "SJWs," social justice warriors. The fake accounts had two additional goals: to create in-group fighting among feminists online, specifically targeting women of color feminists, and to paint feminist politics as extreme and ridiculous. They began in 2013, roughly around the time that Mikki Kendall's hashtag #SolidarityIsForWhiteWomen, which was used to critique the shortcomings of white feminists on issues of race, was receiving widespread attention and bringing longstanding tensions to the fore.

The harassers set up accounts using stock photos of women of color and gave them names such as NayNay Thompson, Aisha Salaam, and Phoebe Kwon. The users spearheading this campaign had at least some loose associations with the Pick-Up-Artist (PUA) movement, an industry dedicated to teaching men how to "attract" women. PUA philosophy is deeply misogynistic and focuses on achieving heterosexual sexual conquest through psychological, and sometimes physical, manipulation. One high-profile PUA, Roosh Valizadeh, has suggested First World men move to impoverished nations to find a woman to manipulate into submission, argued that rape should be legal on private property, and featured pieces such as "5 Reasons to Date a Girl with an Eating Disorder" and "The Intellectual Inferiority of Women" on his now-defunct website, *Return of the Kings*.[24] It was *Return of the Kings* that posted the first known synopsis of the coordinated effort to use sock puppet accounts—fake accounts created to deliberately deceive— to target SJWs, which the post claimed was codenamed "Operation Lollipop." The post even included screen captures of fake accounts, including that of "Phoebe Kwon," that would be instrumental in promoting the fake hashtag #EndFathersDay.[25]

It was in 2014 that a collection of these sock puppet feminists attempted to trend two fake hashtags—#EndFathersDay and #WhitesCantBeRaped. The former included statements such as "men shouldn't be allowed around children" and claimed that Father's Day "celebrates patriarchy and oppression" and should be replaced with "Castration Day."[26] The latter included claims such as "#Rape = #Force + #Privilege. #WhitesCantBeRaped by PoC [person of color], period. #YesAllWoman who are white and don't accept this are racist."[27] In response, @sassy-crass and @so_treu, who are highly visible Black feminists on Twitter, created a hashtag #YourSlipIsShowing that was used to crowdsource a list of accounts that were part of the sock puppet operation and led to the unmasking hundreds of accounts.[28]

These harassment campaigns occurred in tandem with "Gamergate," a coordinated effort to harass women and people of color associated with the video game industry. Gamergate was yet another iteration of the anti-SJW sentiment that had been percolating online for years. It originated and was coordinated on the same message boards as previous harassment campaigns and featured many of the same players. Gamergate participants claimed they were advocating for "ethics in video game journalism." However, their most consistent complaint seemed to be that feminist and antiracist SJWs were ruining the game industry, and thereby their beloved games, with "political correctness." Game developers such as Zoë Quinn and Briana Wu became targets. The ongoing harassment campaign against feminist media critic Anita Sarkeesian, who had been targeted since her 2012 fundraiser to start a YouTube video series critiquing representations of women in gaming, was added to the efforts.[29] These women received death and rape threats and were doxed and harassed across platforms. Sarkeesian had to move out of her home, and even now these women must routinely have bomb sweeps and extra security measures at their speaking engagements. While Gamergate focused the worst of its ire on high-profile women, its perpetrators also targeted and harassed people of color, particularly women of color, on social media. Users ranging from micro-celebrities to unknown users with small followings found themselves swarmed online for various SJW offenses. Even academics were caught in the wake of Gamergate's wrath. Shira Chess and Adrienne Shaw found themselves at the center of Gamergate conspiracy theory after their participation at a Digital Games Research Association (DiGRA) conference, where they allegedly ran a fishbowl that was actually psyops (psychological operation) for the larger SJW conspiracy.[30]

These harassment campaigns were occurring concurrently with the unrest in Ferguson in 2014, and while they were not highly visible in the Black digital networks engaged with Ferguson during the 2014 protests, on the one-year anniversary of Mike Brown's death, hashtags like #Ferguson and #BlackLivesMatter were flooded with what seemed like auto-generated spam tweets, making the hashtag difficult to use as a locus of remembrance or organizing. Notably, the hashtag #FergusonTaughtMe, created by Leslie Mac of the *Ferguson Response Network* and *Interracial Jawn* podcasts remained relatively spam-free despite appearing in the US trending topics that day.[31] It was clear that although anti-racial justice networks had preplanned the spamming of certain hashtags to decrease their efficacy, they had not anticipated #FergusonTaughtMe, leaving it fairly undisturbed. It has since become de rigueur for users tweeting about racial justice to receive waves of harassment. White supremacists have also proliferated on Twitter, periodically trying their hand at fake accounts but mostly just harassing other users.[32]

As the 2016 presidential elections approached, Gamergate participants began turning their efforts to the benefit of Trump. Two high-profile Gamergaters became champions of Trump, as Gamergate morphed and integrated into the "Alt-Right." Right-wing provocateur Milo Yiannopoulos built his online profile through participation in and support for Gamergate, shortly thereafter becoming a writer for Bannon's far-right website Breitbart.[33] While at Breitbart, Yiannopoulos solicited input on his writing for Andrew "weev" Auernheimer, a hacker and open white supremacist who was the system administrator for the neo-Nazi website The Daily Stormer.[34] Mike Cernovich, a lawyer who started out as a blogger writing about how to pick-up women, also moved from being a vocal supporter of Gamegate, which he once called "the most important battle of the culture war this century," to prolifer-ating anti-Clinton conspiracy theories.[35] Self-identified member of the Alt-Right, Cernovich played a major role in proliferating the #PizzaGate conspiracy, which held that Hillary Clinton's campaign manager John Podesta operated a child sex ring out of the basement of Comet Ping Pong, a Washington, DC, pizzeria (in a building that has no basement).[36]

Bannon, Cernovich, Yiannopoulos, and others were able to channel the existing anger, misogyny, and racism of the (predominantly, though by no means exclusively) white men dwelling in the dark corners of the internet. It is easy to see the synergy between Gamergate's distain for "SJWs" and Trump's rejection of "political correctness." The bile of 4Chan, 8Chan, and Reddit users, of PUAs and men's rights activists, and of white supremacists coalesced and were channeled in support of the Trump political platform. In the wake of the 2016 election, there has been a handful of articles pointing to Gamergate as precursor to what is now called the Alt-Right.[37] But, at the time, few outside the networks where it occurred took Gamergate seriously.

Among other activities, these "alt-right" networks attack and harass people of color and women on social media, with particular attention to women of color. This was most severe on Twitter because the platform has been reluctant to curb such behaviors. Such attacks make it more dif-ficult for marginalized people to use Twitter as a counter-public, which is clearly the intention. Alt-right users not only respond to other users with abusive language and vulgar or heinous images, but also coordinate in large swarms, often using bots to amplify the attacks on their targets. The participants at the center of this project have gotten good at identifying and dealing with such attacks, though it still takes a toll in time and en-ergy. While such harassment campaigns are now largely anticipated, what has come as more of a surprise is the extent to which Russian intelligence seems to have participated in or at least amplified such hostilities.

Russians? Seriously?

There were warnings about Russian interference in the 2016 elections prior to election day, but those warnings went largely unheeded, and it was not until after the election that the full extent of Russia's operation and reliance on social media was widely recognized. Russian intelligence used Facebook, Instagram, and Twitter to spread misinformation and exacerbate existing social and especially racial tensions in the United States.[38] Russian accounts on Facebook included Blacktivist and Black Matters, both of which posted pro-Black content and information about protests; and Twitter accounts had handles such as black4unity, BlackerTheBerr5, BlackGirls2017, and BLMSoldier.[39] A study of Russian Twitter accounts by Leo G. Stewart, Ahmer Arif, and Kate Starbird showed that they exploited the polarization of digital networks and created ideologically tailored content to inject into aligned clusters.[40]

The most recent reports have indicated that Russia targeted Black Americans with messages designed to demobilize the Black vote, often advocating for Black voters to stay home or to vote for Green Party candidate Jill Stein. It is difficult to know how successful these campaigns were. Black voter turnout decreased 7 percent from the previous election, a significant drop. However, the 2016 Black turnout of 59.6 percent is only slightly lower than the pre-Obama turnout from 2004. Thus, there is a compelling argument to be made that the campaigns had little effect on regular voters and that the record 2008 and 2012 turnout was an anomaly resulting from the excitement generated by having a Black candidate on the ballot. Further, it is important to remember that 2016 was the first election since the Supreme Court gutted the Voting Rights Act in 2013 and that there had been a sustained effort to close polling places, limit early voting, require voter IDs, and place other barriers to voting that would discourage or prevent Black Americans from voting.

It is also difficult to know how widely Black Americans were taken in by these fake accounts. Kevin Winstead, in his analysis of the Russian-run Twitter account @Crystal1Johnson, finds that the account never called for specific action or promoted rallies and never tweeted radical political critiques. Thus, while the account was convincing enough to infiltrate and successfully engage with Black Twitter, it participated mostly in ways that reiterated common political discourses in Black American communities, only occasionally pushing out a Kremlin-approved post.[41] Thus, it is still unclear what impact these Russian accounts had on the networks they penetrated, even though it is clear that some of the accounts were fairly believable.

Still, Black activists tend to maintain a healthy skepticism about newcomers, given the history of government informants and agent provocateurs penetrating past movements. Between 2014 and 2016, it was common to see suspicion about possible infiltration of the Movement for Black Lives, often citing the mid-twentieth-century FBI operations that targeted activists in the Civil Rights and Black Power Movements. This suspicion played out with the fake Facebook account of Blacktivist, a page that had over 360,000 likes, which was more than the official Black Lives Matter page. While the page did a good job at maintaining believability, real activists remained skeptical. The Blacktivist page particularly targeted issues around the death of Freddie Gray in Baltimore, yet no one in the city seemed to know who was running the account. Heber Brown III, a Baltimore pastor and organizer, contacted the page and had an exchange with the person running it, which he later posted on Facebook. Brown thought Blacktivist was someone from out of town looking to exploit the cause.[42] Activist Jamye Wooten thought perhaps it was an undercover police officer acting as surveillance.[43] While it is doubtful anyone suspected Russian intelligence, these accounts, despite the number of followers or likes, do not go unquestioned.

Further, we now know that Russian sock puppet accounts were involved in stoking tensions between Hillary Clinton and Bernie Sanders supporters during the contentious 2016 primary, during which time many Twitter users complained of harassment from professed Sanders supporters. While it is indisputable that some of the over-zealous Sanders supporters were earnest and legitimate, many in the network I write about here suggested the involvement of manufactured sock puppet accounts and bots.[44] They noted the Sanders supporters, nicknamed "Bernie Bros," used tactics that were remarkably similar to the campaigns coordinated by Gamergate and other anti-SJW networks and suggested that some of the Bernie Bros were likely part of the kind of 4Chan and Reddit coordinated harassment campaigns that had been in operation for years. But even as there was some suspicion that these online interactions stemmed from a malicious source and were not entirely organic, no one suspected that Russian intelligence had set up the accounts.

While it is not known how many of the accounts defending Sanders were Russian, it is apparent that some such accounts amplified existing discourses that have long been at the heart of racial tensions in the progressive movement. Because of this, and despite Russian participation, I stand by my analysis of #BernieSoBlack. My aim was to investigate how this network uses technologies to negotiate their experiences as racialized subjects. Russian accounts that participated in #BernieSoBlack did not create novel discourses, which would have had little effect. Instead they recycled longstanding tropes that were familiar to the participants in the network I write about. Thus, for the users who are the focus on this project—who I am confident are not Russian plants—this was a real exigency, to which they responded with strategies and discourses that accurately reflect their attitudes regardless of their interlocutors.

Although Congress has released a list of fake Russian-operated Twitter accounts, it is unclear as to how much traction these accounts actually had with Black users. While the sock puppet accounts have been deleted, it is still possible to search their username and see the tweets @-replied to them. There appears to be little interaction with the accounts or predominantly automated retweets or replies. Given the centrality of conversational engagement in the Black Twitter network, this strikes me as a sign that these accounts were only superficially involved in the network. This anecdotal evidence also leaves me with questions about the effectiveness of the mimicry in fooling Black Americans. A deeper, systematic analysis would be fruitful. It seems quite possible that Russian accounts had a much narrower range of behaviors available to them to pass effectively in Black networks. Black Americans, who have more experience using alternative information networks and a historically necessitated skepticism of unknown entities, likely possess skills that could bolster the broader US public's ability to vet information.

Further, as such hostilities and antagonisms have intensified, I have seen a shift toward increased sequestration of networked enclaves. It was during 2015, when presidential primaries were in full swing—coinciding with more open racial hostilities, a contentious primary between Sanders and Clinton, and an intense Russian intelligence operation—that podcasts began creating closed Facebook groups, and it was in the aftermath of the 2016 election that more and more people in the network made their Twitter accounts private, allowing only approved followers to see their tweets and preventing retweeting. This strategy preserves access to their existing network but prevents the addition of new followers and limits the circulation of their posts. Twitter has shown little will to curb harassment on their platform, and I anticipate that more sequestration efforts will continue, with the behavior of this network presaging larger digital media trends.

The Interstitial Hustle

Another change that has occurred since I have completed my research is that TWiB! has scaled back operations significantly, so that by the end of 2017, it had returned to its origins as a largely solo project of its founder, Elon James White. The reasons for this are complex, though overall TWiB!'s trajectory underscores the instability of the interstitial modes of production upon which endeavors like it are built.

Prior to 2017, TWiB! employed production techniques that are common among independent digital content creators. Media studies scholars have chronicled the financial precarity, the ad hoc and improvisational production process, and the necessity for creators to fulfill multiple production roles simultaneously.[45] This practice closely resembles what Hamid Naficy has termed an "interstitial mode production" in his work on filmmakers living in exile. Used "to operate both within and astride the cracks and fissures of the system, benefiting from its contradictions, anomalies, and heterogeneity," this mode of production is deployed by marginalized creatives who are outside traditional industry structures and lack access to those resources, and it manifests in three concrete areas: language, financing, and labor.[46] For now, I am bracketing language in favor of focusing on financing and labor.[47] Financially, creators of a project such as a podcast must invest their own money, raise funds from private and public sources, and/or make use of the resources available by working in "technical or routine capacities in the media and entertainment industries." Essentially, creators have to hustle, paying out of pocket and finding donations and investments where and how they can, and, rather than having clear labor roles, those involved in the project take on multiple roles, often simultaneously, as needed. As Naficy observes, the interstitial mode of production is characterized by a "multiplication or accumulation of labor (especially on behalf of the director) instead of a division of labor."[48] Thus, the main creator of a project, White in the case of TWiB!, often does all the work that large-scale corporate media have entire infrastructures to accomplish, and so while the interstitial mode of production allows the projects of marginalized creators to be made, it is exceedingly difficult to maintain indefinitely.

At its height, TWiB! produced *TWiB! Prime* and *TWiB! in the Morning* four days a week, Monday through Thursday, along with six weekly podcasts plus a show on FreeSpeechTV. This was financed, in addition to what White paid for personally, through audience donations and, starting in 2014, subscriptions, as well as small ad spots from companies like Bevel Shaving, revenue as an Amazon affiliate, and occasionally producing media for organizations such as Netroots Nation.[49] As with most independent media projects, TWiB! always suffered from financial precarity. TWiB! personnel worked hard and produced a great deal of high quality content, at first for free and eventually for pay, though never enough for anyone to quit their "day job." They did this largely because they believed in the project, though some also wanted to learn skills to move into the media industry. People can sustain that for a period of time, but not indefinitely. A finite project, such as a film or a web series with a set number of episodes in a season, can be produced using an interstitial mode, but it is difficult to produce a podcast four days a week *indefinitely* that way.

Of course, the hustle to create these media is intended to to achieve sustainable and monetized media production, either as an independent entity or through partnership with existing media companies. That the internet offers potential opportunity for enterprising content creators to bypass industry gatekeepers is apparent, but, despite commonly held beliefs, monetizing online content is extremely difficult, and online visibility does not readily translate into financial prosperity. Even on YouTube, the platform with the clearest way for content creators to monetize via ad revenue, most creators make hardly anything. While a channel can be in the top 3 percent of channels that garner 85 percent of the views, it is not likely generate enough revenue to put its creator above the poverty line.[50] Wildly popular platforms such as Twitter, Reddit, and Soundcloud have yet to find a way to turn a profit. What are the chances that users fare better than the platforms that hosts their content? This means that the vast majority of online independent media projects could forever remain in the interstitial hustle, which seems to be unsustainable, particular at the scale of TWiB!, which at times had as many as a dozen people involved.

While TWiB! grew quickly and faced challenges due to its reliance on a mode of production that was ill-suited to support the scale of the endeavor, the other Chitlin' Circuit podcasts have grown more slowly. They have also taken to crafting a monetization strategy based on maximizing the support of a small but dedicated audience. The most successful of these has been The Black Guy Who Tips. Rod and Karen started their show in 2010, while both were working fulltime jobs. In early 2013, Rod was laid off, and they decided to try to monetize the podcast with what became their freemium service. Accordingly, the ten most recent episodes of *The Black Guy Who Tips* podcast were free and available through various podcatcher apps and an RSS feed, while early *TBGWT* episodes and their new premium shows—*The Nerd Off, Balls Deep Sports*, and *Medium Talk*—were subscription-only at a cost of $15 a month. The plan worked, and within a month they exceeded their goal of one hundred subscribers, bringing in enough money for Rod to make the podcast his fulltime job. Over the last five years, the franchise has continued to grow, adding subscribers and receiving regular ad placements from companies such as Tweeked Audio, Bevel, Adam and Eve, Loot Crate, and Shadow Dog Productions.

Other podcasts networks have also begun moving to a freemium model. As of 2018, both the Movie Trailer Review (MTR) Network and Where's My 40 Acres? have freemium services. The MTR Network maintains five free podcasts—*Insanity Check, Character Corner, Secret Sauce, Super Tuesday*, and *Unanimous Decision*—that are available via podcatchers and RSS and increasingly via YouTube. Additionally, for an $8 monthly subscription fee, subscribers get access to nine premium shows, including a science show called *Molecules and Shit*, a book club style show for comic books called *Comic Book Club*, and two nostalgia-based movie reviews of older movies called *Nostalgia Review* and *Scarestalgia*. MTR shows also receive ad placements from many of the same advertisers as TBGWT. While its content consists heavily of audio podcasts, MTR also maintains a robust website featuring written reviews and commentary and is introducing short videos via YouTube. Phenom Blak, of Where's My 40 Acres? has also joined MTR and works with Kriss to do reviews and create content, as the MTR network seems to be taking a turn toward hope labor, the investment of time and energy with the goal of building a professional and monetizable endeavor.

Where's My 40 Acres? uses a similar model. While WM40A? continues to produce free shows—*Where's My 40 Acres?*, *EarGasm*, and *BoobTube*—for a monthly subscription fee, fans also get access six premiums shows, including review shows such as the super hero–focused *Podvengers* and the action film–focused *Say Yes to Death*, as well as *Wifey Material*, a show featuring Phenom Blak's fiancée, Ashley, and *Behind the Ratchet*, which includes conversations among the hosts before and after the flagship show. For premium subscriptions WM40A? uses Patreon, a website that enables people to become patrons of creators by pledging a monthly fee, and allows for tiers of pledges of increasing size, with rewards increasing as amounts increase (similar to GoFundMe). WM40A? lists pledges from $2 to $100, with $10 being the minimum for full premium access and larger amounts adding extra rewards such as picking the topic of an episode, having co-host Deirdre send the subscriber a "special box" of goodies (which often contains baked goods), or being a guest on the show.[51] Like that of MTR, WM40A?'s content is primarily audio podcasts, but, in association with its premium show *Craft Beer Killahs*, WM40A? has begun posting beer reviews on Instagram, featuring an image of the beer with a description and review in the comments.[52]

Other podcasts are also using Patreon. *3 Guys On*, featuring DC-based comedians Randolph Terrance, Andy Kline (who is white), and Tim Miller, offers a weekly premium episode, in addition to a regular free episode, for $3 a month. The Black Astronaut Podcast (BAP) Network started producing premium content in early 2017, offering Patreon tiers ranging from $3 to access past BAP episodes to $10 to participate in a monthly live-stream chat.[53] The Cold Slither Podcast Network (CSPN), which as of 2018 produced seventeen different podcasts (though not all always in regular production), is also on Patreon offering tiers of $1, $3, and $5, with $3 being the minimum for premium access to "lost podcast episodes, special interviews, behind-the-scenes features and outtakes and more." CSPN also hosts nine affiliate links on their website, including Amazon, Blue Apron, and Audible, under the heading "Keep Our Podcasts Free." When listeners make a purchase, sometimes with an associated discount, CSPN receives a small fee.

The Patreon accounts yield only a few hundred dollars a month, mainly to help with covering production costs such as equipment and hosting. For example, the Black Astronauts' Patreon reads, "Hitting our goal of 500 dollars a month would allow me to purchase better equipment, pay our web hosting fees and allow me to focus on the podcast network full time. This would also allow me to expand into premium content."[54] WM4oA?, which has a Patreon goal of $1,500 a month, tells fans, "Nobody would be able to quit their day job, BUT we would be able to get an equipment upgrade, more designs for shirts, hoodies, socks, and tumblers, a much needed upgrade to the website, and a travel fund for live events like NegroCon, Essence Festival, Dragon Con, Podcon, and more. We want to bring 40 Acres to your city."[55]

These podcasts share heavily overlapping audiences, and their strategy seems to be to produce large amounts of content, covering a variety of topics, to super-serve that audience. The strong sense of social connection and collectivity has played a major role in supporting the Chitlin' Circuit podcasts up until this point. Audiences are loyal and donate for equipment or travel needs. Listeners have even donated to help hosts in personal financial crises. TBGWT has noted on more than one occasion that guests on the show report a significant benefit from such appearances, since TBGWT audience members then buy what they are promoting or attend their shows, and the support they receive significantly outstrips what they receive from appearances on larger more mainstream shows.

However, it remains to be seen how much revenue these strategies can generate. Though the scale of these podcasts allows them to avoid some of the pitfalls of the interstitial hustle, even after anywhere from five to ten years of podcasting, most are still working toward covering their costs. Their Patreon accounts range from 11 to 184 patrons. Barring greater growth, producing premium shows for such a small audience may not have much longevity. Further, though the subscription fees are relatively low, listeners will only support so many podcasts, as costs add up. Hence, the freemium model will only be viable for a finite number of podcasts. It also remains to be seen how the repeal of net neutrality might impact these content creators, as internet service providers become free to block and throttle content, most likely the that of sites that don't pay to avoid slowed download speeds.

Conclusion

Despite the mutation of colorblind discourses, the persistent harassment on Twitter, and the challenges of financial sustainability for content creators, the network remains vital. Even as Twitter becomes increasingly hostile, with alt-right harassers bolstered by Russian intelligence, it still serves as a crucial resource. The Black Twitter network has been cultivated over the course of nearly a decade now. Many of the connections made there are longstanding and have proliferated to other platforms and even moved offline. Users have well-honed strategies for negotiating and mitigating harassment and abuse, and their transplatform connections make many of the subnetwork "neighborhoods" of Black Twitter less reliant on the platform.

The podcast Chitlin' Circuit continues to flourish, though they haven't referred to themselves with this term for a while now. New podcasts and podcast networks, featuring many familiar and beloved individuals, continue to emerge from the network. As of this writing, Aaron Rand Freeman and Dacia Mitchell have founded their own podcast network—Unreasonable Fridays (UNF)—which features six podcasts. N'Jaila Rhee, former host of TWiB!'s sex-positive podcast *TWiB! after Dark* now hosts UNF's *Cuntcast*, and Shane Paul Neil, who worked with TWiB! in a variety of capacities, now hosts *SPN Writes*, which is a short podcast featuring Neil's writing and stories about his life. A range of familiar guests cycle through UNF's podcast episodes—from Rashanii from *Single Simulcast* reading Neil's poems to TBGWT's Karen and *Three Fifs* co-host Justin Jones. Imani Gandy is now the co-host of Rewire's legal podcast *Boom! Lawyered*, while Dara M Wilson, a longtime contributor to TWiB! and co-host of *TWiB!* Prime in its last couple of years, is now co-host and co-producer of the video series and podcast, *Next Big Thing with Courtney and Dara*. MTR's premium show *Molecules and Shit* is hosted by long-time network participants Coqui Negra and P Funk, whose participation via the channels for listener engagement created by TWiB! and the other Chitlin' Circuit podcasts often made them interlocators and contributors to the shows and the community.

Black users will continue to innovate and adapt, as they always have, as the cultural and technological landscape shifts. The people who comprise this networked public continue to expand, adapt, and craft their technological space. It's difficult to say what will come—with the resurgence of overt white supremacy, the hard-right-wing control of the government, and the possibility of even greater corporate control over web content. But, participants in this network will continue to reimagine the affordances of the technologies available to them so that they can keep each other as safe and sane as possible.

ACKNOWLEDGMENTS

First and foremost, I owe the existence of this book to Elon James White and Emily Epstein-White, who, when a random white lady from Wisconsin contacted them in 2012, responded by inviting her into their home studio. I am particularly indebted to White, with whom I spent many hours talking about TWiB!'s operations and who was not only open to, but excited about this project. I am also grateful to all the TWiB! personnel I met and spent time with—Aaron Rand Freeman, L. Joy William, Dacia Mitchell, Imani Gandy, Dara M Wilson, Bassey Ikpi, N'Jaila Rhee, Shane Paul Neil, Robyn Jordan, and Amber Flame—who were kind and generous from the first day. I also want to acknowledge Feminista Jones, David von Ebers, Anthea Butler, Fahnon Bennett, and Rachel Parenta, all of whom I became acquainted with over the course of my research and whose contributions I appreciate.

There are so many podcasts and internet friends that contributed to this project that I am sure I will leave someone out. I am grateful to Rod and Karen Morrow, whose generosity of spirit is unmatched. I appreciate all the people who took time to look at and respond to the drafts I sent—Phenom Blak (who even alerted me to a typo in a draft of the first article I published from this research); Nic and Reggie from *What's the Tea?*; Ashlee of Graveyard Shift Sisters; Amber P. of *Black, Sexy, Geeky, and Mental*; Blair L. M. Kelley (who provided insightful feedback); Feminista Jones; Darryl from *Straight Outta LoCash*; Aaron B. from The Black Astronauts; Kriss from Movie Trailer Reviews; *Whiskey, Wine, and Moonshine*; Kalief Adams and Shareef Jackson of *Spawn on Me*; Coqui Negra, and P Funk of MTR's *Molecules & Shit*; De Ana, JP Fairfield, Jamie Nesbit-Golden, Kia, and Roxie_Moxie of Nerdgasm Noire Network; and Patient C.

I'm grateful to André Brock and Catherine Knight Steele, two of my most generous and rigorous scholarly interlocutors without whom my thinking would be undeniably poorer. I am grateful to Miriam Sweeney, whose sharp insights always help me cut through to core issues, and Kishonna Gray, whose positivity and pragmatism always keep me on course. It is difficult to overstate the impact these four scholars, trailblazers in the study of race and technology, have had on my work and in simulating and pushing my thinking. They, along with Jenny Korn, Khadijah Costly White, and Lois Scheidt have been my metaphorical and literal backchannel, serving as sounding board, peer-reviewers, and support system.

I want to thank Mary L. Gray for pushing me to nuance my engagement with the concept of affordances, which strengthened my core argument tremendously. I'm also grateful to Bambi Haggins, who helped me think through the racial shifts that occurred after the 2016 presidential election and whom I can always count on to nerd-out about podcasts with me. I owe a debt to Yeidy Rivero. When I transitioned to my doctoral work, fresh from an MA in musicology, and knew nothing of media studies, she mentored and supported me. Without her, I doubt I would be where I am today. I'm also grateful to Jane Goodman, who shepherded me through my dissertation, and to Portia Maultsby, who taught me to understand the aesthetic nuances of Black American music in new and profound ways that shaped my thinking.

I am grateful to and humbled by the scholars who have supported me. I owe much to Lisa Nakamura and Anna Everett. I am thankful for their support and for their pioneering work on race and digital technologies. Without them, and their willingness to forge a path, this book and my career would likely not exist. I'm also grateful to Aswin Punathambekar, whose dedication to supporting scholars doing work on race and media invaluably enriches our profession and whose feedback strenghtened this project. Thank you to Lisha Nadkarni, who guided this project, and me, through the editorial process. Finally, the senior women scholars of the Society for Cinema and Media Studies Black Caucus have had a greater impact on me than they might know.

This book would not exist were it not for the support of the A.W. Mellon Postdoctoral Fellowship at the Institute for Research in the Humanities at the University of Wisconsin-Madison. The fellowship provided me with two years, without the tenure clock ticking in the background, to develop this project. Without this time, I doubt I would have taken the risk to turn what started as a chapter about Black podcasting into this monograph. While in Wisconsin, I also benefited from the input of Robert Glenn Howard and the other postdoctoral fellows—Brian Goldstein, Deagan Miller, Mary Murell, Amanda Rogers, and Jerome Tharaud. The input of the faculty in the Department of Communication Arts at UW-Madison also shaped this project considerably. I am grateful to Karma Chavéz, Jonathan Gray, Michelle Hilmes, Eric Hoyt, Derek Johnson, Jenell Johnson, Lori Kido Lopez, Sara McKinnon, and Jeremy Morris, who all in various ways aided my thinking and my work.

The revisions for the final draft of this book were done in large part in the co-working space of the Nexus Digital Research Coop, spearheaded by Jacque Wernimont. I am grateful to her for creating this space and introducing me to so many amazing women and femme scholars on the Arizona State University campus. I also want to thank Liz Grumbach and Nikki Stevens, whose friendship, feedback, and encouragement saw me through the last push of the revision process.

Finally, I want to thank my family and friends, without whose support I would be lost. I am grateful to my sister, Beth, and father, Bob, for their ongoing support and encouragement. I owe a profound debt to my mother, Barbara, and my grandparents, Melvin and Francis Fesser. Though I cannot share this with you, I know you would be proud. I am grateful to my longtime friend Bianca Mandity. I don't know what I'd do without you. Thank you to Kasia Chmielewska, Konrad Budziszewski, Jeremiah Donovan, Bryan-Mitchell Young, and Meghan Midgely, who saw me through graduate school and without my life would be poorer. Finally, thank you to my husband, Rob Kolhouse. You know what you did.

METHODOLOGICAL APPENDIX

I am frequently asked how I came to do this research. Often this question is grounded in historically informed concerns about white scholars exploiting communities of color and creating distorted representations of them through their research. The question also speaks to how the perspectives and knowledge of people of color about their own lives have often been obscured in favor of the work of white researchers and the structures of white supremacy that privileges white voices. In this appendix, I attempt of answer this oft-asked question by offering the narrative of how I came to this project and why I chose to do this work despite the very real problematics of my positionality. I then explore how I grappled with and attempted to mitigate the power dynamics inherent in being a white researcher writing about Black cultural practices.

My participation in this network did not come from my research agenda; rather, it was vice versa. I had joined Twitter in early 2010. At the time, US Twitter users numbered roughly 10 million, far fewer than the 67 million Americans using the platform by the end of 2016.[1] A *Mashable* report from the end of that year touted Twitter's growth by pointing to increased activity on the site: "Twenty-one percent of Twitter users now follow more than 100 people—that's up from 7% last year—and 16% now have more than 100 followers."[2] These numbers are laughably small by today's standards, when users routinely have follower counts in the tens of thousands. Twitter felt like a much smaller place. Or, as Elon James White tweeted in 2009, "Realizing my Twitter game is not up to par. Everybody knows everybody. I feel like I'm the new kid in H.S."[3]

Upon joining, I followed a handful of academics, journalists, and Hip-hop artists. I gradually started following people I saw retweeted often and people I thought were interesting. I found many people through the Follow Friday hashtag, #FF. At the time, despite being only 13 percent of the US population, Black Americans comprised 25 percent of US Twitter users.[4] The relative intimacy of Twitter in those days combined with a substantial Black presence and their conversational usage of the platform meant that following a few Black users quickly made a much larger Black network visible to me. Because of this, I found comedians and commentators like White and Baratunde Thurston and performers such as poet Bassey Ikpi. I followed other people who were not public figures in the traditional sense but who were known for their smart and funny commentary. That summer, I realized that many Twitter users were, like me, watching season 3 of *The Boondocks* while scrolling through their timelines, as evidenced by *Boondocks*-related phrases dominating the trending topics each Sunday night.

When journalists and bloggers started talking earnestly about "Black Twitter" in mid-2010 and referring to people I followed and conversations or jokes I remembered, it began to dawn on me that I might be on "Black Twitter." I was inspired by Thurston's 2010 South by Southwest (SXSW) talk, in which he described the hashtag #howblackareyou as a digital iteration of the Dozens, a game of ritualized insult that has long been part of the Black oral tradition. His astute observation was the starting point for my own thinking, exploring how in digital environments, where the corporeal signifiers of race are absent or obscured, communicative practices and cultural competencies functioned as important performances of identity.

It was through the serendipity of Twitter that I discovered that White and Ikpi co-hosted a podcast, *Blacking It Up!* (*BIU*). While writing my dissertation, I would take midday breaks Monday through Thursday to listen to *BIU* as it streamed live. I gradually began participating in the chatroom that accompanied these live streams, and as the community around the show grew, our interactions moved to the *BIU* discussion forums, where we exchanged Twitter handles and began connecting on social media. I learned of other podcasts through these interactions around *BIU*. Rod and Karen from *The Black Guy Who Tips* would participate in the chatroom, and Rod regularly snuck away from his office job to call into the show, starting each call by responding, "Chillin' chillin'" regardless of how White greeted him. Kriss of the *Insanity Check* podcast, which has since grown into the Movie Trailer Review Network, was a frequent guest and posted on the *BIU* forums. I learned of *Where's My 40 Acres?* from a thread on the forums about Black podcasts, of which there were only a handful at the time. Gradually, members of the *BIU* audience and chatroom participants began creating their own projects. In March 2011, De Ana, JP Fairfield, Jamie Nesbit-Golden, Kia, and Roxie_Moxie started their nerd culture podcast *Nerdgasm Noire*, which quickly developed into a podcast network and blog. Later that year the Nerdgasm Noire Network added *Operation Cubicle*, a podcast focused on life as an office worker, co-hosted by Fairfield, Shareef Jackson, and BCole, and *Character Select*, a video series focused on gaming hosted by Fairfield, Jackson, and 8BitAnimal. By 2012, a handful of independent Black podcasters were embedded in a robust digital and social media network that I believed warranted scholarly attention.

I include this narrative to make clear that I did not go out and look for some Black folks to study. Rather, independently of my research project at the time, I developed a set of relationships and connections with a network of Black Americans whom I saw to be early adopters and innovators. I watched them pioneer digital practices that are now conventional in the internet landscape—such as live-tweeting television and anticipating the podcast boom by at least two years. At the same time, they were all but invisible to most digital media scholars. This project arose out of my desire to make visible what I believe to be important and innovative digital practices.

However, while I believe my intentions were in the right place, this does not mean my research is unproblematic. Good intentions are all but useless in the face of white supremacy and do very little to undermine the way racism structures our world. More than good intentions, I realized that I needed rigorous ethical standards for myself and my work. I developed two core and interrelated principles that guided my approach—minimize harm and be accountable.

BAD CHOICES AND SLIGHTLY LESS BAD CHOICES

When operating within systems of dominance, such as our current heteronormative white supremacist patriarchy, we often have only bad choices and somewhat less bad choices. By taking on this project, I reproduce the historic power dynamics of white scholars writing about people of color rather than letting them speak for themselves, something I don't want to do. But, choosing not to do this project would perpetuate the erasure of Black Americans in inquiries about digital media and reify the notion that race and the cultures and practices racialized people should be of interest only to people of color—also something I don't want to do.

When I began this project in the fall of 2012, there were few scholars writing about Black Americans and digital media. Seven years later, many young scholars of color are emerging from graduate programs doing important work, and senior scholars of color from a variety of disciplines have turned their attention to digital media. Under the circumstances, I might make a different decision today. But at the time I undertook this project few people were exploring the practices of Black digital networks. Although they did receive some attention in the scholarly writings of Anna Everett, André Brock, and Adam Banks, the public intellectual work of Kimberly Ellis and Tara Conley, and the commentary of public figures such as Thurston, White, and others, no scholarship or analysis was being produced about Black podcasts. So I decided that the "less bad" choice was for me to move forward with the research. I sincerely believed it was the only way this work would be done. I quickly realized this choice, between harmful and less harmful, would come to characterize every element of my work.

Another prominent double bind I encountered involved the politics of citation and voice. I sought to foreground and prioritize the voices of the people I was writing about. I also wanted to give proper credit to people for their ideas and creativity. To do this, I made the choice to cite heavily, avoiding summaries and paraphrasing as much as I could, given the limitations of space. Additionally, in an effort to preserve people's original voices, whenever possible, I quoted from sources that have the most permanence and are the most widely available. I privileged podcasts and Twitter as sources of quotations because, unlike public chatrooms, personal communications, or interviews, they are the most easily retrievable—thereby both ensuring my accuracy and allowing readers access to the context and the larger discussion from which the quotes were drawn.

There is growing debate around the ethics of citing digital media produced by marginalized groups, particularly social media. While citation and quotation seem positive, they also have the potential for harm. First, there is a concern with exploitation. Many social media users and public figures from marginalized groups have critiqued the notion that it is appropriate to use their words and ideas, even with proper attribution, just because they are publicly visible. Bound up in this are issues of ownership, agency, and control of intellectual production, as well as a fundamental question about the point at which such quotation verges into the territory of exploitation and intellectual colonialism. (Think of how many "This is what Twitter is talking about" articles you've read online that are composed of an introductory blurb and a long series of tweets.) And there is the very real and concrete harm that can come from citation. Many marginalized people, particularly Black women, are relentlessly harassed and targeted on social media platforms. For them, a well-meaning attempt to preserve their voice and give proper attribution to their ideas might functionally translate into a surge in abuse.

To mitigate this, I attempted to limit quotations as much as possible to podcasts and to the social media of people who are public figures or micro-celebrities. Despite the social, collective, and participatory character of the podcasts discussed here, podcasts are ultimately understood by their creators to be mass media. The notion of circulation and public visibility is inherent in this model. When quoting and citing social media, I confined myself to public figures and micro-celebrities as much as possible, assuming that my work would not substantially increase their visibility and therefore not expose them to increased hostility. While I believe this research is important, I am also realistic enough to know that Imani Gandy's more than 136,000 Twitter followers dwarfs the number of people who will see a quotation from her Twitter timeline in this book. If someone's tweets are published in the *Washington Post* or put on Buzzfeed listicles, my work will probably do little to expose them to further scrutiny.

THE COMPLEXITIES OF ACCOUNTABILITY

Because of the tensions and pitfalls above, I developed a set of standards for myself, which would also allow me to be accountable to the people I write about. I began simply by requesting permission. Hence, I contacted White in the fall of 2012 to ask if he and the other members of TWiB! would be comfortable with my doing research focused on them. I visited TWIB!'s Brooklyn studio (that is, White and Emily Epstein-White's apartment), in the spring of 2013, and then I attended both Netroots Nation meetings in 2013–2016 and the 2019 Democratic National Convention with them, serving as an extra pair of hands where

I could. This gave me insight into TWiB!'s production practices. But, perhaps more importantly, it gave TWiB! personnel an opportunity to get to know me in a way that helped build trust. This, along with my existing relationships with the TWiB! community of listeners, many of whom were also content creators in their own right, helped create a good working relationship.

I have committed to a set of ethical standards, some of which are norms in academia and some that exceed them, when writing about social media. As per the human subjects regulations, I excluded any social media that was not publicly available. This includes closed Facebook groups, group chats I was included in, and Twitter accounts that are private. I mention such closed spaces only to the extent they are discussed in other publicly available media. For example, I refer to the existence of The Black Guy Who Tips and TWiB!'s closed Facebook communities and to statements made about them on the podcasts or via public Twitter accounts. But beyond this, I do not include or refer to any posts or interactions that took place there. I had joined both communities as part of my own personal fandom and social media use, and I have refrained from joining others until this project is completed to avoid the appearance that I am systematically joining groups as part of my research.

In addition to such restrictions, I have created a set of standards for how I treat publicly available social media posts, asking permission before quoting or citing a post by anyone who is not a public figure. Traditionally academics have considered anything publicly available online as "published." Therefore, no permissions are required to cite this material. But while this is an accepted standard among researchers, it is not universally agreed upon by social media users, many of whom feel that citing their tweets is equivalent to eavesdropping on a personal conversation or even intellectual property theft. This has emerged as an ongoing debate with little consensus.

Because social media blurs the lines between public and private, producer and audience, and mass and interpersonal communication, users have complicated and often contradictory beliefs about how their social media timelines should be viewed and potentially used by researchers.[5] Twitter is a particular challenge because it so commonly functions as a one-to-many style of communication. Politicians and celebrities rarely hold official press conferences anymore. They instead make statements via social media, particularly Twitter. Many Twitter users see their tweets as contributions to a larger public discourse and often describe them in terms of intellectual labor and/or property. At the same time, Twitter is *social* media and retains some of the expectations of social interaction. Users see many of their conversations and interactions as expressions of sociality, not forms of mass communication, and consequently, quoting or referencing these tweets is viewed as similar to quoting a conversation that was overheard. Users in the same networks, at times even the same users, interpret Twitter in these contradictory ways. Thus, while my inclination has been to adopt the standards of the network I am writing about, this has been difficult at best.

Unlike many social media platforms, Twitter's terms of service does not grant the platform copyright of users' content. According to Twitter, "You retain your rights to any Content you submit, post or display on or through the Services. What's yours is yours."[6] Traditionally, the rights and regulations of intellectual property have been governed by a set of federal laws that outline who can use ideas, how, and under what circumstances. Section 107 of the Copyright Act allows for unlicensed use of copyrighted material for commentary and criticism, parody, news and reporting, teaching, scholarship, and research.[7] Academics are covered under several of these categories, making direct citation permissible with proper attribution.

However, although that is the legal standard, in the age of massive media conglomerates the de facto standard for fair use has depended on which entities have the resources for legal action. For example, academics are routinely forced to pay licensing fees to cite song lyrics in their work. Under fair use, quotation of song lyrics should be permissible as commentary, criticism, or scholarship. However, since the music industry began aggressively pursuing peer-to-peer file-sharing and other intellectual property issues in the early 2000s, fair use has come to seem null and void when it comes to materials owned by this industry. Publishers of academic books and journals simply can't afford to be embroiled in a legal conflict with large media corporations and will instead require that authors get permission for quotations. Obtaining this permission generally involves the author paying a licensing fee that can be several hundred dollars *per line* of lyrics. This phenomenon is not confined to academia. Stephen Colbert did several segments on

The Colbert Report in which he joked about his inability to use footage of NFL games or even the trademarked phrase "Super Bowl" because Comedy Central's parent company, Viacom, was unwilling to take the legal risk. Thus, while there are legal standards, ultimately copyright and usage are matters of power, not legality, and I try to approach them as such in my work.

Some Twitter users express attitudes about intellectual property and quotation that are in line with fair use, merely wanting their ideas attributed to them. However, some users express a belief that on the surface is more in line with the licensing model embraced by the music industry or the NFL and feel that they should be compensated when their words are used regardless of the context. In part this is grounded in the ways that marginalized people, particularly Black women, are systematically denied the opportunity to benefit from their intellectual contributions. Outlets often seem eager to quote marginalized people's ideas while rarely giving them opportunities to write professionally. Thus, this licensing-style approach to quotation seems to grow out of this inequality. Often, these users are criticized and derided for claiming intellectual property rights that far exceed those granted by law or norm. But, given that the enforcement of intellectual property rights has become largely about power, rather than legal standing, demanding compensation for quotation can be understood not only as an attempt to rectify an economic imbalance, but also as an attempt to reclaim power. Users from marginalized groups have long had little say in how they were written about and how their ideas were used. Demands for remuneration when they are quoted are both an amelioration of inequitable material circumstances and an assertion of agency.

All of this makes Twitter difficult ethical terrain for a researcher trying to produce scholarship while minimizing the harm inherent to systems of privilege and oppression. Often, the ethnographic answer is to use the standards of the community about which one is writing to guide ethical choices. Here, however, there is not one unified normative standard. Consequently, I created guidelines that I believe negotiate these tensions and uncertainties as best as possible. These are not universal, and each research project requires the examination of the particularities of the context.

First, as mentioned above, I gave preference to public figures and micro-celebrities when choosing quotations. This is not only because their existing visibility is usually greater than what my work would generate, but also because doing so helped me to navigate the otherwise unclear boundary between mass and interpersonal communication. A Twitter user with fifty thousand followers understands that his or her statements might receive scrutiny and circulate beyond the intended audience. A mother of a Black teenager expressing her distress and feelings of helplessness to her two hundred followers after the acquittal of George Zimmerman likely does not think about her words being quoted in an academic research project. Thus, I tried to avoid statements that were likely made with the intention that only the user's immediate network would see them. However, sometimes tweets were so relevant to my argument that I asked permission to quote them. Second, I also asked permission to quote publicly available social media produced by micro-celebrities. People often just want to know if someone is writing about them and appreciate being shown the respect of being contacted prior to publication. However, given the lack of consensus about the issue of quotation, it is ethically appropriate to actively seek explicit permission to quote anyone, and I did so.

Third, I shared drafts pre-publication, often when asking permission to quote someone. This allowed these individuals to see the larger context in which their words were being used. I also sent drafts to all the content creators about whom I was writing, usually concurrently with the peer review process—the principle being that when something is "out for review" by my academic colleagues, it is also "out for review" by the people I have written about. Hence, I provided them with drafts, solicited feedback, and indicated that I was willing to make changes before publication.

But here, too, there is a double-bind. Asking the people I was writing about to read drafts was asking for their time and energy. (I always feel a little like I'm popping up in people's inboxes to give them homework.) While I wish I had the personal or institutional resources to pay each person an honorarium, like most academics, I don't. So, here again, I tried to choose the least-bad options. Hence, when I sent the drafts to various individuals, I made their contributions as easy as possible for them to access by giving page numbers or even cutting and pasting relevant paragraphs directly into the email. I also made it clear that I had no expectation that recipients read the portions in question; instead, I indicated that I wanted to give them the opportunity to do so and that I was open to their input. Some people read what I sent; some didn't. But, it was incumbent on me to give them the choice.

Of course, the reality of research is that it is never as tidy as one plans, and though I feel ethically obligated to contact the people I write about and quote, that can prove challenging at times. First, some people are difficult to find contact information for. This is likely deliberate, given the hostility and harassment Black users face online. For some users, even those with large follower counts, I was unable to find an email address, which is my preferred method of contact. If there is no email address, I attempt to use other methods to contact them – Twitter direct messages, Facebook messages, contact forms on their websites. Even still, I was unable to contact some people.

Second, even when there was a way to contact them, not everyone responds. Many podcasters and micro-celebrities respond. But, if they do not, I have notified them and provided them with an opportunity to do so. For everyday users, I generally only send a few sentences with a link to what I want to quote and an offer to provide more information. In the case of such users, who do not have the highly visible public profile of commentators, professional writers, content creators, activists, or media professionals, I do not quote them without explicit permission.[8] This led me to omit some examples from this book because I was unable to contact the person or did not get a response. While this is disappointing, it is preferable to exposing a marginalized person to potential harm (e.g., possible harassment that they might suffer as a result of the additional visibility) or removing their agency to determine how their words and social interactions are used.

However, in my experience, most people merely want the courtesy of being asked. Several highly visible Twitter users thanked me for asking, explaining that they often run across their own words used in a variety of contexts without their knowledge. I have come to believe that asking is a recognition of humanity; it demonstrates that I view the people I write about as people and not merely research objects. To this point, I have never had anyone say no. At most, I've been asked for minor revisions that, honestly, strengthened the work.

Had anyone disputed my description or interpretation of an event, I would have adjusted the manuscript accordingly. If they provided new information that changed my understanding, I would have revised to reflect this. If, after considering views that differed from mine, I still stood by what I wrote, I would have integrated them into the text, indicating that they disagree with my views, while also explaining the rationale behind them. This would have allowed my analysis and that of others to exist side by side, rather requiring me to make changes that I believed compromised my analysis or substituting my voice for theirs. Although this was ultimately never an issue, I made this decision in advance and had a plan in place that allowed me to be accountable should the need arise.

While I applied these guidelines rigorously with respect to the network itself, I did not always follow them with those outside the network. There were two reasons for this. First, I put these procedures in place to build trust and to mitigate the power dynamics of being a white researcher writing about Black cultures and networks. I did not feel the same need to do this with all users. For example, I did not contact, ask permission, or provide drafts to users on Twitter who, for example, were harassing the people about whom I was writing. Given that there is not a history of white academics writing in problematic and exploitative ways about white people who use Twitter to chastise Black people for their political opinions, I did not feel the need for such measures.

Second, I eschew false equivalencies that fail to acknowledge power structures and thereby reinforce inequalities. Often US culture operationalizes equity as identical treatment. This is at the core of colorblindness, where the notion that everyone is to be treated the same obscures and ultimately reinforces an uneven playing field. The set of standards I created for myself were designed to minimize harm and prevent me from repeating historical patterns of misrepresentation and exploitation. Homophobes such as Reverend Manning, white progressives who refuse to divest from their whiteness, and white users who harass people of color on Twitter did not warrant such consideration; in fact, to give them to such people would merely reinforce hierarchies I was seeking to undermine through this project. These individuals have forwarded positions that have dominance in US culture, and I refused to treat their statements as equivalent to the voices and perspectives of marginalized people speaking out for social justice. Nor did I send them drafts, solicit feedback, or integrate their differing interpretations into this book where they could exist alongside those of the people that are its focus. Their perspectives already permeate our culture and did not need me to make space for them here.

Finally, I attempted to be guided by my humanity and the recognition of the humanity of others. In particular, I was careful about what I included and excluded when discussing the deaths of Black Americans during encounters with the police. When recounting the ways that digital and social media were used in relationship to these issues, I attempted to be respectful about both the topic and how and what I cited. Thus, for example, while some Ferguson residents posted to Twitter and Instagram in the immediate aftermath of Brown's death, including photos of his body, I noted such posts in my discussion, but out of respect I did not cite the specific social media posts.

I strive to always make the "least bad" of the bad choices offered me by the oppressive systems we all must navigate. I certainly do not claim to have answers or perfect solutions. My research methods are ever evolving, a constant process of learning and changing. In large part, I owe my ability to analyze and address these challenges to my training in ethnographic methods. Ethnographers have long been forced to grapple with complicated and uneven power dynamics in their research. Researchers looking to navigate the complicated terrain of social media research that engages with user content would be well served to familiarize themselves with ethnographic approaches to digital media.

NOTES

INTRODUCTION

1 Tef Poe (@TefPoe), Twitter post, August 9, 2014 (7:35 p.m.), https://twitter.com/TefPoe/status/498251204389269505/photo/1?ref_src=twsrc^tfw.

2 The Black Guy Who Tips, "Ep. 760 #IGotTheTalk," *The Black Guy Who Tips*, Podcast Audio, August 10, 2014. http://theblackguywhotips.podOmatic.com/rss2.xml.

3 "We ARE ALL #MikeBrown, We ARE ALL #Ferguson," *Straight Outta LoCash*, Podcast Audio, August 14, 2014. https://straightolc.podbean.com/feed.xml.

4 This Week in Blackness, "#FergusonDispatch: Gassed (Snippet)," YouTube, Online Video Clip, August 19, 2014, https://www.youtube.com/watch?v=DA4IT-rGNDg; "The Effects of Tear Gas," *Melissa Harris-Perry Show*, August 24, 2014, http://www.msnbc.com/melissa-harris-perry/watch/the-effects-of-tear-gas-321564227633.

5 I make a distinction here between "transmedia" and "transplatform." I use "media" to refer to sound, text, and image in line with the concept of transmedia storytelling as worldbuilding and narrative spanning across multiple media. The term "transplatform" foregrounds technological elements of the discussion—materiality, interface, devices, and so on. I am not using the term "platform" in the strict computational sense, as the underlying programmable infrastructure that allows additional computing to be done. I instead employ the term as it has commonly come to be used—to refer to a range of digital services. This common usage is a structural metaphor that melds the computational definition of platform with nontechnological meanings that include the architectural meaning—"raised level surface on which people or things can stand, usually a discrete structure intended for a particular activity or operation"—and the figurative meaning—"the ground, foundation, or basis of an action, event, calculation, condition, etc." It is important to remember, as Tarleton Gillespie highlights, that this structural metaphor is not neutral, but does discursive work that constructs platforms as "open, neutral, egalitarian and progressive support for activity." (Tarleton Gillespie, "The Politics of 'Platforms,'" *New Media and Society* 12, no. 3 [2010]: 347–63.)

6 Henry Jenkins, *Convergence Culture: Where Old and New Media Collide* (New York: New York University Press, 2006).

7 Matthew Freeman and Renira Rampazzo Gamabarato, *The Routledge Companion to Transmedia Studies* (New York: Routledge, 2019).

8 Aymar Jean Christian, *Open TV: Innovation beyond Hollywood and the Rise of Web Television* (New York: New York University Press, 2018); Elizabeth Ellcessor,

"Tweet @Feliciaday: Online Social Media, Convergence, and Subcultural Stardom," *Cinema Journal* 51, no. 2 (2012): 46–66; Lori Kido Lopez, *Asian American Media Activism: Fighting for Cultural Citizenship* (New York: New York University Press, 2016); Nancy K. Baym, *Playing to the Crowd: Musicians, Audiences, and the Intimate Work of Connection* (New York: New York University Press, 2018).

9 Stuart Cunningham and David Craig, *Social Media Entertainment: The New Intersection of Hollywood and Silicon Valley* (New York: New York University Press, 2019), 5.

10 André Jansson and Karin Fast, "Transmedia Identities: From Fan Cultures to Liquid Lives," in *The Routledge Companion to Transmedia Studies*, ed. Matthew Freeman and Renira Rampazzo Gamabarato,340–49 (New York: Routledge, 2019), 304.

11 Jillian M. Báez, "Spreadable Citizenship: Undocumented Youth Activists and Social Media," in *The Routledge Companion to Latina/O Media*, ed. Maria Elena Cepeda and Dolores Inés Casillas (New York: Routledge, 2016).

12 Manuel Castells, "A Network Theory of Power," *International Journal of Communications* 5 (2011): 776.

13 André Brock, Jr."Beyond the Pale: The Blackbird Web Browser's Critical Reception," *New Media and Society* 13, no. 7 (2011): 1085–1103.

14 Miriam E. Sweeney, "The Ms. Dewey 'Experience': Technoculture, Gender, and Race," in *Digital Sociologies*, ed. Jessie Daniels, Karen Gregory, and Tressie McMillan Cottom (Chicago: Polity Press, 2017), 403.

15 Miriam E. Sweeney, "The Intersectional Interface," in *The Intersectional Internet*, ed. Safiya Umoja Noble and Brendesha M. Tynes (New York: Peter Lang, 2016), 215.

16 Peter Nagy and Gina Neff, "Imagined Affordances: Reconstructing a Keyword for Communication Theory," *Social Media + Society* 1, no. 2 (2015): 5.

17 Lori Kendall coined the term "deep data" during the Q&A at the "'Small Data' in a 'Big Data' World" panel at the 2013 International Congress of Qualitative Inquiry (May 17). Objecting to the use of the term "small data" as the qualitative counterpart to "big data," Kendall instead suggested using the descriptor "deep." She argued, "There is nothing small about ethnographic data." Tricia Wang has used the term "thick data" to refer similarly to robust but nonquantitative data. See Wang, "Why Big Data Needs Thick Data," *Ethnography Matters*, January 20, 2016, https://medium.com/ethnography-matters/why-big-data-needs-thick-data-b4b3e75e3d7.

18 Anna Everett, *Digital Diaspora: A Race for Cyberspace* (Albany: State University of New York Press, 2009), 1–20.

19 David Harvey, *A Brief History of Neoliberalism* (New York: Oxford University Press, 2005): 2.

20 Individualism, including Lockean individualism, which conceptualizes individual freedom as the freedom of "individuals to pursue profit in a marketplace," has long been a strain of thought in US culture. But it was traditionally tempered by other discourses, including patriotism, civic republicanism, the labor movement,

and other conceptualizations of individualism. See Thomas Streeter, *The Net Effect: Romanticism, Capitalism, and the Internet* (New York: New York University Press, 2011), 72.

21 Charles Gallagher, "Color-Blind Privilege: The Social and Political Functions of Erasing the Color Line in Post-Race America," *Race, Gender, and Class* 10, no. 4 (2003) 1–17.

22 Catherine Squires et al., "What Is This 'Post-' in Postracial, Postfeminist . . . (Fill in the Blank)?," *Journal of Communication Inquiry* 34, no. 3 (2010): 167; see also David Goldberg, *The Threat of Race: Reflections on Racial Neoliberalism* (Malden, MA: Wiley-Blackwell, 2009), 334–35; Nisha Kapoor, "The Advancement of Racial Neoliberalism in Britain," *Ethnic and Racial Studies* 36, no. 6 (2013): 1034.

23 Herman Gray, *Cultural Moves: African Americans and the Politics of Representation* (Berkeley: University of California Press, 2005), 142–44.

24 Gallagher, "Color-Blind Privilege, 9."

25 Michael Omi and Howard Winant, *Racial Formations in the United States*, 3rd ed. (New York: Routledge, 2014), 129; emphasis in the original.

26 Richard Delgado and Jean Stefancic, *Critical Race Theory: An Introduction* (New York: New York University Press, 2001), 35–36.

27 Henry Giroux, "Spectacles of Race and Pedagogies of Denial: Anti-Black Racist Pedagogy under the Reign of Neoliberalism," *Communication Education* 52, no. 3/4 (2003): 200.

28 Harvey, *A Brief History of Neoliberalism*, 23.

29 Harvey, *A Brief History of Neoliberalism*, 41.

30 Eduardo Bonilla-Silva, *Racism without Racists: Color-Blind Racism and the Persistence of Racial Inequality in America*, 5th ed. (Lanham, MD: Rowman and Littlefield, 2018), 26–28; Delgado and Stefancic, *Critical Race Theory*, 23–24.

31 Bonilla-Silva, *Racism without Racists*, 62–63.

32 Kent Ono, "Postracism: A Theory of the 'Post' as Political Strategy," *Journal of Communication Inquiry* 34, no. 4 (2010): 227–33.

33 Cathy J. Cohen, *Democracy Remixed: Black Youth and the Future of American Politics* (New York: Oxford University Press, 2010), 46.

34 Cohen, *Democracy Remixed*, 46.

35 Michael I. Norton and Samuel R. Sommers, "Whites See Racism as a Zero-Sum Game That They Are Now Losing," *Perspectives on Psychological Science* 6, no. 3 (2011): 215–18.

36 I use the term "Hispanic" here because that is the designation used by both the US Census and the Pew Research Center. However, it is important to note that this term is problematic. It was created by the US government in the 1970s as a way to capture the number of people in the country who trace their roots to Spanish-speaking countries. Research from the Pew Research Center indicates that a slight majority of people in this artificial category identify most often by their family's country of origin, with only 24 percent preferring a panethnic label. I place the term "Hispanic" in quotation marks to indicate its contested nature.

Paul Taylor, Mark Hugo Lopez, Jessica Martínez, and Gabriel Velasco,"When Labels Don't Fit: Hispanics and Their Views of Identity," Pew Research Center, April 3, 2012, www.pewhispanic.org.

37 Jens Manuel Krogstad, "One-in-Four Native Americans and Alaska Natives Are Living in Poverty," Pew Research Center, June 13, 2014, www.pewresearch.org; National Congress of American Indians, "Education," accessed December 9, 2018, www.ncai.org.

38 "Demographic Trends and Economic Well-Being," Pew Research Center, June 27, 2016, accessed December 9, 2018, www.pewsocialtrends.org.

39 "Unemployment on Indian Reservations at 50 Percent: The Urgent Need to Create Jobs in Indian Country," Hearing before the Committee on Indian Affairs, United States Senate, Transcript, January 28, 2010. https://www.indian.senate.gov. https://www.indian.senate.gov/sites/default/files/upload/files/January2820102.pdf.

40 John Gramlich, "The Gap between the Number of Black and Whites in Prison Is Shrinking," Pew Research Center, January 12, 2018, accessed December 9, 2018, www.pewresearch.org.

41 Gustavo López, Neil G. Ruiz, and Eileen Patten, "Key Facts about Asian Americans, a Diverse and Growing Population," Pew Research Center, September 8, 2017, www.pewresearch.org.

42 Cohen, *Democracy Remixed*, 46.

43 Matt Ford and Adam Chandler, "'Hate Crime': A Mass Killing at a Historic Church." *The Atlantic*, June 19, 2015. www.theatlantic.com.

44 Manoucheka Celeste, *Race, Gender, and Citizenship in the African Diaspora: Traveling Blackness* (New York: Routledge, 2016), 14.

45 Lopez, *Asian American Media Activism*, 5.

46 Chris Atton, "Reshaping Social Movement Media for a New Millennium," *Social Movement Studies* 2, no. 1 (2003); Yochai Benkler, *The Wealth of Networks: How Social Production Transforms Markets and Freedom* (New Haven, CT: Yale University Press, 2006); Jenkins, *Convergence Culture*; Sonia Livingstone, "What Is Media Literacy?," *Intermedia* 32, no. 3 (2004): 18–20.

47 Jenkins, *Convergence Culture*.

48 Henry Jenkins, Sam Ford, and Joshua Green, *Spreadable Media: Creating Value and Meaning in a Networked Culture* (New York: New York University Press, 2013).

49 André Brock, Jr. "'Who Do You Think You Are?!': Race, Representation, and Cultural Rhetorics in Online Spaces," *POROI [Project on Rhetoric of Inquiry]* 6, no. 1 (2009): 346.

50 Wendy Chun, *Programmed Visions: Software and Memory* (Cambridge, MA: MIT Press, 2011), 8–10.

51 Lisa Nakamura, *Digitizing Race: Visual Cultures of the Internet* (Minneapolis: University of Minnesota Press, 2008), 2–3.

52 Streeter, *The Net Effect*; Richard Barbrook and Andy Cameron, "The Californian Ideology," *The HRC Archive*, accessed December 9, 2018, www.imaginaryfutures.net.

53 Gabriella E. Coleman, *Coding Freedom: The Ethics and Aesthetics of Hacking* (Princeton, NJ: Princeton University Press, 2013), 72–73.

54 Alice Marwick, *Status Update: Celebrity, Publicity, and Branding in the Social Media Age* (New Haven, CT: Yale University Press, 2013), 50–51.

55 Marwick, *Status Update*, 5.

56 Lee Rainie and Barry Wellman, *Networked: The New Social Operating System* (Cambridge, MA: MIT Press, 2012).

57 Marwick, *Status Update*, 5–7, 17.

58 W. Lance Bennett and Alexandra Segerberg, "The Logic of Connection Action: Digital Media and the Personalization of Contentious Politics," *Information, Communication, and Society* 15, no. 5 (2012): 739–40.

59 Sherry Turkle, "Who Am We?" Wired. Janurary 1, 1996. www.wired.com; see also N. Katherine Hayles, *How We Became Posthuman* (Chicago: University of Chicago Press, 1999), 634–48; Sherry Turkle, "Cyberspace and Identity," *Contemporary Sociology* 28 (1999): 643–48.

60 Kalí Tal, "The Unbearable Whiteness of Being: African American Critical Theory and Cyberculture," *Wired*, October 1996.

61 Lisa Nakamura, "Race in/for Cyberspace: Identity Tourism and Racial Passing on the Internet," in *Reading Digital Culture*, ed. David Trend (Malden, MA: Blackwell, 2001), 228.

62 Nakamura, "Race in/for Cyberspace," 227–30.

63 Lopez, *Asian American Media Activism*, 149–56.

64 Ralina L. Joseph, *Postracial Resistance: Black Women, Media, and the Uses of Strategic Ambiguity* (New York: New York University Press, 2018), 2–15; emphasis in original.

65 Lopez, *Asian American Media Activism*, 19.

66 Jennifer Stoever, *The Sonic Color Line: Race and the Cultural Politics of Listening* (New York: New York University Press, 2016), 19.

67 Stoever, *The Sonic Color Line*, 231–34; emphasis in original.

68 Kishonna L. Gray, *Race, Gender, and Deviance in Xbox Live: Theoretical Perspectives from the Virtual Margins* (New York: Routledge, 2014).

69 Marisa Parham, "Sample, Signal, Strobe," lecture, *Digital Blackness in the Archive: A Documenting the Now Symposium*, Ferguson/St. Louis, MO: DocNow, December 11, 2017. https://www.youtube.com/watch?v=taCxTq5pdeY.

70 Paul Gilroy, *The Black Atlantic: Modernity and Double Consciousness* (Cambridge, MA: Harvard University Press, 1993); Tal, "The Unbearable Whiteness of Being."

71 Tal, "The Unbearable Whiteness of Being."

72 Catherine Knight Steele, "Black Bloggers and Their Varied Publics: The Everyday Politics of Black Discourse Online" *Television and New Media* 19, no. 2 (2018): 113.

73 Mark Dueze, "Participation, Remediation, Bricolage: Considering Principle Components of Digital Culture," *Information Society* 22, no. 2 (2006): 63–75.

74 Portia Maultsby, "Africanisms in African-American Music," in *Africanisms in American Culture*, ed. Joseph Holloway, 156–76 (Bloomington: Indiana University Press, 2005).

75 Henry Louis Gates Jr., *Signifying Monkey: A Theory of African-American Literary Criticism* (New York: Oxford University Press, 1988), xxx; Veit Erlmann, "Communities of Style: Musical Figures of Black Diasporic Identity," in *The African Diaspora: A Musical Perspective*, ed. Ingrid Monson, 92–109 (New York: Routledge, 2003).

76 Limor Shifman, *Memes in Digital Culture* (Cambridge, MA: MIT Press, 2013); Jenkins, *Convergence Culture*.

77 Parham, "Sample, Signal, Strobe."

78 I had initially defined the parameters of the study as including only noncommercial podcasts. But several of the podcasts I write about here have begun monetizing through subscriptions and donations, rendering the label inaccurate.

79 The Loud Speaker Network (LSN) was created by Reggie Osse, aka Combat Jack, and his partner, Chris Morrow, in 2013, after a few years of Osse hosting his online radio show, *The Combat Jack Show*, for PNC Radio. They started LSN with $500 and built it into a fully independent, profitable venture, commanding advertising fees in the five figures. Despite this, I have opted to exclude it from this project, because although in many ways LSN fits the parameters I have outlined, Osse and Morrow's connections to and understanding of media industries make LSN qualitatively different from the Chitlin' Circuit podcasts. Prior to LSN, Osse was an entertainment lawyer who worked with top Hip-hop artists and a former manager for *Source Magazine*; Morrow had experience in radio and had ghost written for celebrities such as Russell Simmons. Consequently, both men had access to significant social and cultural capital that facilitated their generation of financial capital. In this way, LSN stands apart from the other podcasts discussed here.

80 Meredith Clark, "To Tweet Our Own Cause: A Mixed-Method Study of the Online Phenomenon 'Black Twitter.'" (PhD diss., University of North Carolina-Chapel Hill, 2014).

81 André Brock, Jr. "From the Blackhand Side: Twitter as a Cultural Conversation," *Journal of Broadcasting and Electronic Media* 56, no. 4 (2012): 529–49; Clark, "To Tweet Our Own Cause"; Sarah Florini, "Tweets, Tweeps, and Signifyin': Communication and Cultural Performance on 'Black Twitter,'" *Television and New Media* 15, no. 3 (2014): 223–37.

82 "The Podcast Consumer 2012," Edison Research, accessed March 1, 2015. www.edisonresearch.com.

83 Maeve Duggan, Nicole B. Ellison, Cliff Lampe, Amanda Lenhart, and Mary Madden, "Demographics of Key Social Networking Platforms," Pew Research: Internet and Technology, January 9, 2015, accessed June 10, 2015, www.pewinternet.org.

84 Aaron Smith, "African Americans and Technology: A Demographic Portrait," Pew Internet and American Life Project, accessed August 30, 2015. www.pewinternet.org.

85 John Hartley, *Creative Industries* (London: Blackwell, 2005).

86 Jean Burgess and Joshua Green, *Youtube: Online Video and Participatory Culture* (Cambridge, MA: Polity, 2009), 58; Lopez, *Asian American Media Activism*, 157–63.

87 Baym, *Playing to the Crowd*; Christian, *Open TV*; Ellcessor, "Tweet @Feliciaday"; Lopez, *Asian American Media Activism*.

88 Clemencia Rodríguez, *Fissures in the Mediascape: An International Study of Citizens' Media* (Cresskill, NJ: Hampton Press, 2001), 20.

89 Cunningham and Craig, *Social Media Entertainment*, 5–6.

90 Brooke Erin Duffy, *(Not) Getting Paid to Do What You Love: Gender, Social Media, and Aspirational Work* (New Haven, CT: Yale University Press, 2017); Kathleen Kuehn and Thomas F. Corrigan, "Hope Labor: The Role of Employment Prospects in Online Social Production," *Political Economy of Communication* 1, no. 1 (2013): 9–25; Gina Neff, *Venture Labor: Work and the Burden of Risk in Innovative Industries* (Cambridge, MA: MIT Press, 2012).

91 Lopez, *Asian American Media Activism*, 149.

92 Cunningham and Craig, *Social Media Entertainment*, 266–67.

93 Earl Ofari Hutchinson, *Blacks and Reds: Race and Class Conflict 1919–1990* (East Lansing: Michigan State University, 1995); Ann Garland Mahler, *From the Tricontinental to the Global South: Race, Radicalism, and Transnational Solidarity* (Durham, NC: Duke University Press, 2018); Timothy Tyson, *Radio Free Dixie: Robert F. Williams and the Roots of Black Power* (Chapel Hill: University of North Carolina Press, 1999); Robeson Taj Frazier, *The East Is Black: Cold War China in the Black Radical Imagination* (Durham, NC: Duke University Press, 2015).

94 Kristian Davis Bailey, "Black-Palestinian Solidarity in the Ferguson-Gaza Era," *American Quarterly* 67, no. 4 (2015): 1017–26.

95 Alicia Garza, "A Herstory of the #BlackLivesMatter Movement by Alicia Garza," *Feminist Wire*, accessed October 7, 2017, www.thefeministwire.com; President Lecture Series, Ted Constant Convocation Center, Old Dominion University, February 2, 2016.

96 There is conflict over the role of "Black Lives Matter" in Ferguson. Garza has said that she, Cullors, and Tometi used their resources to participate in the Black Lives Matter Freedom Ride (www.colorlines.com) and bring journalists, creatives, and others to Ferguson. Some of the Ferguson protestors, however, have argued that this Black Lives Matter contingent spent time in the streets only when it was safe, stayed in their hotel, and coopted the momentum of the Ferguson movement.

97 Abby Phillips, "Clinton to meet with Black Lives Matter Activists in Cleveland," *Washington Post*, October 21, 2016, www.washingtonpost.com.

98 Alicia Garza (@aliciagarza), Twitter post, July 27, 2017 (7:52 p.m.), https://twitter.com/aliciagarza/status/625816117307678720; Twitter post, July 28, 2015 (4:57 p.m.), https://twitter.com/aliciagarza/status/626134367094575108; Deray McKesson (@deray), Twitter post, August 17, 2015 (9:21 a.m.), https://twitter.com/deray/sta-

tus/633267373534019584; Bernie Sanders (@BernieSanders), Twitter post, August 17, 2015 (11:29 a.m.), https://twitter.com/BernieSanders/status/633299592365350913.

99 Barbie Zelizer, "Reading the Past against the Grain: The Shape of Memory Studies," *Critical Studies in Mass Communication* 12, no. 2 (1995): 213–39.

CHAPTER 1. MAPPING THE TRANSPLATFORM NETWORK

1 @nicju, Twitter post, January 28, 2016 (3:28 p.m.), https://twitter.com/nicju/status/692806382123245568.

2 Harlem Pride, Inc. (@HarlemPride), Twitter post, January 28, 2016 (3:09 p.m.), https://twitter.com/HarlemPride/status/692801655826305024.

3 Nancy K. Baym, "Fans or Friends?: Seeing Social Media Audiences as Musicians Do," *Particpations: Journal of Audience and Reception Studies* 9, no. 2 (2012): 286–316; Manuel Castells, "Communication, Power and Counter-Power in the Network Society," *International Journal of Communcation* 1 (2007): 773–87 ; Henry Jenkins, *Convergence Culture: Where Old and New Media Collide* (New York: New York University Press, 2006); Alice Marwick and danah boyd, "I Tweet Honestly, I Tweet Passionately: Twitter Users, Context Collapse, and the Imagined Audience," *New Media and Society* 13, no. 1 (2010): 114–33.

4 General William T. Sherman's Special Field Order No. 15, issued in 1865, stipulated that land should be redistributed in forty-acre plots to emancipated slaves in the wake of the Civil War. Though Sherman issued the order, the idea originated with twenty Black ministers in Savannah, Georgia. In a later order, Sherman stipulated that the Army could lend mules to the Black farmers—thus the well-known phrase "forty acres and a mule." Sherman's Order was overturned by President Andrew Johnson. Black landowners were displaced and the land returned to the white Southern plantation owners. (Henry Louis Gates, Jr., "The Truth Behind 40 Acres and a Mule," *PBS*, accessed May 16, 2019, www.pbs.org.)

5 Kris Markman, "Doing Radio, Making Friends, and Having Fun: Exploring the Motivations of Independent Audio Podcasters," *New Media and Society* 14, no. 4 (2012) 547–565; Dennis Mocigemba and Gerald Riechmann, "International Podcastsurvey: Podcasters-Who They Are, How and Why They Do It," 2007, accessed September 18, 2014. http://podcastersurvey/ipcs07.pdf.

6 Richard Berry, "Will the Ipod Kill the Radio Star?: Profiling Podcasting as Radio," *Convergence* 12, no. 2 (2006): 146.

7 The Black Guy Who Tips, "Ep. 683 Loving Black Women," *The Black Guy Who Tips*, Podcast audio, April 14, 2014. http://theblackguywhotips.podOmatic.com/rss2.xml.

8 "Ep. 46 Nerd Outrage," *What's the Tea?*, Podcast audio, April 7, 2014. http://whatsthet.podomatic.com/rss2.xml.

9 The Black Astronauts, "Friends of the Show," accessed November 17, 2015, www.blackastronauts.com.

10 "Ep. 46 Nerd Outrage." *What's the Tea?*

11 "Ep. 126 Support Ya Own!" *Single Simulcast*, Podcast audio, November 20, 2013. http://singlesimulcast.com/category/episodes/feed/.

12 "The Podcast Consumer 2012," Edison Research, accessed March 1, 2015. www. edisonresearch.com.

13 *The Infinite Dial 2014*, Edison Research and Triton Digital, 2014, www.edisonre-search.com.

14 Rodimus Prime (@rodimusprime), Twitter post, June 19, 2015 (7:35 a.m.), https:// twitter.com/rodimusprime/status/611859942685847555.

15 Rodimus Prime, (@rodimusprime), Twitter post, June 19, 2015 (7:39 a.m.), https:// twitter.com/rodimusprime/status/611860901969293312; Twitter post, June 19, 2015 (7:40 a.m.), https://twitter.com/rodimusprime/status/611861026196197376.

16 Rodimus Prime, (@rodimusprime), Twitter post, June 19, 2015 (7:41 a.m.), https:// twitter.com/rodimusprime/status/611861392174542848.

17 *Whiskey, Wine, and Moonshine*, "Ep. 84: #WWMPod Reviews #BeingMary-Jane Pt. 1," Podcast audio, January 9, 2015, http://whiskeywineandmoonshine. podomatic.com/rss2.xml; "Ep. 86: @WWMPod Reviews #BeingMaryJane Pt. 2," *Whiskey, Wine, and Moonshine*, Podcast audio, January 17, 2015; "Ep. 87: #WWM-Pod Reviews #BeingMaryJane Pt. 3," *Whiskey, Wine, and Moonshine*, Podcast audio, January 22, 2015; "Ep. 89: #WWMPod Reviews #BeingMaryJane Pt. 4," *Whiskey, Wine, and Moonshine*, Podcast audio, February 1, 2015; "Ep. 97: Prime-Time Review of #BeingMaryJane," *Whiskey, Wine, and Moonshine*, Podcast audio, April 15, 2015; "Ep. 99: #BeingMaryJane Season 2 Finale Review," *Whiskey, Wine, and Moonshine*, Podcast audio, May 2, 2015.

18 The Black Guy Who Tips, "Ep. 975: Don't Save Rachel," *The Black Guy Who Tips*, Podcast audio, June 20, 2015. http://theblackguywhotips.podOmatic.com/rss2. xml.

19 Kristen J. Warner, *The Cultural Politics of Colorblind TV Casting*. (New York: Routledge, 2015).

20 This Week in Blackness, "Ep. 102: Question Everything," *Blacking It Up!*, Podcast audio, June 28, 2011. "Ratchet," a term from Black Vernacular English, is used to refer to the practices, tastes, and aesthetics commonly characterized by dominant cultures as excessive, improper, and inappropriate. The term is also often used in a derogative manner to describe ways of being common among low-income Black women. TWiB! has since stopped using the term because of its sexist and classist implications.

21 This Week in Blackness, "Ep. 102."

22 Elon James White. Personal Communication. n.d.

23 This Week in Blackness, "Ep. 536: Daddy Doesn't Care about Sports," *TWiB! Prime*, Podcast audio, June 16, 2014. http://feeds.feedburner.com/twibradio.

24 Tracie Powell, "The Demise of NPR's *Tell Me More* Can Be Traced to Member Stations," *Columbia Journalism Review*, June 5, 2014, accessed November 17, 2015. www.cjr.org.

25 This Week in Blackness, "Ep. 536."

26 Gina Neff, *Venture Labor: Work and the Burden of Risk in Innovative Industries* (Cambridge, MA: MIT Press, 2012), 16.

27 Kathleen Kuehn and Thomas F. Corrigan, "Hope Labor: The Role of Employment Prospects in Online Social Production," *Political Economy of Communication* 1, no. 1 (2013): 9–25.

28 Brooke Erin Duffy, *(Not) Getting Paid to Do What You Love: Gender, Social Media, and Aspirational Work* (New Haven, CT: Yale University Press, 2017).

29 This Week in Blackness, "Ep. 536: Daddy Doesn't Care About Sports," *TWiB! Prime*, June 16, 2014. http://feeds.feedburner.com/twibradio.

30 The Black Guy Who Tips, "Ep. 998: Hillary 2016," *The Black Guy Who Tips*, Podcast audio, July 21, 2015. http://theblackguywhotips.podOmatic.com/rss2.xml.

31 Pew Research, "Portrait of a Twitter User: Status Update Demographics," October 21, 2009, www.pewinternet.org.

32 Bloggers such as Choire Sicha, who wrote a blog post for *The Awl* titled "What Were Black People Talking about on Twitter Last Night?" and Alan Wolk, who wrote "What 'Thuglife' Can Teach Us about Twitter" in *Advertising Age*, were among the first to note "Black Twitter." In 2011, *Slate*'s Farhad Manjoo wrote "How Black People Use Twitter," starting a heated conversation about the Black presence on the platform.

33 André Brock, Jr. "From the Blackhand Side: Twitter as a Cultural Conversation," *Journal of Broadcasting and Electronic Media* 56, no. 4 (2012) 529–49.

34 Meredith Clark, "To Tweet Our Own Cause: A Mixed-Method Study of the Online Phenomenon 'Black Twitter,'" (PhD diss., University of North Carolina-Chapel Hill, 2014).

35 Clark, "To Tweet Our Own Cause," 88.

36 Clark, "To Tweet Our Own Cause," 85.

37 Brock, "From the Blackhand Side."

38 Zoe Fox, "Travyon Martin Petition Is Fastest-Growing in Change.org History," *Mashable*, March 28, 2012, http://mashable.com/.

39 Fox, "Travyon Martin Petition."

40 The Black Guy Who Tips, "Ep. 975: Don't Save Rachel."

41 *New York Magazine*, July 27–August 9, 2015, www.nymag.com; Rachel Zarrell, "#DudesGreetingDudes Is One Guy's Flawless Takedown of Catcalling," *Buzzfeed*, November 5, 2014, www.buzzfeed.com; Nina Bahadur, "#DudesGreetingDudes Hilariously Proves Catcalling Isn't 'Just a Compliment,'" *Huffington Post*, November 4, 2014, www.huffingtonpost.com; Heidi Stevens, "#DudesGreetingDudes Skewers Catcalling, with Gleeful Success," *Chicago Tribune*, November 5, 2014, www.chicagotribune.com; Wyatt Massey, "Cosby Cover Sparks #TheEmptyChair Discussion," CNN, July 27, 2015, www.cnn.com; Lindsey Bever, "#TheEmptyChair on NY Magazine's Cosby Cover Takes on a Life of Its Own," *Washington Post*, July 28, 2015, http://www.washingtonpost.com; "#TheEmptyChair Amplifies Conversation about Sexual Assault," *Morning Edition*, NPR, July 31, 2015, www.npr.org.

42 Imani Gandy (@AngryBlackLady), Twitter post, July 19, 2015 (10:23 a.m.), https://twitter.com/AngryBlackLady/status/622773873100980224.

43 Rodimus Prime (@rodimusprime), Twitter post, July 19, 2015 (10:24 a.m.), https://twitter.com/rodimusprime/status/622774029796012032.

44 Imani Gandy, (@AngryBlackLady), Twitter post, July 19, 2015 (10:37 a.m.), https://twitter.com/AngryBlackLady/status/622777372547284992.

45 Rodimus Prime (@rodimusprime), Twitter post, July 19, 2015 (10:38 a.m.), https://twitter.com/rodimusprime/status/622777579800412161; Twitter post, July 19, 2015 (10:41 a.m.), https://twitter.com/rodimusprime/status/622778233092620288; Twitter post, July 19, 2015 (10:43 a.m.), https://twitter.com/rodimusprime/status/622778730100854784.

46 Lena Masri, "Sander Hit by #BernieSoBlack," Reuters, July 20, 2015, http://blogs.reuters.com; Martin Pengelly, "O'Malley and Sanders Take on Police Brutality after Protests Disrupt Forum," Guardian, July 19, 2015, www.theguardian.com; Arti John, "What #BernieSoBlack Can Teach Bernie Sanders and His Supporters," Bloomberg, July 19, 2015, www.bloomberg.com; Andrea Beasley, "#BernieSoBlack Becomes Trending Topic in Wake of Netroots," MSBNC, July 19, 2015, www.msnbc.com; Jamelle Bouie, "More Than a Food Fight: Why Hillary Should Take the Black Lives Matter Netroots Fracas Seriously," Slate, July 20, 2015, www.slate.com.

47 Dara Lind, "#BernieSoBlack Creator Explains Why He's So Frustrated with Sanders's Supporters," Vox, July 20, 2015, www.vox.com; Dexter Thomas, "Just How Black Is Bernie Sanders?" Los Angeles Times, July 19, 2015, www.latimes.com; Dan Merica, "How Hillary Clinton Will Go After Bernie Sanders on Race," CNN, August 4, 2015, www.cnn.com; Asawin Suebsaeng, "#BlackTwitter Turns On Bernie Sanders," Daily Beast, July 19, 2015, www.thedailybeast.com.

48 Jonathan Sterne, Jeremy Morris, Michael Brendan Baker, and Ariana Moscote Freire, "The Politics of Podcasting," Fiberculture Journal, no. 13 (2008), http://thirteen.fibreculturejournal.org/fcj-087-the-politics-of-podcasting/.

49 Richard Rogers, "Debanalising Twitter: The Transformation of an Object of Study," in Twitter and Society, ed. Katrin Weller, Axel Bruns, Jean Burgess, Merja Mahrt, and Cornelius Puschmann (New York: Peter Lang, 2014), xv.

50 Jay Rossen. "Help Me Explain Twitter to Eggheads," Press Think, January 4, 2009, http://archive.pressthink.org.

51 Kate Crawford, "Following You: Disciplines of Listening in Social Media," Continuum: Journal of Media and Cultural Studies 23, no. 4 (2009): 527.

52 Nancy K. Baym and danah boyd, "Socially Mediated Publicness: An Introduction," Journal of Broadcasting and Electronic Media 56, no. 3 (2012): 322–23.

53 Baym and boyd, "Socially Mediated Publicness," 322–23.

54 Marwick and boyd, "I Tweet Honestly, I Tweet Passionately."

55 Anamik Saha, Race and the Cultural Industries (Cambridge, MA: Polity, 2018), 136.

56 Christian, Open TV, 99.

57 Catherine Squires, "Black Talk Radio: Defining Community Needs and Identity," *Harvard International Journal of Press/Politics* 5, no. 2 (2000): 78.

58 William Barlow, *Voice Over: The Making of Black Radio* (Philadelphia: Temple University Press, 1999), 296.

59 Squires, "Black Talk Radio," 78–82.

60 Laurence A. Breiner, "Caribbean Voices on the Air: Radio, Poetry, and Nationalism in the Anglophone Caribbean," in *Communities of the Air: Radio Century, Radio Culture*, ed. Susan Merrill Squier 93–108 (Durham, NC: Duke University Press, 2003); Susan Douglas, *Listening In: Radio and the American Imagination* (Minneapolis: University of Minnesota Press, 2004); Jason Loviglio, "Vox Pop: Network Radio and the Voice of the People," in *Radio Reader: Essays in the Cultural History of Radio*, ed. Michele Hilmes and Jason Loviglio 89–112 (New York: Routledge, 2002).

61 Douglas, *Listening In*, 24.

62 Vorris Nunely, *Keepin' It Hushed: The Barbershop and African American Hush Harbor Rhetoric* (Detroit, MI: Wayne State University Press, 2011), 30–31.

63 Jennifer Stoever, *The Sonic Color Line: Race and the Cultural Politics of Listening* (New York: New York University Press, 2016), 14.

64 Loviglio, "Vox Pop," 91.

65 Squires, "Black Talk Radio," 77–78.

66 Lisa Reichelt, "Ambient Intimacy," *Disambiguity*, March 1, 2007, www.disambiguity.com.

67 Crawford, "Following You," 528.

68 Jan-Hinrik Schmidt, "Twitter and the Rise of Personal Publics," in *Twitter and Society*, ed. Katrin Weller, Axel Bruns, Jean Burgess, Merja Mahrt, and Cornelius Puschmann (New York: Peter Lang, 2014).

69 Schmidt, "Twitter and the Rise of Personal Publics," 8–10.

70 Axel Bruns and Hallvard Moe, "Structural Layers of Communication on Twitter," in *Twitter and Society*, ed. Katrin Weller, Axel Bruns, Jean Burgess, Merja Mahrt, and Cornelius Puschmann, 15–28 (New York: Peter Lang, 2014).

71 Melissa Harris-Lacewell, *Barbershops, Bibles, and Bet: Everyday Talk and Black Political Thought* (Princeton, NJ: Princeton University Press, 2004), 1.

72 ATLAH Worldwide, "White Homosexual Takes Black Woman's Man," YouTube, Online Video Clip, February 25, 2014, https://www.youtube.com/watch?v=2JCJEoHaFek#t=185.

73 This Week in Blackness, "Blackness. Today: #Homodemons," YouTube, Online Video Clip, February 27, 2014, https://www.youtube.com/watch?v=g4j3MUURMkc.

74 ATLAH Worldwide, "Mrs. Elon James White," YouTube, Online Video Clip, March 6, 2014, https://www.youtube.com/watch?v=_SMut_sFirc.

75 Elon James White (@elonjames), Twitter post, March 6, 2014 (12:32 p.m.), https://twitter.com/elonjames/status/441627503543582720; Twitter post, March 6, 2014 (11:10 p.m.), https://twitter.com/elonjames/status/441787934270701568; This

Week in Blackness, "Dear 'Dr.' James David Manning . . . A.K.A. Dr. #Homode-
mons," YouTube, Online Video Clip, March 7, 2014, https://www.youtube.com/
watch?v=pYGmdZlkors.

76 Rodimus Prime (@rodimusprime), Twitter post, March 6, 2014 (1:58 p.m.),
https://twitter.com/rodimusprime/status/441648955353743360.

77 Rodimus Prime (@rodimusprime), Twitter post, March 6, 2014 (2:01 p.m.),
https://twitter.com/rodimusprime/status/441649773066846208.

78 "Questions about the Real Mrs. Elon James White: Dr. #Homodemons Gives
Rod of The Black Guy Who Tips Podcast, and ALL of Us, a Thing or 21 to Think
About," Storify, March 2014.

79 The Black Guy Who Tips, "Ep. 657 #DrManningBars," *The Black Guy Who Tips*,
Podcast audio, March 9, 2014. http://theblackguywhotips.podOmatic.com/rss2.
xml.

80 In Hip-hop, "diss," a shortened iteration of the word "disrespect," is used to refer
to insult or harsh criticism. Hip-hop MCs, who have a long tradition of verbal
sparring and braggadocio, may release what is known as a "diss track," a song
that insults or attacks another MC. In the late 1990s and early 2000s, Hip-hop
stars Jay-Z and Nas released a series of diss tracks attacking and disparaging one
another. Among these was Nas's "Ether," which has become one of the most well-
known and influential diss tracks in American Hip-hop.

CHAPTER 2. ENCLAVES AND COUNTER-PUBLICS

1 Jürgen Habermas, *The Structural Transformation of the Public Sphere*, trans.
Thomas Burger and Frederick Lawrence (Cambridge, MA: MIT Press, 1991); Sonia Livingstone, "On the Relation between Audiences and Publics," in *Audiences
and Publics: When Cultural Engagement Matters for the Public Sphere*, ed. Sonia
Livingstone (Portland, OR: Intellect, 2005), 17.

2 Nancy Fraser, "Rethinking the Public Sphere: A Contribution to the Critique of
Actually Existing Democracy," *Social Text*, no. 25/26 (1990): 68–69; Michael Warner, *Publics and Counterpublics* (Cambridge, MA: MIT Press, 2002).

3 André Brock, Jr., "Black Joy as Frame for Digital Practice: A Libidinal Economic
Approach to Black Online Culture," lecture, Arizona State University, May 18,
2017; Catherine Knight Steele and Jessica Lu, "Defying Death: Black Joy as Resistance," paper presented at International Communication Association, Prague,
May 28, 2018.

4 danah boyd, "Social Networking Sites as Networked Publics: Affordances, Dynamics, and Implications," in *Networked Self: Identity, Community, and Culture on
Social Networking Sites*, ed. Zizi Papacharissi, 47-66 (New York: Routledge, 2010),
39; emphasis added.

5 danah boyd, "Why Youth <3 Social Networking Sites: The Role of Networked
Publics in Teenage Social Life," in *Youth Identity and Digital Media*, ed. D
Buckingham, 119–42 (Cambridge MA: MIT Press, 2007); Ganaele Langlois, Greg
Elmer, Fenwick McKelvey, andZachary Devereaux, "Networked Publics: The

Double Articulation of Code and Politics on Facebook," *Canadian Journal of Communication* 34, no. 3 (2009) https://cjc-online.ca/index.php/journal/article/view/2114/3031; Zizi Papacharissi and Maria de Fatima Oliveira, "Affective News and Networked Publics: The Rhythms of News Storytelling on #Egypt," *Journal of Communication* 62, no. 2 (2012) 266–282; Bjarki Valtysson, "Facebook as a Digital Public Sphere: Processes of Colonization and Emancipation," *Journal for a Global Sustainable Information Society* 10, no. 1 (2012) 77–91; McKelvey Karissa, Joseph DiGrazia, and Fabio Rojas, "Twitter Publics: How Online Political Communities Signaled Electoral Outcomes in the 2010 US House Election," *Information, Communication & Society* 17, no. 4 (2014) 436–50; Schmidt, "Twitter and the Rise of Personal Publics," 4–13; Axel Bruns and Jean Burgess, "Twitter Hashtags from Ad Hoc to Calculated Publics," in *Hashtag Publics: The Power and Politics of Discursive Networks*, ed. Nathan Rambukkana 13–28 (New York: Peter Lang, 2015); Bryce J. Renninger, "'Where I Can Be Myself . . . Where I Can Speak My Mind: Networked Counterpublics in a Polymedia Environment," *New Media and Society* 17, no. 9 (2015) 1513–1529; Alexander Cho, "Queer Reverb: Tumblr, Affect, Time," in *Networked Affect*, ed. Ken Hillis, Susanna Paasonen, and Michael Petit 43–58 (Cambridge, MA: MIT Press, 2015).

6 Catherine Squires, "Rethinking the Black Public Sphere: An Alternative Vocabulary for Multiple Public Spheres," *Communication Theory* 12, no. 4 (2002): 448, 463.

7 Catherine Squires, "Black Talk Radio: Defining Community Needs and Identity," *The Harvard International Journal of Press/Politics* 5, no. 2 (2000): 91. emphasis original.

8 Squires, "Rethinking the Black Public Sphere," 464.

9 Catherine Knight Steele, "Black Bloggers and Their Varied Publics: The Everyday Politics of Black Discourse Online," *Television and New Media* 19, no. 2 (2017): 112–27.

10 James C. Scott, *Domination and the Arts of Resistance: Hidden Transcripts* (New Haven, CT: Yale University Press, 1990); Squires, "Rethinking the Black Public Sphere."

11 Karma Chávez, "Counter-Public Enclaves and Understanding the Function of Rhetoric in Social Movement Coalition-Building," *Communication Quarterly* 59, no. 1 (2011): 3.

12 Melissa Harris-Lacewell, *Barbershop, Bibles, and Bet: Everyday Talk and Black Political Thought* (Princeton, NJ: Princeton University Press, 2004); Quincy T. Mills, *Cutting along the Color Line: Black Barbers and Barber Shops in America* (Philadelphia: University of Pennsylvania Press, 2013).

13 Mark Anthony Neal, *What the Music Said: Black Popular Music and Black Public Culture* (New York: Routledge, 1999).

14 Vorris Nunely, *Keepin' It Hushed: The Barbershop and African American Hush Harbor Rhetoric* (Detroit, MI: Wayne State University Press, 2011), 18–19.

15 Nunely, *Keepin' It Hushed*, 2–4.

16 Nunely, *Keepin' It Hushed*, 7–13.

17 The Black Guy Who Tips, "Ep. 979: Black on Black Love," *The Black Guy Who Tips,* June 24, Podcast audio, 2015. http://theblackguywhotips.podOmatic.com/rss2.xml.

18 The Black Guy Who Tips, "Ep. 979."

19 Deltagal2, "3 Guys on Podcast Game Changer!" iTune review, October 7, 2014, https://itunes.apple.com/us/podcast/three-guys-on/id357001831?mt=2.

20 The Black Guy Who Tips, "Ep. 844: 5 Star Reviews for Christmas," *The Black Guy Who Tips*, Podcast audio, 2014. http://theblackguywhotips.podOmatic.com/rss2.xml.

21 its_always_golden, "Country Play Cousin," iTunes review, September 4, 2012, https://itunes.apple.com/us/podcast/the-black-guy-who-tips-podcast/id349830668?mt=2.

22 Deltagril29, "Love you all!" iTunes review, April 24, 2019, https://itunes.apple.com/us/podcast/whiskey-wine-and-moonshine/id664691796?mt=2.

23 RawWhite24, "Great Show!" iTunes review, November 4, 2014, https://itunes.apple.com/us/podcast/whats-the-tea/id648598889?mt=2.

24 JayKing717, "Great Content & Crew!" iTunes review, June 2, 2014, https://itunes.apple.com/us/podcast/black-astronauts-podcast/id592681501?mt=2; ElliRed, "Love LL," iTunes review, August 25, 2014, https://itunes.apple.com/us/podcast/black-astronauts-podcast/id592681501?mt=2.

25 P. Andre Joseph, "Break Out Those Good Plates!" iTunes review, January 19, 2014, https://itunes.apple.com/us/podcast/whats-the-tea/id648598889?mt=2.

26 This Week in Blackness, "Ep. 63: Barbershop," *Blacking It Up!*, Podcast audio, 2011. http://feeds.feedburner.com/twibradio.

27 @CarlTheHaitan, "Barber Shop (or Beauty Shop) Talk for You [sic] iPod and MP3 Player," iTunes review, May 6, 2011, https://itunes.apple.com/us/podcast/the-black-guy-who-tips-podcast/id349830668?mt=2.

28 cor3na, "am i in the barber shop?!" iTunes review, December 19, 2014, https://itunes.apple.com/us/podcast/three-guys-on/id357001831?mt=2.

29 Shane Paul Neal, "Black Podcasts Bring the Barbershop to the Internet," *Huffington Post*, March 13, 2013, www.huffingtonpost.com.

30 TAYREL713, "Now Listen," iTunes review, May 9, 2014, https://itunes.apple.com/us/podcast/whats-the-tea/id648598889?mt=2.

31 real-ness, "What can I say," iTunes review, January 22, 2014, https://itunes.apple.com/us/podcast/whats-the-tea/id648598889?mt=2.

32 Harris-Lacewell, *Babershop, Bibles, and Bet*.

33 Douglas, *Listening In*, 30.

34 Jomokee, "Cool, cool, cool," iTunes review, January 16, 2013, https://itunes.apple.com/us/podcast/straight-outta-lo-cash/id482570636?mt=2.

35 Alexander Weheliye, *Phonographies: Grooves in Sonic Afro-Modernity* (Durham, NC: Duke University Press, 2005).

36 Shuhei Hosokawa, "The Walkman Effect," *Popular Music* 4 no. (1984): 165–80; Mack Hagood, "Quiet Comfort: Noise, Otherness, and the Mobile Production of

Personal Space," *American Quarterly* 63, no. 3 (2011) 573–89; Alex V. Blue, "'Hear What You Want': Sonic Politics, Blackness, and Racism-Canceling Headphones," *Current Musicology* nos. 99–100 (2017) 87–106.

37 Michael Bull, "iPod Use, Mediation, and Privatization in the Age of Mechanical Reproduction," in *The Oxford Handbook of Mobile Music Studies*, vol. 1, ed. Sumanth Gopinath and Jason Stanyek (New York: Oxford University Press, 2014), 105.

38 Bull, "iPod Use, Mediation, and Privatization," 115.

39 Hagood, "Quiet Comfort," 574; emphasis in original.

40 Hagood, "Quiet Comfort," 581.

41 Nunely, *Keepin' It Hushed*, 156.

42 Nunely, *Keepin' It Hushed*, 47.

43 Hagood, "Quiet Comfort," 585.

44 Hagood, "Quiet Comfort," 582.

45 André Brock, Jr. "'Who Do You Think You Are?!': Race, Representation, and Cultural Rhetorics in Online Spaces," *POROI [Project on Rhetoric of Inquiry]* 6, no. 1 (2009): 346.

46 André Brock, Jr. "From the Blackhand Side: Twitter as a Cultural Conversation," *Journal of Broadcasting and Electronic Media* 56, no. 4 (2012) 529–49.

47 boyd, "Social Networking Sites."

48 Elon James White (@elonjames), Twitter post, August 7, 2015 (9:55 p.m.), https://twitter.com/elonjames/status/629833209371607040.

49 @SayDatAgain, Twitter post, July 12, 2015 (5:25 p.m.), https://twitter.com/SayDatAgain/status/620343547900768256.

50 @SayDatAgain,, Twitter post, July 12, 2015 (5:30 p.m.), https://twitter.com/SayDatAgain/status/620344425621798912.

51 The Black Guy Who Tips, "Ep. 1025: Are You Pressed?" *The Black Guy Who Tips*, Podcast audio, September 6, 2015.

52 Squires, "Rethinking the Black Public Sphere: An Alternative Vocabulary for Multiple Public Spheres," 460.

53 Susannah Fox, Kathryn Zickuhr, and Aaron Smith, "Twitter and Status Updating, Fall 2009," Pew Research Center, October 21, 2009, www.pewinternet.org.

54 Bloggers such as Choire Sicha, who wrote a blog post in 2009 titled, "What Were Black People Talking about on Twitter Last Night?" and Farhad Manjoo, who wrote "How Black People Use Twitter" in 2010, started a heated conversation about the Black presence on the platform. Manjoo's article was accompanied by the image of what has become known as the "Brown Twitter Bird," a brown bird in a fitted baseball cap holding a cell phone, presumably tweeting. One of the primary criticisms of Manjoo's article was that it was reductive, homogenizing Black users and treating them as an undifferentiated monolith. The critique manifested in the response from the blog *Instant Vintage* and its readers, who photoshopped the Brown Twitter Bird with a variety of different hats, hairstyles, accessories, and backgrounds to represent the fullness of Black life. By

2011, the *Root* was writing regular articles about Black Twitter, and in 2012 Dr. Goddess presented her panel "The Bombastic Brilliance of 'Black Twitter'" at SXSW (South by Southwest). Choire Sicha, "What Were the Black People Talking about on Twitter Last Night?" *The Awl*, November 11, 2009, www.theawl.com; Farhad Manjoo, "How Black People Use Twitter," August 10, 2010, www.slate. com; ". . . oh, Slate . . ." *Instant Vintage*, August 10, 2010, www.innyvinny.com; Kimberly Ellis, "The Bombastic Brilliance of 'Black Twitter,'" presented at South by Southwest (SXSW), March 9, 2012.

55 Tracy Clayton, "The 21 Biggest #Blacktwitter Moments of 2013," Buzzfeed, December 23, 2013, www.buzzfeed.com.

56 Axel Bruns and Hallvard Moe, "Structural Layers of Communication on Twitter," in *Twitter and Society*, ed. Katrin Weller, Axel Bruns, Jean Burgess, Merja Mahrt, and Cornelius Puschmann, 15–28 (New York: Peter Lang, 2014).

57 Alain Sherter, "In Day of Protests, 'Occupy Wall Street' Faces Police Violence," *CBS News*, November 17, 2011, www.cbsnews.com; Laurie Penny, "Occupy Wall Street: Police Violence Reveals a Corrupt System," *Guardian*, November 15, 2011, www.theguardian.com; Michael Tracey, "The NYPD's Violent Crackdown on Occupy Wall Street Protestors," *Mother Jones*, October 6, 2011, www.motherjones. com; Rania Khalek, "Why Are Police Attacking Peaceful Protesters? How OWS Has Exposed the Militarization of US Law Enforcement," AlterNet, October 20, 2011, www.alternet.org.

58 Elon James White (@elonjames), Twitter post, November 17, 2011 (1:53 p.m.), https://twitter.com/elonjames/status/137241989417668608.

59 Elon James White, "Dear OWS: Welcome to Our World," *Root*, November 29, 2011, www.theroot.com.

60 Elon James White (@elonjames), Twitter post, November 29, 2011 (10:49 a.m.), https://twitter.com/elonjames/status/141544281776201728; Twitter post, November 29, 2011 (11:41 a.m.), https://twitter.com/elonjames/status/141557285561438208; Twitter post, November 29, 2011 (2:22 p.m.),https://twitter.com/elonjames/status/141597870217379840.

61 @popfreeradio, Twitter post, November 29, 2011 (10:10 a.m.), https://twitter.com/popfreeradio/status/141534581869395968.

62 @LJbouge, Twitter post, November 29, 2011 (5:12 p.m.), https://twitter.com/LJbouge/status/141640719587753984.

63 @V3rsus, Twitter post, November 29, 2011, deleted.

64 @Belle_Todrani, Twitter post, November 29, 2011 (10:12 p.m), https://twitter.com/Belle_Todrani/status/141716194792185856.

65 Elon James White (@elonjames), Twitter post, November 29, 2011 (3:45 p.m.), https://twitter.com/elonjames/status/141618916458889219.

66 @solbutterfly, Twitter post, November 29, 2011 (4:06 p.m.) accessed September 19, 2017 https://twitter.com/solbutterfly/status/141624149654245376.

67 Elon James White (@elonjames), Twitter post, November 29, 2011 (4:09 p.m.), https://twitter.com/elonjames/status/141624897276346368; Twitter post, Novem-

ber 29, 2011 (5:16 p.m.), https://twitter.com/elonjames/status/141641670520344576; Twitter post, November 29, 2011 (5:29 p.m.), https://twitter.com/elonjames/status/141644863132278784; Twitter post, November 29, 2011 (5:32 p.m.), https://twitter.com/elonjames/status/141645793084964864; Twitter post, November 29, 2011 (5:56 p.m.), https://twitter.com/elonjames/status/141651682714071040.

68 This was prior to the addition of features that allowed easy creation of threads on Twitter. In 2014, Twitter added a reply feature that connected a tweet with the one to which it was a reply. At this point, users began replying to their own tweets to connect the tweets in their tweetstorms. In 2017, Twitter added the ability to thread the tweets of tweetstorms together, and similar practices are now often referred to as a "thread."

69 Blair L. M. Kelley (@profblmkelley), Twitter post, November 29, 2011 (11:02 p.m.), https://twitter.com/profblmkelley/status/141728727200567296; Elon James White (@elonjames), Twitter post, November 29, 2011 (11:04 p.m.), https://twitter.com/elonjames/status/141729163471101953; Blair L. M. Kelley (@profblmkelley), Twitter post, November 29, 2011 (11:04 p.m.), https://twitter.com/profblmkelley/status/141729258841178113; Elon James White (@elonjames), Twitter post, November 29, 2011 (11:05 p.m.), https://twitter.com/elonjames/status/141729547837128705.

70 Rebecca Wanzo, "African American Acafandom and Other Strangers: New Genealogies of Fan Studies," *Transformative Works and Cultures* 20 (2015) https://doi.org/10.3983/twc.2015.0699.

71 Mel Stanfill, "Doing Fandom, (Mis)Doing Whiteness: Heteronormativity, Racialization, and the Discursive Construction of Fandom," *Transformative Works and Cultures* 8 (2011) https://doi.org/10.3983/twc.2011.0256; Wanzo, "African American Acafandom and Other Strangers."

72 Mary Bucholtz, "The Whiteness of Nerds: Superstandard English and Racial Markedness," *Journal of Linguistic Anthropology* 11, no. 1 (2001) 84–100; Ron Eglash, "Race, Sex, and Nerd: From Black Geeks to Asian American Hipsters," *Social Text* 20 (2002) 49–64; Lori Kendall, "'White and Nerdy': Computers, Race and the Nerd Stereotype," *Journal of Popular Culture* 44, no. 3 (2011) 505–24.

73 Lori Kendall, "'Oh No! I'm a Nerd!': Hegemonic Masculinity on an Online Forum," *Gender and Society* 14, no. 2 (2000) 256–74.

74 Kristen J. Warner, "ABC's Scandal and Black Women's Fandom," in *Cupcakes, Pinterest, and Ladyporn: Feminized Popular Culture in the Early Twenty-First Century*, ed. Elana Levine (Champaign: University of Illinois Press, 2015), 37.

75 Warner, "ABC's Scandal and Black Women's Fandom," 35.

76 Often the network participates as part of the larger Black Twitter. Since 2009, the annual BET Awards has dominated the national Trending Topics on Twitter. In fact, it was this event that began to bring the Black Twitter network to greater attention. For example, the 2009 BET Awards' domination of the Trending Topics sparked commentary on what many white users felt was a surprising and inappropriate use of Twitter by Blacks.
    Several of the problematic responses were cataloged at the website "OMG! Black People!" which had the stated purpose of highlighting "some

of the interesting reactions to the trending topics related to the 2009 BET Awards." Tweets highlighted on the site include comments such as "The trending topics a disturbing today. BET awards [sic] are number 1!" and "i'm [sic] sad that the first 7 of 10 trending topics on twitter have to do with the BET awards [sic]." The overtly racist tone of some tweets highlight the perils of Black users engaging in visible fan practices—"Did anyone see the new trending topics? I don't think this is a very good neighborhood. Lock the car doors kids" and "wow!! too [sic] many negros in the trending topics for me. I may be done with this whole twitter thing." https://omgblack-people.wordpress.com.

77 Black Girl Nerds, "About," accessed November 15, 2017, http://blackgirlnerds.com.

78 FiyaStarter, audio podcast, July 7, 2012; @TheREALHeemDee, Twitter post, May 13, 2012 (9:06 p.m.), https://twitter.com/TheREALHeemDee/status/201840833136308224.

79 The Black Guy Who Tips, "Ep. 315: Girls and Dem Thrones," *The Black Guy Who Tips*, Podcast audio, May 31, 2012. http://theblackguywhotips.podOmatic.com/rss2.xml; "Ep. 443: Return of #Demthrones," *The Black Guy Who Tips*, Podcast audio, April 4, 2013.

80 Ava DuVernay (@ava), Twitter post, May 4, 2014 (9:03 p.m.), https://twitter.com/ava/status/463121761387941889; Netta Elzie, Twitter post, account deactivated, accessed September 19, 2017.

81 Sarah Florini, "Enclaving and Cultural Resonance in Black 'Game of Thrones' Fandom," *Transformative Works and Cultures*, vol. 29, 2019. https://doi.org/10.3983/twc.2019.1498.

82 Sidney Fussell, "If You're Using the 'Game of Thrones' Hashtag, You're Missing out on the Show's Best Commentary," *Business Insider*, May 16, 2016. www.businessinsider.com.

83 The Gadsden flag is the iconic yellow flag depicting a coiled snake inscribed with the phrase, "Don't Tread on Me." It gets its name from Christopher Gadsden who designed it during the American Revolutionary War.

84 @Wes_St_Clair, Twitter post, May 8, 2016 (9:44 p.m.), https://twitter.com/Wes_St_Clair/status/729487272354172929.

85 Bipartisan Report (@Bipartisanism), Twitter post, July 19, 2015 (12:07 p.m.), https://twitter.com/Bipartisanism/status/622800050440122368.

86 Roderick Morrow (@rodimusprime), Twitter post, July 21, 2015 (10:46 p.m.), https://twitter.com/rodimusprime/status/623685519155683328.

87 The Black Guy Who Tips, "Ep. 997: Brought to You By HRC and the Kock Bros," *The Black Guy Who Tips*, Podcast audio, July 20, 2015. http://theblackguywhotips.podOmatic.com/rss2.xml.

88 Brock, Jr. "From the Blackhand Side"; Sarah Florini, "Tweets, Tweeps, and Signifyin': Communication and Cultural Performance on 'Black Twitter,'" *Television and New Media* 15, no. 3 (2014) 223–37.

89 The Black Guy Who Tips, "Ep. 997: Brought to You by HRC and Koch Bros," *The Black Guy Who Tips*, Podcast audio, July 20, 2015. http://theblackguywhotips. podOmatic.com/rss2.xml.

90 @saleemjourney, Twitter post, July 19, 2015 (5:04 p.m.), https://twitter.com/saleemjourney/status/622874692492374016.

91 @MJGWrites, Twitter post, July 19, 2015 (5:14 p.m.), https://twitter.com/MJG-Writes/status/622877156167696384.

92 @kidfick, Twitter post, July 19, 2015 (5:17 p.m.), https://twitter.com/damonfick/status/622877990934986752.

93 @trayNTP, Twitter post, July 19, 2015 (12:00 p.m.), https://twitter.com/trayNTP/status/622798198365683713.

94 Lena Masri, "Sanders Hit by #BernieSoBlack," Reuters, July 20, 2015, http://blogs. reuters.com; Martin Pengelly, "O'Malley and Sanders Take on Police Brutality after Protests Disrupt Forum," *Guardian,* July 19, 2015, http://www.theguardian. com; Andrea Beasley, "#BernieSoBlack Becomes Trending Topic in Wake of Netroots," MSNBC, July 19, 2015, www.msnbc.com; Jamelle Bouie, "More Than a Food Fight: Why Hillary Should Take the Black Lives Matter Netroots Fracas Seriously," *Slate*, July 20, 2015, www.slate.com.

95 Dara Lind, "#BernieSoBlack Creator Explains Why He's So Frustrated with Sanders's Supporters," *Vox*, July 20, 2015, www.vox.com; Dexter Thomas, "Just How Black Is Bernie Sanders?," *Los Angeles Times*, July 19, 2015, www.latimes. com/; Dan Merica, "How Hillary Clinton Will Go after Bernie Sanders on Race," CNN, August 4, 2015, www.cnn.com; Asawin Suebsaeng, "#BlackTwitter Turns on Bernie Sanders," *Daily Beast*, July 19, 2015, www.thedailybeast.com.

96 The Black Guy Who Tips, "Ep. 996: #BernieSoBlack," *The Black Guy Who Tips*, Podcast audio, July 19, 2015. http://theblackguywhotips.podOmatic.com/rss2.xml.

97 Rita, Spreecast Chatroom Post, "Ep. 996: #BernieSoBlack," *The Black Guy Who Tips, July 19, 2015.*

98 Cedric, Spreecast Chatroom Post, "Ep. 996: #BernieSoBlack," *The Black Guy Who Tips*, July 19, 2015.

99 The Black Guy Who Tips, "Ep. 996: #BernieSoBlack."

100 The Black Guy Who Tips, "Ep. 996.

101 The Black Guy Who Tips, "Ep. 1000: Twiterary Genius," *The Black Guy Who Tips*, Podcast audio, July 25, 2015. http://theblackguywhotips.podOmatic.com/rss2.xml.

102 The Black Guy Who Tips, "Ep. 996: #BernieSoBlack."

103 The Black Guy Who Tips, "Ep. 999: Bernie Marched Way in the Back," *The Black Guy Who Tips*, Podcast audio, July 22, 2015. http://theblackguywhotips.podO-matic.com/rss2.xml.

104 Marisa Kabas, "Twitter Takes Aim at Bernie Sanders' Minority Strategy with #BernieSoBlack," *Daily Dot*, July 19, 2015, www.dailydot.com; "#BernieSoBlack: Sanders' Supporters Tout His Civil Rights Record, #Blacktwitter Cracks Jokes," *NewsOne*, July 19, 2015, https://newsone.com; David Ferguson, "Twitter Users Debate Bernie

Sanders' Civil Rights Credibility with #BernieSoBlack Hashtag," *Raw Story*, July 19, 2015, http://www.rawstory; Beasley, "#BernieSoBlack Becomes Trending Topic in Wake of Netroots"; Tom McKay, "Here's What Happened When #BlackLivesMatter Activists Confronted Bernie Sanders," *Mic*, July 19, 2015, https://mic.com; D. L. Chandler, "Black Twitter Goes in with #BernieSoBlack," *Hip-Hop Wired*, July 19, 2015, http://hiphopwired.com; Dara Lind, "#BernieSo-Black: Why Progressives Are Fighting about Bernie Sanders and Race," *Vox*, July 20, 2015, https://www.vox.com.

105 The Black Guy Who Tips, "Ep. 997: Brought to You by HRC and Koch Bros."

106 The Black Guy Who Tips, "Ep. 998: Hillary 2016," *The Black Guy Who Tips*, Podcast audio, July 21,2015. http://theblackguywhotips.podOmatic.com/rss2.xml.

107 The Black Guy Who Tips, "Ep. 997: Brought to You by HRC and Koch Bros."

108 The Black Guy Who Tips, "Ep. 997."

109 The Black Guy Who Tips, "Ep. 997."

110 For example, Karen tweeted, "Some of them Bernie stands [sic] through they were gonna get in our private Facebook group? Hahahahahahahahahahahahahaha-hahahahahahahahahahaha" (@SayDatAgain, Twitter post, August 10, 2015 [9:21 p.m.], https://twitter.com/SayDatAgain/status/630911915930226688).

111 The Black Guy Who Tips, "Ep. 999: Bernie Marched Way in the Back," *The Black Guy Who Tips*, Podcast audio, July 22, 2015. http://theblackguywhotips.podOmatic.com/rss2.xml.

112 The Black Guy Who Tips, "Ep. 999."

113 The Black Guy Who Tips, "Ep. 999."

114 The Black Guy Who Tips, "Ep. 999."

115 The Black Guy Who Tips, "Ep. 999."

116 The Black Guy Who Tips, "Ep. 999."

117 The Black Guy Who Tips, "Ep. 999."

118 The Black Guy Who Tips, "Ep. 999."

CHAPTER 3. "MLK, I CHOOSE YOU!"

1 This Week in Blackness, "Ep. 21.5: Even Professors Dougie," *Blacking It Up!*, Podcast audio, January 28, 2011. http://feeds.feedburner.com/twibradio.

2 This Week in Blackness, "Ep. 21.5."

3 Astrid Erll, "Cultural Memory Studies: An Introduction," in *Cultural Memory Studies Reader: An International and Interdisciplinary Handbook*, ed. Astrid Erll and Ansgar Nügging, 38–65 (New York: Walter de Gruyter, 2008).

4 Pierre Nora, "Between Memory and History: *Les Lieux De Mémoire*," *Representations* 26 (1989): 8.

5 Erll, "Cultural Memory Studies: An Introduction," 6–7.

6 Melvin Dixon, "The Black Writer's Use of Memory," in *History and Memory in African-American Culture*, ed. Geneviéve Fabre and Robert O'Meally (New York: Oxford University Press, 1994), 19.

7 Stuart Hall, "Cultural Identity and Diaspora," in *Theorizing Diaspora*, ed. Jana Evans Braziel and Anita Mannur 35–47 (Malden, MA: Blackwell, 2003). It is important to note that Hall also emphasizes the fluid and ever-changing nature of identity. These points of identification are by no means static or stable.

8 Jean-Christophe Marcel and Laurent Mucchielli, "Maurice Halbwach's Mémoire Collective," in *Cultural Memory Studies Reader: An International and Interdisciplinary Handbook*, ed. Astrid Erll and Ansgar Nügging (New York: Walter de Gruyter, 2008), 142; Barbie Zelizer, "Reading the Past against the Grain: The Shape of Memory Studies," *Critical Studies in Mass Communication* 12, no. 2 (1995): 218–19.

9 Patrick H. Hutton, "Collective Memory and Collective Mentalities: The Halbwachs-Aries Connection," *Historical Reflections/Reflexions Historique* 15, no. 2 (1988): 314.

10 Michael Schudson, *Watergate in American Memory: How We Remember, Forget, and Reconstruct the Past* (New York: Basic Books, 1992), 53.

11 Barry Schwartz, "Memory as a Cultural System: Abraham Lincoln in World War II," *American Sociological Review* 61, no. 5 (1996): 911.

12 Erll, "Cultural Memory Studies," 5.

13 Emily S. Rosenberg, *A Date Which Will Live: Pearl Harbor in American Memory* (Durham, NC: Duke University Press, 2003), 4.

14 Zelizer, "Reading the Past against the Grain." 227–29.

15 Schwartz, "Memory as a Cultural System."

16 Zelizer, "Reading the Past against the Grain," 227–29.

17 Peniel E. Joseph, *Dark Days, Bright Nights: From Black Power to Barack Obama* (New York: Basic Civitas, 2010); Manning Marable, *Beyond Black and White: From Civil Rights to Barack Obama*, 2nd ed. (Brooklyn, NY: Verso, 2009).

18 Eduardo Bonilla-Silva, *Racism without Racists: Color-Blind Racism and Racial Inequality in Contemporary America*, 3rd ed. (New York: Rowman & Littlefield, 2010).

19 Michael Kammen, *Mystic Chords of Memory: The Transformation of Tradition in American Culture* (New York: Knopf, 1991).

20 Edward P. Morgan, "The Good, the Bad, and the Forgotten: Media Culture and Public Memory of the Civil Rights Movement," in *Interpreting the Civil Rights Movement: Contradiction, Confirmation, and the Cultural Landscape*, ed. Renee Romano and Leigh Raiford 5–27 (Athens: University of Georgia Press, 2006).

21 Jennifer Fuller, "Debating the Present through the Past: Representations of the Civil Rights Movement in the 1990s," in *Interpreting the Civil Rights Movement: Contradiction, Confirmation, and the Cultural Landscape*, ed. Renee Romano and Leigh Raiford 167-96 (Athens: University of Georgia Press, 2006).

22 I draw on Foucault's descriptors of "dominant" versus "counter-" to indicate how differing versions the past relate to larger sociocultural relations of power. I refer to versions of the past that emerge from and perpetuate hegemonic power relations and dominance as "dominant" histories, while I term accounts of the past

that make visible and challenge these hierarchies of power "counter-histories." Neither dominant histories nor counter-histories are monolithic, unified constructions. Both are complex, multilayered, contingent, and in constant dialectic interaction with one another. Given the role of remembering in our interpretation of the present, the interactions and tension between histories and counter-histories are central to the maintenance or transformation of social relationships. Foucault, Michel. "Nietzsche, Genealogy, History," *Language, Counter-Memory, Practice: Selected Essays and Interviews with Michel Foucault*. Edited and with introduction by Donald F. Bouchard. Translated from French by Donald F. Bouchard and Sherry Simon, 139-64. (New York: Cornell University Press, 1977).

23 Manning Marable, *Living Black History: How Reimagining the African-American Past Can Remake America's Racial Future* (New York: Civitas Books, 2011): 9–13.

24 Marable, *Living Black History*, 12.

25 This Week in Blackness, "Ep. 74: A Life of Reinvention," *Blacking It Up!*, Podcast audio, May 10, 2011. http://feeds.feedburner.com/twibradio.

26 Blair L. M. Kelley, *Right to Ride: Streetcar Boycotts and African American Citizenship in the Era of Plessy v. Ferguson* (Chapel Hill: University of North Carolina Press, 2010).

27 This Week in Blackness, "Ep. 23: Historical Beef," *Historical Blackness*, Podcast audio, April 23, 2015. http://feeds.feedburner.com/101619781770377.

28 This Week in Blackness, "Ep. 23: Historial Beef."

29 This Week in Blackness, "Ep. 14: The Red Pill," *Historical Blackness*, Podcast audio, September 26, 2014. http://feeds.feedburner.com/101619781770377.

30 This Week in Blackness, "Ep. 14."

31 This Week in Blackness, "Ep. 14."

32 This Week in Blackness, "Ep. 14."

33 This Week in Blackness, "Ep. 14."

34 This Week in Blackness, "Ep. 2: We've Been Here Before," *Historical Blackness*, Podcast audio, Februrary 26, 2014. http://feeds.feedburner.com/101619781770377.

35 This Week in Blackness, "Ep. 2."

36 Renee Romano, "Narratives of Redemption: The Birmingham Church Bombing Trials and the Construction of Civil Rights Memory," in *The Civil Rights Movment in American Memory*, ed. Renee Romano and Leigh Raiford (Athens: University of Georgia Press, 2006), 122–24, 40.

37 Owen Dwyer, "Interpreting the Civil Rights Movement: Contradiction, Confirmation, and the Cultural Landscape," in *The Civil Rights Movement in American Memory*, ed. Renee Romano and Leigh Raiford (Athens: University of Georgia Press, 2006).

38 Jacquelyn Dowd Hall, "The Long Civil Rights Movement and the Political Uses of the Past," *Journal of American History* 91, no. 4 (2005): 1234.

39 Morgan, "The Good, the Bad, and the Forgotten."

40 Hall, "The Long Civil Rights Movement," 1254.

41 Hall, "The Long Civil Rights Movement," 1255.

42 Hall, "The Long Civil Rights Movement," 1234.

43 Nikhil Pal Singh, *Black Is a Country: Race and the Unfinished Struggle for Democracy* (Cambridge, MA: Harvard University Press, 2004), 5.

44 Marable, "Living Black History," 6.

45 Fred Powledge, *Free at Last* (New York: Harper Collins, 1991), xiv.

46 Morgan, "The Good, the Bad, and the Forgotten," 141; Hall, "The Long Civil Rights Movement," 1234.

47 Cited in Morgan, "The Good, the Bad, and the Forgotten," 141–42.

48 Morgan, "The Good, the Bad, and, the Forgotten," 143.

49 Hall, "The Long Civil Rights Movement," 1237.

50 Hall, "The Long Civil Rights Movement," 1238.

51 Denise M. Bostdorff and Steven R. Goldzwig, "History, Collective Memory, and the Appropriation of Martin Luther King Jr.: Reagan's Rhetorical Legacy," *Presidential Studies Quarterly* 35, no. 4 (2005): 662.

52 Bostdorff and Goldzwig, "History, Collective Memory, and the Appropriation of Martin Luther King Jr.," 670.

53 Hall, "The Long Civil Rights Movement," 1252.

54 Bostdorff and Goldzwig, "History, Collective Memory, and the Appropriation of Martin Luther King Jr.," 675.

55 Bostdorff and Goldzwig, "History, Collective Memory, and the Appropriation of Martin Luther King Jr.," 674.

56 Morgan, "The Good, the Bad, and the Forgotten," 143.

57 Drew D. Hansen, *The Dream: Martin Luther King Jr. and the Speech That Inspired a Nation* (New York: Harper Collins, 2003), 222, 676.

58 Morgan, "The Good, the Bad, and the Forgotten," 146.

59 This Week in Blackness, "Ep. 451: The 'This Motherf*cker Right Here' Hour," *TWiB! Radio*, Podcast audio, July 17, 2013. http://feeds.feedburner.com/twibradio.

60 Kate Zernike, "Where Dr. King Stood, Tea Party Claims His Mantle," *New York Times*, August 27, 2010, www.nytimes.com.

61 Zernike, "Where Dr. King Stood."

62 Kathleen McKinley (@KatMcKinley), Twitter post, August 27, 2010, (10:04 a.m.), https://twitter.com/KatMcKinley/status/22269254956.

63 In 2011, the state of Wisconsin saw massive protests over collective bargaining rights of state workers. The Republican governor, Scott Walker, supported a bill that would lessen budget shortfalls by limiting raises for public employees and by taking away the rights of state workers, with the exclusion of law enforcement, to collectively bargain for pensions and healthcare benefits. Protests against the bill lasted for months and, at their height, reached crowd sizes of up to 100,000 people.

64 AFL-CIO, "King's Call for Worker Justice," accessed March 28, 2011, www.aflcio.org.

65 "Glenn Beck," *Fox News*, April 4, 2011, http://mediamatters.org.

66 "Glenn Beck," *Fox News*, March 21, 2011, http://mediamaters.org.

67 This Week in Blackness, "Ep. 47: MLK <3'ed Unions," *Blacking It Up!*, Podcast audio, March 21, 2011. http://feeds.feedburner.com/twibradio.

68 "Neil Cavuto," Fox News, April 4, 2011, http://mediamatters.org.

69 This Week in Blackness, "Ep. 47: MLK <3'ed Unions."

70 David Sirota (@davidsirota), Twitter post, July 16, 2013 (12:57 p.m.), https://twitter.com/davidsirota/status/357182242864373760; Twitter post, July 16, 2013 (12:54 p.m.), https://twitter.com/davidsirota/status/357181355873935360; Twitter post, July 16, 2013 (12:55 p.m.), https://twitter.com/davidsirota/status/357181751698784256.

71 David Sirota (@davidsirota), Twitter post, July 16, 2013 (11:20 p.m.), https://twitter.com/davidsirota/status/357338918498205698.

72 Martin Luther King Jr., "Beyond Vietnam—Breaking the Silence." April 4, 1967. Riverside Church, New York. *Beyond Vietnam: An Address Sponsored by the Clergy and Laymen Concerned about Vietnam* (Palo Alto, Altoan Press, 1967).

73 David Sirota (@davidsirota), Twitter post, July 16, 2013 (11:24 p.m.), https://twitter.com/davidsirota/status/357340121449771008.

74 Elon James White (@elonjames), Twitter post, July 16, 2013 (11:32 p.m.), https://twitter.com/elonjames/status/357341922731360256; Twitter post, July 16, 2013 (11:35 p.m.), https://twitter.com/elonjames/status/357342696538505219; Twitter post, July 16, 2013 (11:36 p.m.), https://twitter.com/elonjames/status/357342983223382017.

75 David Sirota (@davidsirota), Twitter post, July 16, 2013 (11:30 p.m.), https://twitter.com/davidsirota/status/357343857127591936.

76 This Week in Blackness, "The 'This Motherf*cker Right Here' Hour," *TWiB! Radio*, Podcast audio, July 17, 2013. http://feeds.feedburner.com/twibradio.

77 This Week in Blackness, "The 'This Motherf*cker Right Here' Hour."

78 Eclectablog, "White Progressives Get a Taste of Anger and Frustration as #BlackLivesMatter Activist Upstage Bernie Sanders," July 18, 2015, www.eclectablog.com; Imani Gandy (@AngryBlacklady), Twitter post, July 18, 2015 (9:34 p.m.), https://twitter.com/AngryBlackLady/status/622580210693570561.

79 Triple J (@TripleJ666), Twitter post, Jul7 21, 2015 (9:50 a.m.), https://twitter.com/TripleJ666/status/623535419960000514.

80 Elon James White, "A Message from Elon James White," *Daily Kos*, July 21, 2015, www.dailykos.com.

81 @JamiaStarheart, Twitter post, July 18, 2015 (3:47 p.m.), https://twitter.com/Jamia-Starheart/status/622493030172487681.

82 @yippigirl, Twitter post, July 18, 2015 (12:15 p.m.), https://twitter.com/yippigirl/status/6224847850767974w40.

83 @annagalland, Twitter post, July 18, 2015 (2:25 p.m.), https://twitter.com/annagalland/status/622517671729299456; Brian Stewart, "MoveOn Response to Netroots Nation Presidential Town Hall," July 18, 2015, http://front.moveon.org; @AliAkink, Twitter post, July 18, 2015 (2:30 p.m.), https://twitter.com/AliAkinK/status/622518888283176960.

84 @NifMuhammad, Twitter post, July 18, 2015 (5:25 p.m.), https://twitter.com/NifMuhammad/status/622562984154501120.

85 This Week in Blackness, "Ep. 360: IGNANT-ASS MUSIC," *TWiB! Radio*, Podcast audio, January 22, 2013. http://feeds.feedburner.com/twibradio.

86 This Week in Blackness, "Ep. 451: The 'This Motherf*cker Right Here' Hour."

87 "Community Organizer on Violence in Baltimore Protests," *The Situation Room with Wolf Blitzer*, CNN, accessed September 19, 2017, www.cnn.com.

88 The Black Guy Who Tips, "Ep. 940: Well Just Call Em . . . ," *The Black Guy Who Tips*, Podcast audio, April 28, 2015. http://theblackguywhotips.podOmatic.com/rss2.xml.

89 Marable, "Living Black History," 6.

90 DeRay McKesson, Vine Video, January 17, 2015, https://vine.co/v/Oj69Ori2Qjj.

91 Kathleen McKinkley, Twitter post, January 17, 2015 (6:08 p.m.), tweet deleted.

92 @loltanisha, Twitter post, January 17, 2015 (6:50 p.m.), https://twitter.com/loltanisha/status/556599425167273984; Kathleen McKinley, Twitter post, January 17, 2015 (7:02 p.m.), https://twitter.com/KatMcKinley/status/556602598719897602.

93 Kathleen McKinley, Twitter post, January 28, 2011 (11:13 a.m.), https://twitter.com/KatMcKinley/status/31022122277019648; Twitter post, October 11, 2011 (12:18 p.m.), https://twitter.com/KatMcKinley/status/123794640255188992; Twitter post, October 11, 2011 (3:55 p.m.), https://twitter.com/KatMcKinley/status/123849276215410688; Twitter post, April 16, 2012 (3:36 p.m.), https://twitter.com/KatMcKinley/status/191973320550400000; Twitter post, April 22, 2013 (4:41 p.m.), https://twitter.com/KatMcKinley/status/326435546924732417.

94 Joe Walsh (@WalshFreedom), Twitter post, January 18, 2016 (8:56 a.m.), https://twitter.com/WalshFreedom/status/689083917853429765; Twitter post, January 18, 2016 (10:29 a.m.), https://twitter.com/WalshFreedom/status/689107320538816513; Twitter post, January 18, 2016 (12:17 p.m.), https://twitter.com/WalshFreedom/status/689137165369012229.

95 Joe Walsh (@WalshFreedom), Twitter post, August 28, 2013 (11:24 a.m.), https://twitter.com/WalshFreedom/status/372741605150568449; Twitter post, August 28, 2013 (12:49 p.m.), https://twitter.com/WalshFreedom/status/372762961011437568.

96 Ferguson Action, "Reclaim MLK," accessed September 19, 2017 http://fergusonaction.com.

97 Coalition against Police Violence, Facebook page, accessed September 19, 2017, https://www.facebook.com/TheCAPV/info/?tab=page_info.

98 jpmassar, "New Mayor Gets a Wake-Up Call," *Daily Kos*, January 19, 2015, http://m.dailykos.com.

99 Zizi Papacharissi and Maria de Fatima Oliveira, "Affective News and Networked Publics: The Rhythms of News Storytelling on #Egypt," *Journal of Communication* 62, no. 2 (2012) 266-82.

100 @WyzeChef, Twitter post, January 19, 2015 (5:10 p.m.), https://twitter.com/WyzeChef/status/557299184337174528.

101 This Week in Blackness, "Ep. 729: The Great Oath Keeper Experiment." *TWiB! Prime*, Podcast audio, August 19, 2015. http://feeds.feedburner.com/twibradio.

102 Ferguson Response Network, "Ep. 4: #ReclaimMLK," *Ferguson Response Network Podcast*, Podcast audio, January 9, 2015. http://feeds.feedburner.com/FergusonResponseNetworkPodcast.

103 Martin Luther King Jr., "Beyond Vietnam—Breaking the Silence."

104 Ferguson Response Network, "Ep. 4: #ReclaimMLK."

105 Ferguson Response Network, "Ep. 4: #ReclaimMLK."

106 Ferguson Response Network, "Ep. 4: #ReclaimMLK."

107 This Week in Blackness, "Ep. 729," *TWiB! Prime*. http://feeds.feedburner.com/twibradio.

108 @EbonyDigest, Twitter post, January 13, 2015 (5:57 p.m.), https://twitter.com/ebonydigest/status/555136631166877697.

109 Elon James White (@elonjames), Twitter post, May 12, 2015 (11:31 p.m.), https://twitter.com/elonjames/status/598329590793183232.

110 King Jr, Martin Luther. "Letter from Birmingham Jail." *UC Davis L. Rev.* 26 (1992): 835.

111 This Week in Blackness, "Ep. 721: #EarnThisDamnVoteOrLose," *TWiB! Prime*, Podcast audio, July 28, 2015. http://feeds.feedburner.com/twibradio.

112 Imani Gandy (@AngryBlackLady), Twitter post, August 14, 2015 (9:44 p.m.), https://twitter.com/AngryBlackLady/status/632050160214786048.

113 Imani Gandy, "Dr. King and White Progressives™," *ReWire*, August 13, 2015, https://rewire.news.

114 Imani Gandy, "Dr. King and White Progressives™."

115 This Week in Blackness, "THE BROOKLYN SITUATION," *TWiB! In the Morning*, Podcast audio, March 12, 2013. http://feeds.feedburner.com/amTWIB.

116 This Week in Blackness, "THE BROOKLYN SITUATION." http://feeds.feedburner.com/twibradio.

CHAPTER 4. "THIS IS THE RESOURCE OUR COMMUNITY NEEDED RIGHT NOW"

1 Brent McDonald and John Woo, "They Helped Make Twitter Matter in Ferguson Protests," *New York Times*, August 10, 2015, www.nytimes.com.

2 Kate Crawford, "Following You: Disciplines of Listening in Social Media," *Continuum: Journal of Media and Cultural Studies* 23, no. 4 (2009) 525-35; Alfred Hermida, "From TV to Twitter: How Ambient News Became Ambient Journalism," *M/C Journal* 13, no. 2 (2010) http://journal.media-culture.org.au/index.php/mcjournal/article/view/220.

3 Alfred Hermida, "Twittering the News: The Emergence of Ambient Journalism," *Journalism Practice* 4, no. 3 (2010) 297–308.

4 Hermida, "Twittering the News."

5 Axel Bruns and Jean Burgess, "Researching News Discussion on Twitter," *Journalism Studies* 13, nos. 5–6 (2012): 801.

6 Hermida, "From TV to Twitter."

7 J. D. Lasica, "Blogs and Journalism Need Each Other," Blog post, September 8, 2003, www.jdlasica.com.

8 Mark Deuze, "The Changing Context of News Work: Liquid Journalism and Monitorial Citizenship," *International Journal of Communcation* 2 (2008): 852.

9 Axel Bruns, *Gatewatching: Collaborative Online News Production* (New York: Peter Lang, 2005), 17.

10 John Zaller, "A New Standard of News Quality: Burglar Alarms for the Monitorial Citizen," *Political Communication* 20, no. 2 (2003): 122.

11 Hermida, "Twittering the News," 301.

12 Hermida, "From TV to Twitter."

13 Farhad Manjoo, "How Black People Use Twitter," *Slate*, August 10, 2010, www.slate.com.

14 Topix San Francisco (@topix_sf), Twitter post, January 2, 2009 (9:30 a.m.), https://twitter.com/topix_sf/status/1091588648; KTVU (@KTVU), Twitter post, January 1, 2009 (10:56 a.m.), https://twitter.com/KTVU/status/1090057212; Twitter post, January 5, 2009 (3:58 p.m.), https://twitter.com/KTVU/status/1097935901; "Video of California Police Shooting Spurs Investigation," CNN, January 7, 2009, www.cnn.com.

15 TWiB! Nation (@TWiBnation), Twitter post, January 6, 2009 (1:00 p.m.), https://twitter.com/TWIBnation/status/1099972399.

16 Mary Grace Anthony and Ryan J. Thomas, "'This Is Citizen Journalism at Its Finest': YouTube and the Public Sphere in the Oscar Grant Shooting Incident," *New Media and Society* 12, no. 8 (2010) 1280–96.

17 Youth Radio, "Oscar Grant Case: Eyewitness Karina Vargas," YouTube video, May 19, 2009, https://www.youtube.com/watch?v=dZ1mCTQx3UI; "What Makes Oscar Grant's Incident Different?" YouTube video, June 15, 2010, https://www.youtube.com/watch?v=kXtVZQwegBI; "Oscar Grant: Protests Lead to Arrests," YouTube video, November 8, 2010, https://www.youtube.com/watch?v=HtASU2HAb-4&list=PL3067F44827CDEBAC.

18 Thandisizwe Chimurenga, "Emancipatory Journalism," n.d., accessed October 12, 2017, http://www.thandisizwe.net/what-is-emancipatory-journalism/.

19 @InvincibleDET, Twitter post, May 16, 2010 (5:22 p.m.), https://twitter.com/invincibleDET/status/14120702131.

20 Erhardt Graeff, Matt Stempeck, and Ethan Zuckerman, "The Battle for 'Trayvon Martin': Mapping a Media Controversy Online and Off-Line," *First Monday* 19, no. 2 (2014) https://doi.org/10.5210/fm.v19i2.4947.

21 Manjoo, "How Black People Use Twitter"; "Why Black Twitter Trending Topics Paint Wrong Picture of Us," *NewsOne*, January 18, 2011, https://newsone.com/985275/why-black-twitter-trending-topics-paint-wrong-picture-of-us/; Nicole Hardesty, "Top 10 All-Time #Blacktwitter Trends," *NewsOne*, December 16, 2011, https://newsone.com/2000035/top-10-all-time-black-twitter-trends/; Jeff Bercovici, "Twitter Gets Even More Popular with Black Users. Why?," June 1, 2011, https://www.forbes.com/sites/jeffbercovici/2011/06/01/twitter-gets-even-more-popular-with-black-users-why/#75cf113fb1b3.

22 "How Blogs, Twitter and Mainstream Media Have Handled the Trayvon Martin Case," Pew Research Center, Journalism and Media, March 30, 2012, www.journalism.org.

23 For example, this exchange: Elon James White (@elonjames), Twitter post, July 5, 2013 (1:23 p.m.), https://twitter.com/elonjames/status/353202403148972032; @HollaBlackGirl, Twitter post, July 5, 2013 (1:29 p.m.), https://twitter.com/HollaBlackGirl/status/353204093965189120.

24 Elon James White (@elonjames), Twitter post, July 11, 2013 (3:27 p.m.), https://twitter.com/elonjames/status/355407952775102466; L. Joy Williams (@ljoywilliams), Twitter post, July 11, 2013 (3:44 p.m.), https://twitter.com/ljoywilliams/status/355412300175384576; Tracy Clayton (@brokeymcpoverty), Twitter post, July 11, 2013 (3:48 pm.), https://twitter.com/brokeymcpoverty/status/355413349162418177; Dacia Mitchell (@daciatakesnote), Twitter post, July 11, 2013 (3:50 p.m.), https://twitter.com/daciatakesnote/status/355413890005352449.

25 @GayPatriot, Twitter post, July 13, 2013 (10:19 p.m.), https://twitter.com/GayPatriot/status/356236430256775172; @KennethWebster3, Twitter post, July 13, 2013 (10:25 p.m.), tweet deleted.

26 This Week in Blackness, "Ep. 452: The TMFRH Hour 2," *TWiB! Radio*, July 18, 2013. http://feeds.feedburner.com/twibradio.

27 Phylis Johnson, "Black Radio Politically Defined: Communicating Community and Political Empowerment through Stevie Wonder's Kjlh-Fm, 1992–2002," *Political Communication* 21, no. 3 (2004): 355.

28 William Barlow, *Voice Over: The Making of Black Radio* (Philadelphia: Temple University Press, 1999), 214.

29 Johnson, "Black Radio Politically Defined."

30 Ghasson Hage, "The Affective Politics of Racial Mis-Interpellation," *Theory, Culture, and Society* 27, nos. 7–8 (2010) 112–29.

31 Hage, "The Affective Politics of Racial Mis-Interpellation," 122.

32 Hage, "The Affective Politics of Racial Mis-Interpellation," 126–27.

33 W. E. B. DuBois, *The Souls of Black Folks* (Oxford, UK: Oxford University Press, 2007).

34 This Week in Blackness, "Ep. 447: #ZimmermanTrial Verdict," *TWiB! Radio*, Podcast audio, July 14, 2013. http://feeds.feedburner.com/twibradio.

35 This Week in Blackness, "Ep. 449: Understanding the Term 'Hiatus,'" *TWiB! Radio*, Podcast audio, July 16, 2013. http://feeds.feedburner.com/twibradio.

36 This Week in Blackness, "Ep. 447: #ZimmermanTrial Verdict."

37 Elon James White (@elonjames), Twitter post, July 13, 2013 (10:21 p.m.), https://twitter.com/elonjames/status/35623459588211972.

38 Monica Roberts (@TransGriot), Twitter post, July 14, 2013 (1:50 a.m.), https://twitter.com/TransGriot/status/35628950279064480.

39 This Week in Blackness, "Ep. 447: #ZimmermanTrial Verdict."

40 This Week in Blackness, "Ep. 447."

41 @lilsoulsista, Twitter post, July 14, 2013 (2:26 am), https://twitter.com/lilsoulsista/
    status/356298604488568832.

42 Jeffrey C. Alexander, "Toward a Theory of Cultural Trauma," in *Cultural Trauma
    and Collective Identity*, ed. Jeffery C. Alexander, Ron Eyerman, Bernard Giesen,
    Neil J. Smelser, and Piotr Sztompka (Berkeley: University of California Press,
    2004), 10, 22.

43 Alexander, "Toward a Theory of Cultural Trauma, 22."

44 Elon James White, personal communication, 2013.

45 Laurence A. Breiner, "Caribbean Voices on the Air: Radio, Poetry, and National-
    ism in the Anglophone Caribbean," in *Communities of the Air: Radio Century,
    Radio Culture*, ed. Susan Merrill Squier 93–108 (Durham, NC: Duke University
    Press, 2003); Susan Douglas, *Listening In: Radio and the American Imagination*
    (Minneapolis: University of Minnesota Press, 2004).

46 André Brock, Jr. "From the Blackhand Side: Twitter as a Cultural Conversation,"
    Journal of Broadcasting and Electronic Media 56, no. 4 (2012); 531–38.

47 This Week in Blackness, "Ep. 447."

48 Elon James White, personal communication, 2013.

49 @AwakeBlackWoman, Twitter post, July 14, 2013 (12:53 a.m.), https://twitter.com/
    AwakeBlackWoman/status/356275256308150274.

50 @CoquiNegra, Twitter post, July 14, 2013 (2:19 a.m.), https://twitter.com/Co-
    quiNegra/status/356477981650194433.

51 This Week in Blackness. "Ep. 447: #ZimmermanTrial Verdict."

52 This Week in Blackness. "Ep. 447."

53 @HaggsBoson, Twitter post, July 14, 2013 (1:23 a.m.), https://twitter.com/Haggs-
    Boson/status/356282739772755968.

54 The Black Guy Who Tips, "Ep. 507: Just Us for Trayvon," *The Black Guy Who Tips*,
    Podcast audio, July 14, 2013. http://theblackguywhotips.podOmatic.com/rss2.xml.

55 "Ep. 11: Justice for Trayvon," *What's the Tea?*, Podcast audio, July 16, 2013. http://
    whatsthet.podomatic.com/rss2.xml.

56 This Week in Blackness, "Ep. 453: The Obama Plantation," *TWiB! Radio*, Podcast
    audio, July 22, 2013. http://feeds.feedburner.com/twibradio.

57 This Week in Blackness, "Ep. 451: The 'This Motherf*cker Right Here' Hour,"
    TWiB! Radio, Podcast audio, July 17, 2013. http://feeds.feedburner.com/twibradio.

58 Elon James White (@elonjames), Twitter post, July 13, 2013 (4:04 p.m.), https://
    twitter.com/elonjames/status/359041295496396800.

59 David Sirota, "George Zimmerman Killed the Presumption of Innocence," *Salon*,
    July 15, 2013, http://www.salon.com.

60 dvnix, "Of Drones, MLK, Condescension, and Snatching Wigs," https://storify.
    com/dvnix/of-drones-mlk-condescension-and-snatching-wigs.

61 Elon James White (@elonjames), Twitter post, July 16 2013 (11:03 p.m.), https://
    twitter.com/elonjames/status/357334816032694272.

62 Elon James White (@elonjames), Twitter post, July 16, 2013 (11:06 p.m.), https://
    twitter.com/elonjames/status/357335558877478912.

63 Elon James White (@elonjames), Twitter post, July 16, 2013 (11:19 p.m.), https://twitter.com/elonjames/status/357338618177658882.

64 This Week in Blackness, "Ep. 451: The 'This Motherf*cker Right Here' Hour."

65 This Week in Blackness, "Ep. 453: The Obama Plantation."

66 The Black Guy Who Tips, "Ep. 509: F#cking with Black People," *The Black Guy Who Tips*, Podcast audio, July 16, 2013. http://theblackguywhotips.podOmatic.com/rss2.xml.

67 Betsy Bruce, "Teenager Shot, Killed in Ferguson Apartment Complex," *Fox 2 Now*, August 9, 2014, http://fox2now.com.

68 Betsy Bruce, "Teenager Shot, Killed in Ferguson Apartment Complex," KPLR11.com, August 9, 2014, http://kplr11.com; Beth O'Malley, "Social Media Posts from Scene of Ferguson Shooting," *St. Louis Dispatch*, August 9, 2014, http://www.stltoday.com; STL Today, Twitter post, August 9, 2014 (5:48 p.m.), https://twitter.com/stltoday/status/498224424688967680.

69 I am deliberately obscuring the details of these posts because of the sensitive nature of their content. As of the time of writing, the tweets were still available and still led to images of Mike Brown's body. Brown's family has publicly requested such images be removed and not circulated. Because of this, and sense of general human decency, I have deliberately made an exception to the citational practices otherwise adhered to throughout and have opted to omit details that could enable readers to seek these posts themselves or tweets that are threaded with others containing these images. These posts are recorded elsewhere and can be found by other means if one feels a strong need to verify my claims. But, I chose not to facilitate their further circulation.

70 Brittany Noble-Jones, Instagram post, August 9, 2014, https://www.instagram.com/p/rfiFVYyqoT/; (@noblejonesonTV) Twitter post, August 9, 2014 (5:31 p.m.), https://twitter.com/noblejonesontv/status/498219985735790592.

71 Wesley Lowery (@WesleyLowery), Twitter post, August 11, 2014 (1:51 p.m.), https://twitter.com/WesleyLowery/status/498889331919290369.

72 Brittany Noble-Jones, Twitter post, August 9, 2014 (8:25 p.m.), https://twitter.com/noblejonesontv/status/498263738013585408; Twitter post, August 9, 2014 (6:42 p.m.), https://twitter.com/noblejonesontv/status/498238132597178368.

73 Ashley Yates (@brownblaze), Twitter post, August 10, 2014 (6:57 p.m.), https://twittcr.com/brownblaze/status/498604009867849728; Twitter post, August 10, 2014 (7:03 p.m.), https://twitter.com/brownblaze/status/498605610418860032; Twitter post, August 10, 2014 (7:05 p.m.), https://twitter.com/brownblaze/status/498605920864043009; Twitter post, August 10, 2014 (7:05 p.m.), https://twitter.com/brownblaze/status/498606065320091648; Twitter post, August 10, 2014 (7:06 p.m.), https://twitter.com/brownblaze/status/498606299441930241; Twitter post, August 10, 2014 (7:08 p.m.), https://twitter.com/brownblaze/status/498606951979163648; @WyzeChef, Twitter post, August 9, 2014 (11:12 p.m.), https://twitter.com/WyzeChef/status/498305962726273024; Twitter post, August 9, 2014 (11:47 p.m.), https://twitter.com/WyzeChef/status/498314736845324288;

Twitter post, August 9, 2014 (11:50 p.m.), https://twitter.com/WyzeChef/status/498315402506539009; Twitter post, August 9, 2014 (11:51 p.m.), https://twitter.com/WyzeChef/status/498315601777934336.

74 T-Dubb-O (@T_DUBB_O), Twitter post, August 9, 2014 (3:19 p.m.).

75 Tef Poe, Instagram post, August 9, 2014.

76 Tef Poe (@TefPoe), Twitter post, August 9, 2015 (5:09 p.m.), https://twitter.com/TefPoe/status/498229501911121920.

77 Feminista Jones (@FeministaJones), Twitter post, August 9, 2014 (7:19 p.m.), https://twitter.com/FeministaJones/status/498247271516225541.

78 Feminista Jones (@FeministaJones), Twitter post, August 9, 2014 (7:21 p.m.), https://twitter.com/FeministaJones/status/498247673741602816.

79 Baratunde Thurston (@baratunde), Twitter post, August 11, 2014 (6:54 p.m.), https://twitter.com/baratunde/status/498965606222139392.

80 Tracy Clayton (@BrokeyMcPoverty), Twitter list, https://twitter.com/brokeymcpoverty/lists/ferguson.

81 Maeve Duggan, Nicole B. Elison, Cliff Lampe, Amanda Lenhart, and Mary Madden, "Demographics of Key Social Networking Platforms," Pew Internet Research Center, January 9, 2015, http://www.pewinternet.org.

82 Michael Calderone, "How Volunteer-Run Argus Radio Broadcast Ferguson Protests Live to the World," *HuffPost*, August 14, 2014, http://www.huffingtonpost.com; Rebelutionary_z LIVE, UStream, http://www.ustream.tv/z; Bassem Masri, Ustream, http://www.ustream.tv/channel/bassemmasri; Boston University School of Theology, Livestream, https://livestream.com/accounts/4958196/Ferguson.

83 Chris McDaniel, Vine post, September 26, 2014, https://vine.co/v/OZKAF-BFFqH3; Ryan Reilly, Vine post, August 13, 2014, https://vine.co/v/MYH3t-mYBn9X.

84 Kyli Singh, "It Would Take You 8 Years to Watch a Vine Video from Every User," *Mashable*, July 16, 2014, http://mashable.com.

85 Tef Poe (@TefPoe), Twitter post, August 9, 2014 (6:21 p.m.), https://twitter.com/TefPoe/status/498232750336643072.

86 @Khan_SHEGOG, Twitter post, August 9, 2014 (10:34 p.m.).

87 https://twitter.com/cjayconrod/status/498247491674836992.

88 C. Jay Conrod (@cjayconrod), Twitter post, August 9, 2014 (8:30 p.m.), https://twitter.com/cjayconrod/status/498265073161220096.

89 C. Jay Conrod(@cjayconrod), Twitter post, August 9, 2017 (3:58 p.m.), https://twitter.com/cjayconrod/status/498196619959889920; Twitter post, August 9, 2014 (8:18 p.m.), https://twitter.com/cjayconrod/status/498262113404461056; Twitter post, August 9, 2014 (8:22 p.m.), https://twitter.com/cjayconrod/status/498262984095846401; Twitter post, August 9, 2014 (8:31 p.m.), https://twitter.com/cjayconrod/status/498265417958191104; Twitter post, August 11, 2014 (10:19 a.m.), https://twitter.com/cjayconrod/status/498836073686913025.

90 C. Jay Conrod(@cjayconrod), Twitter post, August 11, 2014 (10:33 a.m.), https://twitter.com/cjayconrod/status/498839719367561217.

91 C. Jay Conrod(@cjayconrod), Twitter post, August 11, 2014 (10:35 a.m.), https://
    twitter.com/cjayconrod/status/498840052651151360; Twitter post, August 11, 2014
    (10:35 a.m.), https://twitter.com/cjayconrod/status/498840194850635776.

92 C. Jay Conrod(@cjayconrod), Twitter post, August 11, 2014 (10:48 a.m.), https://
    twitter.com/cjayconrod/status/498843482539040769.

93 T-Dubb-O (@T_DUBB_), Twitter post, August 9, 2014 (7:41 p.m.), https://twitter.
    com/T_DUBB_O/status/498252645698506753.

94 T-Dubb-O, Instagram post, August 11, 2014, https://www.instagram.com/p/rk-
    c2a2COFR/.

95 @GeekNStereo, Twitter post, August 9, 2014 (6:26 p.m.), https://twitter.com/
    GeekNStereo/status/498233852523859968; Twitter post, August 9, 2014 (6:28 p.m.),
    https://twitter.com/GeekNStereo/status/498234333056860161.

96 @WyzeChef, Twitter post, August 11, 2014 (4:57 a.m.), https://twitter.com/
    WyzeChef/status/498755102002266112; wyze43, Instagram post, August 11, 2014,
    http://instagram.com/p/rjVbMmBVwO/.

97 @WyzeChef, Twitter post, August 9, 2014 (9:13 p.m.), https://twitter.com/
    WyzeChef/status/498275827130171392.

98 @WyzeChef, Twitter post, August 9, 2014 (9:13 p.m.), https://twitter.com/
    WyzeChef/status/498276031392804864.

99 @STLtoday, Twitter post, August 9, 2014 (5:48 p.m.), https://twitter.com/stltoday/
    status/498224424688967680.

100 Antonio French (@AntonioFrench), Twitter post, August 9, 2014 (6:02 p.m.),
    https://twitter.com/AntonioFrench/status/498227883488587777.

101 "Police's Fatal Shooting of Black Teenager Draws Angry Crowd in St. Louis Sub-
    urb," Guardian, August 10, 2014, www.theguardian.com; "Fatal Police Shooting of
    Michael Brown Sparks Protests in Missouri," NBC News, August 10, 2014, accessed
    December 12, 2018, www.nbcnews.com.

102 Ashley Yates (@brownblaze), Twitter post, August 9, 2014 (11:16 p.m.), https://
    twitter.com/brownblaze/status/498306887557738496.

103 @Vandalyzm, Twitter post, August 10, 2014 (2:38 p.m.), https://twitter.com/Van-
    dalyzm/status/498538839125016576.

104 C. Jay Conrod, Twitter post, August 11, 2014 (9:23 a.m.), https://twitter.com/cjay-
    conrod/status/498821981349752833.

105 C. Jay Conrod, Twitter post, August 11, 2014 (12:59 a.m.), https://twitter.com/cjay-
    conrod/status/498695180958973953.

106 C. Jay Conrod, Twitter post, August 11, 2014 (10:00 a.m.), https://twitter.com/cjay-
    conrod/status/498831277236039680.

107 Ashley Yates, Twitter post, August 10, 2014 (8:22 p.m.), https://twitter.com/
    brownblaze/status/498625549254676485; Twitter post, August 10, 2014 (8:24 p.m.),
    https://twitter.com/brownblaze/status/498625923139137536; Twitter post, August
    10, 2014 (8:25 p.m.), https://twitter.com/brownblaze/status/498626158569615361.

108 C. Jay Conrod, Twitter post, August 11, 2014 (2:51 a.m.), https://twitter.com/cjay-
    conrod/status/498723243927158784; Twitter post, August 10, 2014 (10:54 a.m.),

https://twitter.com/cjayconrod/status/498482409650667520; @GeekNStereo, Twitter post, August 9, 2014 (7:13 p.m.), https://twitter.com/GeekNStereo/status/498245746869547010.

109 This Week in Blackness, "Ep. 557: #Ferguson," *TWiB! Prime*, Podcast audio, August 11, 2014.

110 This Week in Blackness, "Ep. 557: #Ferguson," (http://feeds.feedburner.com/twibradio.)

111 @tealdeer, Twitter post, August 11, 2014 (10:54 a.m.), https://twitter.com/tealdeer/status/498844847776993280.

112 Elon James White (@elonjames), Twitter post, August 11, 2014 (6:55 p.m.), https://twitter.com/elonjames/status/498965982954549248.

113 This Week in Blackness, "Ep. 558: OMG KKK WTF," *TWiB! Prime*, Podcast audio, August 12, 2014.

114 Elon James White (@elonjames), Twitter post, August 12, 2014 (11:10 p.m.), https://twitter.com/elonjames/status/499392534599454720.

115 Brittany Packnett, Twitter post, August 13, 2014 (12:56 a.m.), https://twitter.com/MsPackyetti/status/499419235958132736.

116 @GeekNStereo, Twitter post, August 13, 2014 (12:10 p.m.), https://twitter.com/GeekNStereo/status/499588801980014592.

117 @TheREAL_MBrooks, Twitter post, August 13, 2014 (1:36 a.m.), 2017 https://twitter.com/TheREAL_MBrooks/status/499429187392790528; Twitter post, August 13, 2014 (1:40 a.m.), https://twitter.com/TheREAL_MBrooks/status/499430338125246465.

118 Elon James White (@elonjames), Twitter post, August 13, 2014 (6:30 p.m.), https://twitter.com/elonjames/status/499684402616864768.

119 Elon James White (@elonjames), Twitter post, August 13, 2014 (3:19 p.m.), https://twitter.com/elonjames/status/499636457607540736; Twitter post, August 14, 2014 (1:48 a.m.), https://twitter.com/elonjames/status/499794703475159040.

120 Emily Epstein-White, Instagram post, August 13, 2014, https://www.instagram.com/p/rp_uRezdnl/; Twitter post, August 13, 2014 (7:02 p.m.), https://twitter.com/EmEps/status/499692539889213443.

121 *The Root*, August 14, 2014, http://theroottv.theroot.com/video/Riot-Police-in-Ferguson-MO.

122 This Week in Blackness, "Ferguson Dispatch #1," YouTube video, August 14, 2014, https://www.youtube.com/watch?v=8orYm8-ISrQ; Elon James White (@elonjames), Twitter post, August 14, 2014 (2:28 p.m.), https://twitter.com/elonjames/status/499985828945215488.

123 Elon James White (@elonjames), Twitter post, August 14, 2014 (7:18 p.m.), https://twitter.com/elonjames/status/500058927321858049.

124 Elon James White (@elonjames), Twitter post, August 16, 2014 (2:49 a.m.), https://twitter.com/elonjames/status/500534862168989698.

125 Michael Kolisha and Jessica Roberts, "Selfies: Witnessing and Participatory Journalism with a Point of View," *International Journal of Communication* 9 (2015) 1672–85.

126 Elon James White, Instagram post, August 20, 2014, https://www.instagram.
com/p/r7c5v-D9BY/?taken-by=elonjames.

127 This Week in Blackness, "Ferguson Dispatch #3: #MikeBrown Was Murdered and
We Want Justice," Podcast audio, August 15, 2014. http://feeds.feedburner.com/
twibradio.

128 This Week in Blackness, "Ferguson Dispatch #5: Protestors and Looters Are Different," Podcast audio, August 16, 2014. http://feeds.feedburner.com/twibradio.

129 Emily Epstein-White, Instagram post, August 15, 2014, https://www.instagram.
com/p/rvcO8Ozdiy/; Twitter post, August 15, 2014 (9:47 p.m.), https://twitter.
com/EmEps/status/500458921535229953.

130 This Week in Blackness, "Ferguson Dispatch #3: #MikeBrown Was Murdered and
We Want Justice," Podcast audio, August 15, 2014. http://feeds.feedburner.com/
twibradio.

131 This Week in Blackness, "Ferguson Dispatch #3."

132 This Week in Blackness, "Ferguson Dispatch #5: Protestors and Looters Are Different."

133 This Week in Blackness, "Ferguson Dispatch #5"; Elon James White (@elon-
james), Twitter post, August 16, 2014 (1:22 p.m.), https://twitter.com/elonjames/
status/500694004850511872; Twitter post, August 16, 2014 (2:45 p.m.),https://twit-
ter.com/elonjames/status/500715021383393281.

134 Aaron Rand Freeman (@ANSFreeman), Twitter post, August 16, 2014 (4:50 a.m.),
https://twitter.com/ANSFreeman/status/500565143017639937.

135 Aaron Rand Freeman, Twitter post, August 16, 2014 (4:52 a.m.), https://twitter.
com/ANSFreeman/status/500565635038851072.

136 This Week in Blackness, "Ferguson Dispatch #3."

137 Elon James White (@elonjames), Twitter post, August 19, 2014 (1:34 a.m.), https://
twitter.com/elonjames/status/501603161124372480.

138 This Week in Blackness, "#FergusonDispatch: Gassed (Snippet)," YouTube post,
August 19, 2014, https://www.youtube.com/watch?v=DA4IT-rGNDg.

139 This Week in Blackness, "#FergusonDispatch."

140 Elon James White (@elonjames), Instagram post, August 18, 2014, https://www.
instagram.com/p/r3pCDHj9Ml/?hl=en&taken-by=elonjames.

141 Elon James White (@elonjames), Twitter post, August 19, 2014 (2:39 a.m.), https://
twitter.com/elonjames/status/501619322419425280.

142 Elon James White (@elonjames), Twitter post, August 19, 2014 (2:42 a.m.), https://
twitter.com/elonjames/status/501620132515696640.

143 Elon James White (@elonjames), Twitter post, August 19, 2014 (2:51 a.m.), https://
twitter.com/elonjames/status/501622375361032192.

144 Elon James White (@elonjames), Twitter post, August 19, 2014 (5:10 a.m.) https://
twitter.com/elonjames/status/501657323857657857; This Week in Blackness, "#Fer-
gusonDispatch."

145 Associated Press, "Police: Gunfire, Molotov Cocktails in Ferguson," YouTube
video, August 18, 2014, https://www.youtube.com/watch?v=OCZ6zikvJQo.

146 "The Effects of Tear Gas," *Melissa Harris-Perry Show*, August 24, 2014, www.msnbc.com; "The Physiological Effects of Tear Gas," *Melissa Harris-Perry Show*, August 24, 2014, www.msnbc.com.

147 "The Physiological Effects of Tear Gas."

148 "#BlackLivesMatter," *Nerdgasm Noire Network*, Podcast audio, August 8, 2014.

149 "Ep. 67: The Revolution Will Not Be Televised," *Whiskey, Wine, and Moonshine*, Podcast audio, August 17, 2014. http://whiskeywineandmoonshine.podomatic.com/rss2.xml.

150 Movie Trailer Review Network, "The Black Episode," *Insanity Check*, Podcast audio, August 16, 2014. https://www.mtrnetwork.net/feed/mtr-network/.

151 "Ep. 355: Hands Up, We Are Ferguson," *Where's My 40 Acres?*, Podcast audio, August 16, 2014. http://www.thetearsoforphans.com/feed/podcast.

152 Movie Trailer Review Network, "The Black Episode."

153 "Ep. 67: The Revolution Will Not Be Televised," *Whiskey, Wine, and Moonshine*, Podcast audio, August 17, 2014. http://whiskeywineandmoonshine.podomatic.com/rss2.xml.

154 The Black Guy Who Tips, "Ep. 760 #IGotTheTalk," *The Black Guy Who Tips*, Podcast audio, August 10, 2014. http://theblackguywhotips.podOmatic.com/rss2.xml.

155 Spawn on Me, "Ep. 26: #MikeBrown Lived in Brookago Too," *Spawn on Me*, Podcast audio, August 18, 2014. https://feedpress.me/som.

156 In Deep Show, "Vol. 174," *In Deep Show*, Podcast audio, August 11, 2014. https://indeepshow.podbean.com/feed.xml.

157 Spawn on Me, "Ep. 26: #MikeBrown Lived in Brookago Too."

158 "Ep. 147: I Deserve, Featuring Rod from *The Black Guy Who Tips*," *Fiyastarter Podcast*, Podcast audio, August 20, 2014. http://fiyastarter.podomatic.com/rss2.xml.

CONCLUSION

1 Anne Helmond, "The Platformization of the Web: Making Web Data Platform Ready," *Social Media + Society* 1, no. 2 (2015) https://doi.org/10.1177/2056305115603080; David Nieborg and Thomas Poell, "The Platformization of Cultural Production: Theorizing the Contingent Cultural Commodity," *New Media and Society* 20, no. 11 (2018) 4275-92.

2 Don Norman, *The Design of Everyday Things*, rev. and exp. ed. (New York: Basic Books, 2013).

3 André Brock, Jr., *Distributed Blackness: African American Online Technoculture* (New York: New York University Press, 2019); Farhad Manjoo, "How Black People Use Twitter," *Slate*, August 10, 2010, www.slate.com.

4 Will Oremus, "Why Twitter's Confusing New 'Conversations' Actually Make Sense," *Slate*, August 23, 2013, www.slate.com.

5 André Brock, Jr. "From the Blackhand Side: Twitter as a Cultural Conversation," *Journal of Broadcasting and Electronic Media* 56, no. 4 (2012): 529–49.

6 Lori Kido Lopez, "Mobile Phones as Participatory Radio: Developing Hmong Mass Communication in the Diaspora," *International Journal of Communication* 10 (2016) 2038–55.

7 Lee Rainie and Barry Wellman, *Networked: The New Social Operating System* (Cambridge, MA: MIT Press, 2012).

8 Andrew Theen, "Umpqua Community College Shooting: Killer's Manifesto Reveals Racist, Satanic Views," *Oregonian*, September 8, 2017, www.oregonlive.com; Jessica Valenti, "Elliot Rodger's California Shooting Spree: Further Proof That Misogyny Kills," *Guardian*, May 24, 2014, www.theguardian.com.

9 Hannah Dreier, "I've Been Reporting on MS-13 for a Year. Here Are the 5 Things Trump Gets Most Wrong," ProPublica, June 25, 2018, www.propublica.org; Tessa Berenson, "Donald Trump Calls for 'Complete Shutdown' of Muslim Entry to U.S.," *Time*, December 7 2015, http://time.com; Michael D. Shear and Julie Hirschfeld Davis, "Stoking Fears, Trump Defied Bureaucracy to Advance Immigration Agenda," *New York Times*, December 23, 2017, www.nytimes.com.

10 Hatewatch, "Breitbart Exposé Confirms: Far-Right News Site a Platform for the White Nationalist 'Alt-Right,'" Southern Poverty Law Center, October 6, 2017, www.splcenter.org; Joseph Bernstein, "Here's How Breitbart and Milo Smuggled White Nationalism into the Mainstream," Buzzfeed, October 5, 2017, www.buzzfeednews.com; Alexander Smith and Vladimir Banic, "Sebatian Gorka Made Nazi-Linked Vitezi Rend 'Proud' by Wearing Its Medal," *NBC News*, April 8, 2017, www.nbcnews.com; William D. Cohan, "How Stephen Miller Rode White Rage from Duke's Campus to Trump's West Wing," *Vanity Fair*, May 30 2017, www.vanityfair.com.

11 Ronald Inglehart and Pippa Norris, "Trump, Brexit, and the Rise of Populism: Economic Have-Nots and Cultural Backlash," *Harvard JFK School of Government Faculty Working Papers Series* (2016): 1–52.; Matthew Luttig, Christopher Federico, and Howard Lavine, "Supporters and Opponents of Donald Trump Respond Differently to Racial Cues: An Experimental Analysis," *Research and Politics* 4, no. 4 (2017) 1–8; Brenda Major, Alison Blodorn, and Gregory Blascovich, "The Treat of Increasing Diversity: Why Many White Americans Support Trump in the 2016 Presidential Election," *Group Process and Intergroup Relations*, October 20, 2016; Brian F. Schaffner, Matthew MacWilliams, and Tatishe Nteta, "Explaining White Polarization in the 2016 Vote for President: The Sobering Role of Racism and Sexism," *Political Science Quarterly*, 133, no. 1 (2018): 9-34.

12 "The Year in Hate: Trump Buoyed White Supremacists in 2017, Sparking Backlash among Black Nationalist Groups," Southern Poverty Law Center, February 21, 2018, www.splcenter.org; Hatewatch, "FBI: Hate Crimes Reach 5-Year High in 2016, Jumped as Trump Rolled toward Presidency," Southern Poverty Law Center, November 12, 2017, www.splcenter.org; Richard Cohen, "Hate Crimes Rise for Second Straight Year; Anti-Muslim Violence Soars amid President Trump's Xenophobic Rhetoric," Southern Poverty Law Center, November 13, 2017, www.splcenter.org; Abigail Hauslohner, "Hate Crimes Jump for Fourth Straight Year in

Largest U.S. Cities, Study Finds," *Washington Post*, May 11, 2018, www.washington-post.com.

13 Sabrina Tavernise, "A Boom in Confederate Monuments, on Private Land," *New York Times*, August 30, 2017, www.nytimes.com; John Haltiwanger, "A Record Number of White Nationalists Are Running for National Office in 2018," *Business Insider*, June 1, 2018, accessed December 16, 2018, www.businessinsider.com.

14 Joe Heim, "Charlottesville—Recounting a Day of Rage, Hate, Violence, and Death," *Washington Post*, August 14, 2017, www.washingtonpost.com.

15 "Full Text: Trump's Comments on White Supremacists, 'Alt-Left' in Charlottes-ville," *Politico*, August 15, 2017, www.politico.com.

16 Eduardo Bonilla-Silva, *Racism without Racists: Color-Blind Racism and the Persistence of Racial Inequality in America*, 5th ed. (Lanham, MD: Rowman and Littlefield, 2018).

17 Benjamin Fearnow, "White Woman Arrested after Racist Bus Rant Using N-Word, 'Illegal Immigrant' Deportation Threats," *NewsWeek*, July 5, 2018, www.newsweek.com; Alanne Orjoux, Paul P. Murphy, and Ray Sanchez, "Attorney in Rant That Went Viral Says He's Not a Racist and Offers an Apology," CNN, May 22, 2018, www.cnn.com; Parker Riley, "Video: Man Screams Racial Slurs at Black Man and Says 'White Men Built These Streets," *NewsOne*, June 19, 2018, https://newsone.com; Emily Shugerman, "Woman Fired after Screaming Racist Slurs at Black Couple on California Freeway," *Independent,* July 14, 2018, www.indepen-dent.co.uk.

18 Terrell Jermaine Starr, "White Fox News Guest: 'There's Nothing Worse than Be-ing Called a Racist,'" *Root*, July 14, 2018, www.theroot.com; Stacey Patton, "Sorry, 'Deplorables': Being Called Racists Doesn't Mean You're Being Oppressed," *Wash-ington Post*, September 15, 2016, www.washingtonpost.com.

19 Richard B. Spencer (@RichardBSpenser), Twitter post, January 23, 2017 (10:29 a.m.), https://twitter.com/RichardBSpencer/status/823553243921821697.

20 Imani Gandy, "#Twitterfail: Twitter's Refusal to Handle Online Stalkers, Abusers, and Haters," *Rewire*, August 12, 2014, https://rewire.news.

21 Kishonna L. Gray, "Deviant Bodies, Stigmatized Identities, and Racist Acts: Examining the Experiences of African-American Gamers in Xbox Live," *New Review of Hypermedia and Multimedia* 18, no. 2 (2012) 261-76; Whitney Phillips, "The House That Fox Built: Anonymous, Spectacle, and Cycles of Amplification," *Television and New Media* 14, no. 6 (2012) 494-509.

22 Gandy, "#Twitterfail"; Terrell Jermaine Starr, "The Unbelievable Harassment Black Women Face Daily on Twitter," *AlterNet*, September 16, 2014, www.alternet.org.

23 Imani Gandy, Tumblr post, "Marc Rattay aka @M_Shale is the Man Behind Assholster, Twitter's Most Notorious Troll Account," 2015, http://angryblacklady.tumblr.com/post/120369559471/marc-rattay-assholster-racist-misogynist.

24 Lindy West, "Now Roosh V and His Band of Sad Men in Dark Rooms Know How It Feels to Be Bombarded with Bile," *Guardian*, February 7, 2016, www.theguardian.com.

25 Douglas Heppner, "Black Propaganda in Feminism," *Return of the Kings*, October 4, 2013. https://archive.is/IaCtn.

26 Ryan Broderick, "Here's How a Fake Feminist Hashtag Like #Endfathersday Gets Started and Why It'll Keep Happening," *Buzzfeed News*, June 16, 2014, 018, www.buzzfeednews.com.

27 #WhitesCantBeRaped, Imgur post, June 8, 2014, https://imgur.com/r/TumblrInAction/XzPSSvh.

28 Broderick, "Here's How a Fake Feminist Hashtag Like #Endfathersday Gets Started"; "Activists Are Outing Hundreds of Twitter Users Believed to Be 4chan Trolls Posing as Feminists," *Buzzfeed News*, June 17, 2014, 2018, www.buzzfeednews.com.

29 Kishonna L. Gray, Bertan Buyukozturk, and Zachary G. Hill, "Blurring the Boundaries: Using Gamergate to Examine 'Real' and Symbolic Violence against Women in Contemporary Gaming Culture," *Sociology Compass* 11, no. 3 (2017) https://doi.org/10.1111/soc4.12458.

30 Shira Chess and Adrienne Shaw, "A Conspiracy of Fishes, or, How We Learned to Stop Worrying About #Gamergate and Embrace Hegemonic Masculinity," *Journal of Broadcasting and Electronic Media* 59, no. 1 (2015) 208–20.

31 Leslie Mac (@LeslieMac), Twitter post, August 9, 2015 (3:29 P.M.), https://twitter.com/LeslieMac/status/630460888663859204.

32 Neha Rashid, "The Emergence of the White Troll behind a Black Face," *Codeswitch*, March 21, 2017, www.npr.org.

33 Zack Beauchamp, "Milo Yiannopoulos: Breitbart's Star Provocateur and Trump Champion, Explained," *Vox*, February 20, 2017, www.vox.com.

34 Bernstein, "Here's How Breitbart and Milo Smuggled White Nationalism into the Mainstream."

35 Mike Cernovich, "Why #Gamergate Is Important," *Danger and Play*, November 22, 2014. http://archive.is/QaXCY#selection-441.18-441.71.

36 Gregor Aisch, Jon Huang, and Cecilia Kang, "Dissecting the #Pizzagate Conspiracy Theories," *New York Times*, December 10, 2016, www.nytimes.com.

37 Matt Lees, "What Gamergate Should Have Taught Us about the 'Alt-Right,'" *Guardian*, December 1, 2016, www.theguardian.com; Ian Sherr and Erin Carson, "Gamergate to Trump: How Video Game Culture Blew Everything Up," CNET, November 27, 2017, www.cnet.com.

38 April Glaser, "Russian Trolls Were Obsessed with Black Lives Matter," *Slate*, May 11, 2018, accessed December 16, 2018, https://slate.com.

39 U.S. House of Representatives Permanent Select Committee on Intelligence Democrats, "Exposing Russia's Effort to Sow Discord Online: The Internet Research Agency and Advertisements" (2018). https://intelligence.house.gov/social-media-content/.

40 Leo G. Stewart, Ahmer Arif, and Kate Starbird, "Examining Trolls and Polarization with a between Network" In Proc. *ACM WSDM, Workshop on Misinformation and Misbehavior Mining on the Web*. 2018.

41 Kevin Winstead, "Caping for Crystal: Crystal Johnson, Digital Propaganda, and Black Political Currency," unpublished manuscript.

42 Heber Brown III, Facebook post, April 16, 2016, https://www.facebook.com/photo.php?fbid=10154097683603610&set=a.423996223609.197367.505488609&type=3&theater.

43 Sam Levin, "Did Russia Fake Black Activism on Facebook to Sow Division in the U.S.?," *Guardian*, September 30, 2017, www.theguardian.com.

44 I am certain that some of the conflict around racial lines in the 2016 Democratic primary were stoked by Russian intelligence deploying sock puppet accounts. *Some* of the "Bernie Bros" were real American citizens. Many of the people in the network I write about in this book personally knew some who were arguing with them about Sanders. It would require further analysis, but, I am inclined to believe that Bernie Bots were being deployed to amplify the "Bernie Bros" and exacerbate tension, a known tactic of this Russian campaign.

45 Aymar Jean Christian, *Open TV: Innovation beyond Hollywood and the Rise of Web Television* (New York: New York University Press, 2018), 68–69; Stuart Cunningham and David Craig, *Social Media Entertainment: The New Intersection of Hollywood and Silicon Valley* (New York: New York University Press, 2019).

46 Hamid Naficy, *An Accented Cinema: Exilic and Diasporic Filmmaking* (Princeton, NJ: Princeton University Press, 2001), 134–36.

47 Naficy argues that the interstitial mode of production is multilingual. He is speaking specifically of filmmakers living in exile from their homelands and notes that the films feature the use of two or more languages. This could apply to TWiB!, given that Black Vernacular English is a distinct form of English and one that many consider a dialect. The phenomenon of code-switching, shifting between ways of speaking based on context and audience, is well documented in Black American communities. Given TWiB!'s priority of functioning as a counterpublic, addressing white progressives on issues of race, multiplicity, and language are relevant here, although this characteristics of interstitial modes of production is not immediately relevant to my discussion above. Naficy, *Accented Cinema*.

48 Hamid Naficy, *An Accented Cinema*, 134–36.

49 Amazon's affiliates program pays a small fee to a website if that site refers users to Amazon and they make a purchase. Each affiliate was assigned a unique Amazon link; for TWiB! it was amazon.com/twib, and purchases made by users arriving at Amazon via that link yielded a small percentage for TWiB!. Many of the podcasts in the network used this program to generate revenue, until Amazon changed the program in 2017, causing revenues to decline.

50 Mathias Bärtl, "Youtube Channels, Uploads and Views a Statistical Analysis of the Past 10 Years," *Convergence* 24, no. 1 (2018) 16–32.

51 *Where's My 40 Acres?*, Patreon, accessed August 18, 2018, https://www.patreon.com/bePatron?u=9740083&redirect_uri=https%3A%2F%2Fwww.thetearsoforphans.com%2Fpremium-2%2F&utm_medium=widget.

52 Craft Beer Killah, Instagram, accessed August 18, 2018, https://www.instagram.com/craftbeerkillah/.
53 Black Astronauts Podcast Network, Patreon, accessed August 18, 2018, https://www.patreon.com/Blackastronauts/overview.
54 Black Astronauts Podcast Network, Patreon.
55 *Where's My 40 Acres?*, Patreon.

METHODOLOGICAL APPENDIX

1 Statista, "Number of Monthly Active Twitter Users in the United States from 1st Quarter 2010 to 3rd Quarter 2017," accessed November 10, 2017, https://www.statista.com/statistics/274564/monthly-active-twitter-users-in-the-united-states/.
2 Jennifer Van Grove, "How Twitter Users Changed in 2010," *Mashable*, December 16, 2010, http://mashable.com.
3 Elon James White (@elonjames), Twitter post, January 3, 2009 (2:24 p.m.), https://twitter.com/elonjames/status/1093827706.
4 Nick Saint, "Everything You Need to Know about Who's Using Twitter," *Business Insider*, April 30, 2010, www.businessinsider.com.
5 Nancy K. Baym, "Fans or Friends?: Seeing Social Media Audiences as Musicians Do," *Particpations: Journal of Audience and Reception Studies* 9, no. 2 (2012) 286–316; Manuel Castells, "A Network Theory of Power," *International Journal of Communications* 5 (2011) 773–87; Henry Jenkins, *Convergence Culture: Where Old and New Media Collide* (New York: New York University Press, 2006); Alice Marwick and danah boyd, "I Tweet Honestly, I Tweet Passionately: Twitter Users, Context Collapse, and the Imagined Audience," *New Media and Society* 13, no. 1 (2010).
6 Twitter, Terms of Service, accessed November 10, 2017, https://twitter.com/en/tos#usContent.
7 "More Information on Fair Use," Copyright.gov, accessed November 10, 2017, https://www.copyright.gov/fair-use/more-info.html.
8 Unfortunately, I have not always adhered to this self-imposed ethical guideline. In my earlier work, particularly that written between 2010–12, I followed the academic standard, which holds that anything publicly available online could be quoted. As the issue of citation and quotation was discussed more and more online, I began adjusting my methods in response to the critiques and concerns coming from marginalized users.

INDEX

ABOUT THE AUTHOR

Sarah Florini is Assistant Professor of Film and Media Studies in the Department of English at Arizona State University.

Lightning Source UK Ltd.
Milton Keynes UK
UKHW041228200320
360651UK00014B/420

9 781479 813056